Narrative Devices in the *Shiji*

SUNY series in Chinese Philosophy and Culture

Roger T. Ames, editor

Narrative Devices in the *Shiji*
Retelling the Past

LEI YANG

SUNY PRESS

Published by State University of New York Press, Albany

© 2024 State University of New York

All rights reserved

Printed in the United States of America

No part of this book may be used or reproduced in any manner whatsoever without written permission. No part of this book may be stored in a retrieval system or transmitted in any form or by any means including electronic, electrostatic, magnetic tape, mechanical, photocopying, recording, or otherwise without the prior permission in writing of the publisher.

For information, contact State University of New York Press, Albany, NY
www.sunypress.edu

Library of Congress Cataloging-in-Publication Data

Name: Yang, Lei, 1985– author.
Title: Narrative devices in the Shiji : retelling the past / Lei Yang.
Description: Albany : State University of New York Press, [2024] | Series: SUNY series in Chinese philosophy and culture | Includes bibliographical references and index.
Identifiers: LCCN 2023043090 | ISBN 9781438497204 (hardcover : alk. paper) | ISBN 9781438497228 (ebook) | ISBN 9781438497211 (pbk. : alk. paper)
Subjects: LCSH: Sima, Qian, approximately 145 B.C.–approximately 86 B.C. Shi ji. | China—History—To 221 B.C.—Historiography. | China—History—Qin dynasty, 221–207 B.C.—Historiography. | China—History—Han dynasty, 202 B.C.–220 A.D.—Historiography.
Classification: LCC DS741.3.S683 Y344 2024 | DDC 931—dc23/eng/20240104
LC record available at https://lccn.loc.gov/2023043090

10 9 8 7 6 5 4 3 2 1

To Yongbai Dai and Guoyan Yang

Contents

Acknowledgments	ix
Introduction	1
Chapter 1　The Turn to Textual Unity	19
Chapter 2　Temporal Order: Weaving a Synthesized Causality	47
Chapter 3　Narrative Speed: Elaborating Stairs Ascending to Power	81
Chapter 4　Multiple Points of View: Illuminating Desires and Dynamics	111
Conclusion	141
Notes	147
Bibliography	171
Index	183

Acknowledgments

This book owes a great deal to the mentorship, support, and encouragement that I have received over the years since I started it as my dissertation at the University of Pennsylvania. I would like to extend my heartfelt thanks to my PhD adviser, Paul R. Goldin, for all he has taught me before and after my graduation. He has offered tremendously beneficial guidance at every stage of the project and read multiple versions of the manuscript. I also owe a special debt of gratitude to two other mentors during my graduate study, Gerald J. Prince and Nathan Sivin, both of whom were members of my committee. Professor Prince had a decisive influence in helping me conceptualize and enter the world of narratology. His inspiring and patient analysis of examples in French narrative literature was of significant assistance to me in approaching Chinese historical writings. Prof. Nathan Sivin (who passed away in 2022) provided invaluable training in academic reading and writing. His rich knowledge and ideas about on Chinese history, as well as his dedication to research, have shaped my understanding of what it means to be a scholar. Overall, I was blessed to receive guidance from the three mentors whose works are a constant source of inspiration for me.

I also owe a debt of gratitude to other professors who taught me during my graduate study, namely Nancy S. Steinhardt, Victor H. Mair, and Adam Smith. Our conversations, both in and outside of the class, have established a broad foundation for my future research and career.

I would also like to thank Martin Kern and Michael Puett, who have been generous in supporting my research endeavors throughout the years. Professor Kern's seminar and Professor Puett's research on *Shiji* (Records of the Historian) are particular inspirations for this monograph. Their enthusiasm and commitment to the field have deeply motivated me to continue my academic journey.

Since moving to Minnesota, I have found an amazing intellectual community both within and outside my home institution, Carleton College. I'd like to thank the fellows on the Faculty Research Seminar supported by the Humanities Center at Carleton, including Kathleen Ryor, Asuka Sango, George Shuffelton, Jessica Keating, Alex Knodell, and Austin Mason, all of whom discussed my work with me and provided thoughtful feedback. Outside Carleton, Ann Waltner and Hsiang-Lin Shih read parts of my chapter drafts and deserve special credit for their thought-provoking comments. I also profited immeasurably from conferences, workshops, and conversations with scholars in China. Xu Jianwei, Guo Xi'an, Chen Jianing, Xie Bo, and Luo Yiyi provided resources and suggestions when I was preparing the manuscript.

Over the years, I have benefited from financial support of various institutions. I am a grateful recipient of the Tang Post-Doctoral Research Award in Early China Studies from the Tang Center for Early China at Columbia University. A Princeton University Library Research Grant enabled me to use the rare books collected there. A Large Faculty Development Fellowship Award, Small Faculty Development Endowment Award, and supplementary research funding from Carleton's Provost Office allowed me the leave time to complete the book. Without these grantors' support, this book could not have been written.

An earlier version of chapter 3 appeared as "How versus What: Changes in Narrative Speed from *Zuozhuan* and *Shiji* to *Hanshu*," in *Monumenta Serica: Journal of Oriental Studies* 68, no. 1 (2020): 1–27. I wish to express my gratitude to the publisher Taylor & Francis Ltd. (http://www.tandfonline.com) for permission to republish this article in the present form. I thank the editor Zbigniew Wesołowski SVD and the journal's anonymous referees for their constructive comments and support in publishing the article.

I'm grateful to the anonymous readers of the manuscript for their careful reading and detailed feedback. I would also like to express my debt and admiration for the editorial team at the State University of New York Press. James Peltz was an exemplary editor throughout the process, and Susan Geraghty and Dan Foote were truly helpful in improving the manuscript.

To my family I owe the deepest debt of gratitude, for they have done so much for me. It is their love and support that have nourished my development from an ignorant girl who had no direction to an adult with a deep passion for research. This book is not mine, but ours.

Introduction

In the reign of Emperor Cheng of Han (r. 32–7 BCE), one of the princes within the imperial household, Prince Dongping, paid a statutory visit to the central court of the empire located in its capital, Chang'an. The prince asked the emperor whether he could take copies of philosophical works and *Taishigong shu* 太史公書 (i.e., *Shiji* 史記, *Records of the Historian*) back to his own enfeoffment.[1] Although *Records of the Historian* was completed around 100 BCE, it was not yet widely circulated when the visit occurred. When the emperor consulted his high minister, Wang Feng 王鳳 (d. 22 BCE), the latter pointed out that the requests were against propriety and that the purpose of a statutory visit—as indicated by its name—was to rectify regulations. Wang explained why princes should not be given access to *Taishigong shu*: "It contains the wily and expedient schemes of the diplomats of the Warring States period, the unusual measures resorted to by the advisers at the time of the founding of the Han, and all the strange occurrences in the realm of the heavens, the strategic points in the territorial lords. None of these is appropriate to be possessed by a regional lord."[2] Furthermore, Wang Feng also suggested specific language for the emperor to use when rejecting the prince's request: since the five classics were regulated by the sages and contain the ten thousand affairs, they were enough to rectify oneself; and the prince could request as many books as he wanted as long as they aid understanding the classics. The emperor heeded Wang Feng's advice and declined both of the prince's requests.

The minister's anxiety about *Records of the Historian* decades after it was completed reflects an early understanding of the text. His concern arose primarily from the facts recorded in the book rather than from the character of its author,[3] Sima Qian 司馬遷 (145?–86 BCE), the great Western Han (202 BCE–8 CE) historian. This understanding of the book in the late Western Han is radically different from the biographical interpretation—*Records of the Historian* is a textual vent of Sima Qian's pain and emotion—that has predominated and been widely accepted since the third century CE. Since Sima Qian was the founding father of Chinese historiography and a genius in Chinese literary history, the question of his intention has shadowed "*Shiji* xue" 史記學 (*Shiji* studies) for centuries. However, it is the monumental work—totaling 526,500 Chinese characters—rather than his intention that cemented his reputation. The text is the first universal history of China and one of the largest narrative works to emerge from Chinese historiography, recounting a period from the origins of Chinese civilization to the reign of the historian's own ruler, Emperor Wu of Han (r. 141–87 BCE). The current study jumps out of Sima Qian's shadow and refocuses on the text per se by providing a systematic narratological analysis of *Records of the Historian*. By restoring the Han text to its place in early Chinese textual history and historiographical evolution, this book examines how narrative devices impact the rhetorical functions of *Records of the Historian*. I shall answer why in early China, when writing was much more laborious than today, historians diligently renarrated events that had been covered by earlier works, and how the historians constructed their visions of the past in their narratives.

Here, I use "narrative" to expand our perspectives on Chinese historical writings and reframe our analysis of these texts. I use this term as the narratologist Gerald Prince defines it: "the representation of at least two real or fictive events or situations in a time sequence, neither of which presupposes or entails the other."[4] Accordingly, a narrative can contain one or multiple episodes that are usually short and freestanding accounts of single events. This definition provides three advantages. First, in addition to "history" and "literature," the definition reveals a previously overlooked dimension of *Records of the Historian* and other texts: narrative. Until now, *Shiji* studies have largely fallen into these two camps—that is, history and literature—because of modern scholars' entrenchment in modern disciplines. In fact, such boundaries in early China were much less explicit, because, in general, political affairs were definitely the core subject of early prose.[5] Second, affirming the textual nature of *Records of the Historian* and other historical writings as narratives allows us to view texts from the perspective of narrative tradition, a practice that has not been implemented before. When we put these texts side by side that were formed centuries apart, the evolution of historiography becomes more visible. Finally, the term "narrative" accommodates accounts of varied length, from barebones entries written in a handful of words to long and sophisticated chapters comprising thousands of characters.

The Early China period, from the legendary origin of Chinese civilization to the end of the second century CE, was a critical interval in Chinese textual history. After the fourth century BCE, numerous texts were made and circulated, many of which have come to us through transmission and excavation. Recent archaeological findings have brought to light variant versions of received texts, as well as texts that we had never seen before. Appealing to the past was an efficient way to make an argument in any of these texts, most of which center on political themes.[6] In 221 BCE, the Qin's (221–206 BCE) unification of regional powers marked the beginning of the imperial period, which ended in 1911 CE. Yet the short-lived Qin dynasty was replaced by the Han (202 BCE–220 CE),[7] which lasted long enough to implement and consolidate the social changes established by the Qin. These early empires exerted transformative influence in ideology building and textual production whose traces are visible even today. Recent discoveries in manuscript culture show that, through these centuries, Chinese texts underwent a revolutionary transformation from "open" to "closed," an eye-opening finding based on a large number of recently excavated manuscripts from tombs. By "open," I refer to the fact that texts were not stabilized; they were still fluid in organization and even contents. By "closed," I refer to the fact that texts became locked, no longer subject to further editing.[8]

Within this trajectory of the textual transformation, Sima Qian was not just an adept writer or well-known historian; he was also an active creator of this new trend, forging the form of Chinese texts from the early empires to the present. During Emperor Wu's reign, the court eagerly collected countless texts from every corner of the Han empire. At that time, a major component of historians' responsibility was managing the imperial library and archives. Sima Qian thus had access to a wide range of texts and actively participated in cataloguing them,[9] which enabled him to complete *Records of the Historian*. Through this text, Sima greatly contributed to stabilizing early texts in two ways. First, with a cornucopia of writings at his fingertips, Sima built the concept of authorship by attributing particular titles to individual authors, frequently mentioning or quoting from many texts, from a couple of sentences to thousands of words.[10] Second, *Records of the His-*

torian initiated a new stage of textual history—an era of "closed" texts. Despite its uneven quality from chapter to chapter, the text per se is a result of Sima's attempt to build coherent accounts, an endeavor that had not been observed before. The fragmentation and fluidity of most texts before *Records of the Historian* determined that they would tend to have short, isolated, and self-contained passages. Narrative collections often organized texts according to the chronology, theme, and subject they recounted. Sima Qian broke with previous practices and created a new framework for unified and stabilized accounts. When possible, he streamlined individual episodes into an integrated chapter with a fixed linear structure. He designed his exquisite chapters with a fixed textual sequence that the reader must follow in order to seek meaning. Setting *Records of the Historian* against both excavated and received texts shows that Sima Qian lived at a turning point of Chinese textual history and that during this formative period of new literary concepts, *Records of the Historian* was one of the earliest texts that manifest the role of an author in the modern sense.

Historical writings not only experienced the trend of textual stabilization but also reached their peak within this transformative era. It is within this historical context that I analyze the relationship between the form and rhetorical function of historical writings, new territory in Chinese historiography. In particular, these texts deserve special attention because their primary form, narrative, is heavily subject to structural manipulation, which then leads to shifts in meaning. Although these histories all center on matters of political significance, such as battles, power, morality, and order, and some even recount the same facts, historians imbued their texts with different ideologies within various periods of the trend of textual stabilization. Before *Records of the Historian*, the most influential historical text, *Zuozhuan* 左傳 (*Zuo Commentary*),[11] dated to the fourth century BCE, follows an annalistic framework; after *Records of the Historian*, *Hanshu* 漢書 (*History of the Han*)[12] was completed around 80 CE with an overall structure heavily influenced by *Records of the Historian*. As the linchpin in this evolution, *Records of the Historian* uses *Zuo Commentary* as one of its major sources while providing *History of the Han* with a large amount of material. During the golden age of Chinese historical writings, these histories demonstrate different modes of representing the past.

The central argument of the current study is that historians in different stages of early China employed various narrative devices to retell their own vision of the past. Specifically, the narrative structure of *Records of the Historian* gives rise to its emphasis on overall, interrelated, long-term historical processes—elevating them to a level that they become as important as, or even more important than, the outcome of an event. Earlier and later histories such as *Zuo Commentary* and *History of the Han* primarily focus on single events: the former predominantly explains historical events through the lens of morality and ritual propriety; the latter principally judges historical figures on the basis of isolated facts. It is *Records of the Historian*'s unparalleled emphasis on the processes that makes the text an outlier among early Chinese historical writings, prompting readers to extract their individual lessons from *Records of the Historian*.

The Tradition of Biographical Reading

Although narrative in nature, early historical works have received little attention from a narratological perspective.[13] Beginning with the Six Dynasties (220–589), premodern scholars mostly based their interpretations of *Records of the Historian* on reading Sima Qian's biographical experiences into the text, a result of the long Chinese tradition of emphasizing authorial intent. This method pays close attention to the author's feelings and emotions, using them to interpret literary works, whether poems or prose. This approach holds that authors encode feelings and emotions in their works and thereby convey their intentions to the reader. In this situation, a qualified reader is expected to not only read the words as written but also to grasp the hidden meaning that the author embedded between the lines. This deep communication reaches beyond straightforward reading; it was considered the ultimate way to appreciate the beauty of literature.

This literary tradition of seeking out authorial intent has also been applied in Chinese historiography since the Han. The most prominent example is the Confucian classic *Chunqiu* 春秋 (*Annals of Spring and Autumn*), a laconic chronicle traditionally attributed to Confucius (551–479 BCE) that lists significant events from 722 to 481 BCE. It was believed that the sage composed (or edited) the *Chunqiu* out of political frustration and encoded great righteousness in subtle words (*weiyan dayi* 微言大義) in this book with the intention of criticizing the son of Heaven, restricting the regional lords, and attacking the grandees (貶天子, 退諸

侯, 討大夫) during the turbulent era that he lived in. Commentators from later generations have interpreted the revered classic by searching for Confucius's hidden intention.

This tradition has set the tone for interpreting *Records of the Historian*. For generations, scholars have looked for clues to Sima Qian's intention from his biographical experiences. Two crucial questions have been particularly emphasized: how he started to work on *Records of the Historian* and why he was punished by castration. Together, the underlying events have created Sima Qian's persona as a heroic writer in numerous readers' minds. The first is narrated in the postface (chapter 130) of *Records of the Historian*, "Taishigong zixu" 太史公自序 (The Grand Historian's Self-Narration), which tells us that Sima Qian took over the project from his father. As an earlier historian at Emperor Wu's court, the father had initiated *Records of the Historian* but could not complete it because of a fatal illness; on his deathbed, he entrusted the task of continuing *Records of the Historian* to his son.[14] Later, Sima Qian succeeded to his father's position at the court and completed the book by taking Confucius as his model.

The second key event, Sima Qian's castration, is one of the most famous tragedies in Chinese literary history, yet this incident is not recounted in *Records of the Historian* but in the "Bao Ren An shu" 報任安書 (The Letter in Reply to Ren An),[15] a letter of uncertain authorship[16] but believed to be Sima Qian's response to the contemporary official Ren An (d. 91 BCE). It recalls that General Li Ling 李陵 joined a military campaign against the Xiongnu, a nomadic enemy group in the north. Although he had fought with great courage in a hopeless situation, the general eventually surrendered to the enemy, a fact that the emperor regarded as a stigma on the Han. Sima Qian's defense of the general at court enraged Emperor Wu, causing the throne to charge Sima with *wuwang* 誣罔 (prevarication and deceit).[17] Facing the sentence of death, Sima chose to be castrated as an alternative penalty, even though this was an extreme disgrace for his entire lineage. In order to finish *Records of the Historian*, he did not make the easier decision to commit suicide.[18]

Having records of these two major incidents has made it plausible to infer a relationship between the incidents and Sima Qian's motivation for composing *Records of the Historian*. Since the Six Dynasties, Sima has been cast in three basic roles: a filial son who hopes to redeem himself from the shame of castration; a great historian who follows Confucius's footsteps to promote good order; a suffering writer who wishes to vent his resentment through his composition. Thereafter, *Records of the Historian* has been accordingly interpreted, first, as a text that was written to achieve eternal glory for the Sima family. To establish one's words (*liyan* 立言) was considered a legitimate means to secure the reputation of an author and his family.[19] Second, *Records of the Historian* is an emulation of Confucius's *Annals*, targeted at Emperor Wu or the First Emperor of Qin, who were both believed to have ruled by force. Lastly, Sima Qian used his brush to express the pain resulting from his shameful misfortune; *Records of the Historian* is thus a medium through which to seek true understanding of what it means to be a gentleman (*junzi* 君子).[20] The compatibility of these roles has led scholars of many generations, premodern and modern, to combine them to strengthen their specific interpretations. Their shared use of the biographical approach has not resulted in consensus; however, fundamentally contradictory arguments are common.[21]

The biographical reading offers a psychological lens to examine *Records of the Historian*, providing potential ways to understand it. This model of interpretation, which later became so influential, was not, however, the mainstream understanding of the text in early China. The negative view of *Records of the Historian* expressed by Emperor Cheng's high minister, as seen in the story at the beginning of this introduction—*Records of the Historian*'s contents are not in line with Confucian classics—was dominant by the end of the Western Han. Han scholars such as Yang Xiong (53 BCE–18 CE), Ban Biao (3–54 CE), and Ban Gu (32–92 CE) represent this criticizing view.[22] The Sima Qian discussed in subsequent literary analysis is not the historical Sima but his persona that shifted with the historical context of readers from various periods.[23]

Moreover, it is doubtful that one consistent philosophy can be extracted from the representation of all past events in *Records of the Historian*, as the massive text is heterogeneous and largely consists of two types of accounts, which I shall call the composite and the composed. The descriptions of events from China's legendary beginning to the Qin are mostly based on preexisting materials[24] over which Sima Qian did not have full control, despite his efforts to arrange them in a certain form. Several times in *Records of the Historian* he laments the lack of sources, which prevented him from completely controlling his text in two respects. First, he had meager fragments from texts antedating the dawn of Han and therefore could not integrate the individual components as an organic account. Second, the scarcity of sources prevented the historian from adding his own understanding of the events into *Records of the Historian*; the sources dictated his accounts. These chapters vary in degrees of integration but remain, overall, in a composite form, preventing us from inferring a clear and consistent intention on the part of the historian. Although patchy accounts and dull narratives constitute part of *Records of the Historian*, Sima's reputation as a master of literature has led critics to neglect these chapters.[25]

On the other hand, the chapters devoted to the Qin-Han transition and the Han dynasty are mostly a result of Sima's own composition. As previously noted, as a historian of the Han court, he had access to all kinds of earlier texts, official documents, and archives that the Qin left and the Han preserved in the imperial library. In addition, Sima Qian was not an armchair historian, relying solely on written sources. His position allowed for travel alongside the emperor. Scattered information in *Records of the Historian* suggests the use of oral sources such as transmitted traditions and his personal observations in various regions. Moreover, Sima also sought evidence from other channels, such as interviews with older officials and even their extended families, in order to handle contradictory information critically.[26] With more raw materials collected in many different ways, the "composed" chapters in *Records of the Historian* often exhibit a higher level of textual control than the "composite" accounts. In writing the former, Sima Qian had more freedom in identifying connections between events, interpreting their impacts, and building them into a logical chain that he believed in. *Records of the Historian*'s complexity naturally leads to constant disagreements over Sima Qian's supposed intentions.

More importantly, even if Sima Qian's intentions were consistent and unwaveringly applied—a questionable premise—it still would not follow that biographical reading is the only valid approach to *Records of the Historian*. Indeed, authorial intent is not always achievable. In 1946, William K. Wimsatt Jr. and Monroe C. Beardsley challenged the idea that a poem can always successfully convey the author's intention. Questioning the value of authorial intention for literary criticism, they argued: "One must ask how a critic expects to get an answer to the question about intention. How is he to find out what the poet tried to do? If the poet succeeded in doing it, then the poem itself shows what he was trying to do. And if the poet did not succeed, then the poem is not adequate evidence, and the critic must go outside the poem—for evidence of an intention that did not become effective in the poem."²⁷ This is to say that while the author's intention(s) may have given rise to a poem, such motivations are typically neither available nor desirable as a standard for judging the success of the poem. As soon as a poem has a reader, it belongs to the public, not the author.

In 1975, the German literary critic Hans-Georg Gadamer (1900–2002) analyzed how texts become meaningful to individual readers in the reading process in general. Without denying the possibility that the reader may grasp the author's intention, Gadamer pointed out that the limited capability of language and the reader's impulsive participation during the reading process inevitably cause divergent interpretations of a single text. This is because our understanding or interpretation of objects and events is always conditioned or shaped by our historical situation in ways that are not transparent even to ourselves. A circumstance does not so much impede as enable knowledge and experience; when we comprehend something (a text, for instance), we always understand it differently from the way others understand it, a difference that does not necessarily amount to an error in judgment. Even the same reader may respond differently when he or she reads the same work at different stages of life.²⁸

These twentieth-century insights prompt a reexamination of the goal(s) behind analyzing Sima's authorial intent. He certainly compiled *Records of the Historian* with some intentions in mind, and he may or may not have revised those intentions after his castration (it remains unclear exactly when this incident occurred and whether it was a cause or result of *Records of the Historian*); but this does not imply that there is only one way to understand *Records of the Historian*. The very multiplicity of the debates—whether a word, sentence, or chapter in the text is a satire; whether Emperor Wu or the First Emperor was Sima's target; and so on—corresponds to the divergence of interpretations that Gadamer analyzes. These interpretations are the results of various readers' reactions in their own age and environment.

In sum, this is not to deny the value of the biographical approach as one way to interpret *Records of the Historian*. The meticulous, centuries-long examination of Sima Qian's personal experiences has contributed to our understanding of his role as a prominent historical figure and of the circumstances of the era in which he lived. Yet the extreme richness of *Records of the Historian* demands that the text be opened up to other potential interpretive approaches.

Returning to the Narratives

The current study aims to shift our attention from authorial intention to the text itself. It is the narratives in *Records of the Historian*, rather than Sima Qian's intentions, that establish the text's monumental stature in Chinese historiography and literary history. Instead of reading between the lines to identify hidden intentions, the current study examines the relationship between *Records of the Historian*'s structure and rhetorical function, opening an alternative window to interpret the text.

Sima Qian created a model that organizes *Records of the Historian*'s one hundred and thirty chapters into five divisions: twelve chapters in the form of *benji* 本紀 (Basic Annals) are devoted to early dynasties as well as individual rulers in the Qin-Han era;[29] the ten chapters of *biao* 表 (Tables) list major events chronologically and report the sequence of rulers, famous ministers, and other noteworthy figures; the eight chapters of *shu* 書 (Treatises) cover a wide range of crucial political and administrative topics, including rites, music, military power, the calendar, astrology, sacrifices, topography, and economy; the thirty chapters in the *Shijia* 世家 (Hereditary Houses) section describe promising families of the Zhou and Han dynasties, recounting their rise and fall over generations; and the seventy chapters in the most widely read section, *liezhuan* 列傳[30] (Arrayed Traditions), recall diverse persons, including statesmen, generals, jokesters, fortune tellers, assassins, women, ethnic groups from neighboring lands, and so on. Despite the differentiation of the five sections, all of the chapters consist of narratives; each chapter has a theme and contains one or multiple accounts. The subjects of the accounts vary, but all the accounts primarily center on historical figures within the political realm.

Within the accounts, Sima Qian's most innovative contribution to Chinese historiography and textual tradition was their unprecedented narrative structure. Earlier historical works were largely self-contained episodes of single events organized on annalistic or geographic principles. *Records of the Historian* marks the appearance of the first complete and coherent historiographical accounts assembled from a series of episodes; many scattered and self-contained anecdotes of earlier histories became full accounts following a storyline with a beginning, a middle, and an ending. These storylines usually commence with the subject's birth and end with his or her death, or proceed from the subject's rise and fall seen from some particular perspective. This creative linear sequence that frames many accounts enables meticulous arrangement and correlation between multiple episodes to illuminate a subject's life journey. The biographical accounts of historical figures in the *liezhuan* section heralded biography as a genre in Chinese textual history.

Narratology analyzes how structural changes affect meanings of what is narrated, integrating contents and form seamlessly. This focus on the relationship between textual structure and narrative meaning allows us to put aside Sima Qian's intention and return to *Records of the Historian*. In this study, I apply narratological theories from Gérard Genette (1930–2018), who examined the common features of narratives by focusing on their structures. By placing *Records of the Historian* and other influential narrative texts into this framework, I systematically examine three dimensions of these texts: how the sequence of events builds causality, what is slowed down and sped up to control information, and how the text provides multiple perspectives to view the same events.

Genette treats narrative as an assemblage of information regarding one or more events. In order to reveal a narrator's manipulation of a narrative, Genette distinguishes "between the narrative text, the story it recounts, and the narrating instance (the producing narrative act—as inscribed in the text—and the context in which that act occurs)."[31] Genette points out that "analysis of narrative discourse is essentially a study of three sets of relations between narrative and story, between narrative and narrating, and (to the extent that they are inscribed in the narrative discourse) between story and narrating."[32] Through these three sets of relations, the theorist reveals the differences between story and narrative, revealing which structural changes affect the writer's feeding of information to the reader.

Historians' task is to narrate, turning bygone events into narratives. As Hayden White points out, "Histories (and philosophies of history as well) combine a certain amount of 'data,' theoretical concepts for 'explaining' these data, and a narrative structure for their presentation as an icon of sets of events presumed to have occurred in times past."[33] It is unsurprising that the same events can be represented in remarkably different ways in texts; when narrating the past, historians inevitably bring their personal perceptions and the historical context of their age into their accounts. In doing so, historians need not change the basic facts, such as the major participants, their actions, and the outcome; nor are they allowed by custom to do so. Any single technique or combination of these—connecting two events with a different logic, controlling the amount of information, and changing the perspective—already suffices to shift the emphasis or even brings to bear an opposite reading of the same events, consciously or unconsciously. Thus, a historian's retelling is only one possible version of the past.

Among the dimensions of narrative that Genette examined, three are of particular value to historical writing. The first deals with temporal distortions (that is, manipulation of the chronological order of events), which affect relationships of linking, alternation, and/or embedding among the different lines of action that make up the story. Regarding the sequence in which events actually occurred and their order in the narrative, there are four types of relationships: chronological order, prolepsis (prophecy), analepsis (flashback), and the sequenced reporting of simultaneous scenes. Through these temporal manipulations, early Chinese historians integrated moral codes, obedience to rules of ritual, inner qualities of historical figures, and other elements into a cause-and-effect chain in a narrative, building the causality of the past.

The second dimension is about narrative information management. The narrator controls the narrative "representation," or, more precisely, narrative information. For example, how many details should be furnished? In what way(s)? Like other narrators, historians inevitably need to decide what can be omitted, what deserves to be included, and to what degree they want to elaborate on details when reporting episodes. When historians speed up their narration, readers receive less information; when the narration slows down, readers have access to more details. Comparisons between *Records of the Historian* and both earlier and later histories shed light on its pattern of abbreviating and expanding, helping us see where the historians spend their valuable energy and clarifying their emphases in the text.

The third dimension that is particularly inspiring for analyzing historical writings is point of view, which filters information through the perspective of the narrator or a character. When a narrative describes an event, the reader receives information through one or more points of view, whether from a character within an account or from the historian who narrates the story. Point of view is conditioned by identity, social status, perception of political issues, and many other factors. Through a character's speeches and thought, historical writings present one or more perspectives of the participants who act within various relationships in the political realm. The interactions and correlations among characters inspire readers to contemplate their own explanation of the reported history.

My application of theories originating from a non-Chinese tradition may trouble some readers. Admittedly, Chinese historiography has been a long-lasting practice and has developed its own characteristics; and Genette's theories are based on French literary works. However, his framework is not affected by the language in which the tale is told but, rather, analyzes generic structural dimensions that mold a narrative regardless of its media and originating culture. It is exactly the exotic origin of this framework that allows us to break free of certain entrenched constraints.

This new approach entails four methodological shifts. First, Genette's framework refocuses attention from the author's intention and biographical experiences to the narratives per se, letting the historical writings speak for themselves. Despite the impressive work that scholars have done to infer Sima Qian's motivations, such inferences remain speculative or vague in many cases. In contrast, Sima Qian's editorial traces are a solid reflection of the narrative devices that he used. Moreover, this new approach permits the interpretation of narrative texts of unknown or imprecise authorship. A large number of texts dated to early China are not connected to an author or are results of multiple hands across a long period of time; and even for those with widely accepted authorship, the attribution may be anachronistic.[34]

Second, we leave behind the notion of *"Chunqiu" bifa* 春秋筆法 (lit., the method of writing the *Annals of Spring and Autumn*), which is based on the traditional belief that Confucius carefully selected the words of the *Annals* to convey his penetrating criticism. Although the question of whether the canon has systematically applied this method of writing remains unresolved, many historians have followed (their conception of) Confucius's model. Some late imperial and modern scholars have asserted that *Records of the Historian* also adopts this method;[35] but there have been no systematic studies of the extent of its application. On the contrary, the detailed descriptions, creative structure, and complex narratives of *Records of the Historian* reveal Sima Qian's heavy divergence from the classic, and the ideal of reading *Records of the Historian* as some kind of latter-day *Chunqiu* is not compatible with the rich narrative features of *Records of the Historian* that I have listed.

Third, the narrative approach advances the study of complicated texts. In moving away from applying authorial intention, we can render contradictory facts and disconnected records in histories more amenable to analysis. Admitting that historians do not fully control their sources, we would not look for a tidy narration, attempt to rationalize patchy or inconsistent accounts, or select some pieces of "evidence" and ignore others. Our scope of examination extends from the chapters that are commonly regarded as compositional models to the accounts that are less unified and are seldom analyzed by literary scholars, for all the imperfections within these chapters disclose the difficulties facing historians and the arduous processes of editing that are elided in more integrated accounts. It is the imperfect accounts *and* the exquisite ones, taken together, that restore the true role that Sima Qian played at the turning point of Chinese textual history.

Fourth, examining *Records of the Historian* from the narratological perspective empowers us to transcend the arbitrary boundaries set by premodern concepts and modern disciplines. Despite the common narrative nature of history and *xiaoshuo* 小說 (fiction; lit., lesser speech—i.e., speech of lesser moral value), both of which require imaginative descriptions, premodern Chinese scholars deliberately drew a borderline between them. In premodern China, history was practiced and revered from private literary circles all the way to the imperial court, whereas *xiaoshuo*'s humble purpose of entertainment concealed their shared nature. Moreover, conservative critics bristle at the very suggestion of comparing history with *xiaoshuo*, on the grounds that one is truth and the other fiction. But treating them both as narrative allows us to draw an evolutive outline of the structural development of narrative texts.

Placing Sima Qian into the full context of Chinese historiography allows me to redefine his role in a broad sense. He was much more than a historian who edited and composed a historical work; nor was he simply a master of literature who built his reputation through literary skills. Rather, he was one of the pioneers who played a key role in turning fluid and fragmented passages into connected, coherent, fully formed compositions. Thereafter, unification and coherence became the common features for any full accounts, completely transforming the practice of reading and composition. With a stabilized textual sequence, literary techniques such as character development, creating suspense 懸念, and structural correspondence 結構呼應 all became possible. The examination of *Records of the Historian*'s place among early Chinese texts illuminates Sima Qian's defining influence in literary history and textual studies.

By showing Sima Qian's use of narrative devices in *Records of the Historian* and their effects in differentiating *Records of the Historian* from *Zuo Commentary* and *History of the Han*, this broad picture raises a missing subject in the current scholarship on Chinese historiography: the relationship between narrative structure and the rhetorical functions of Chinese historical writings. This issue deserves our attention. Early historians retold the past in different forms and styles, at times even rewriting historical events. Yet—in part due to the "*Chunqiu*" *bifa*'s reinforcement of the moral and didactic dimensions of historical writings—scholars have seldom analyzed what functions are fulfilled by historical writings. From the preimperial period to the Han dynasty, Chinese historical writings developed three major models—represented by *Zuo Commentary*, *Records of the Historian*, and *History of the Han*—all demonstrating textual characteristics and thereby causing divergences in their primary functions. The narratological analysis of these works allows us to understand how historians' manipulation of narrative structure affects the texts' rhetorical functions. The majority of entries in *Zuo Commentary* highlight the strong correspondence between causes and outcomes, promoting morality and ritual-obedience as the internal drive of historical direction. A large number of narratives in *History of the Han* mainly emphasize a character's performances in individual events, which, when assembled, provide a foundation of facts for a rational judge of moral standing. In contrast with these texts, *Records of the Historian* prioritizes the complicated and logical historical process that a dynasty, a state, a lineage, a historical person always experiences from rise to decline, prompting readers to extract their own lessons.

    The discrepancy between the primary rhetorical functions of *Records of the Historian* and those of *History of the Han* elucidates the development of narrative literature and dynastic histories. *Records of the Historian*'s exposition of a story's progression affords a prototype for Chinese narrative texts, particularly novels and fiction produced in the late imperial period. Numerous scholars and writers admirably emulated its structure and style to tell an interesting tale, whose reading pleasure comes from experiencing the process rather than merely knowing the outcome of events or what triggered that outcome. As the first dynastic history, *History of the Han* is a powerful model as it establishes standards of right and wrongdoings. Many later dynastic histories were modeled after *History of the Han*, rather than *Records of the Historian*, in their judgments of historical figures' actions. For these works, an interlocked and logical process is of less importance than connecting morality with political legitimacy, which is more practical and efficient in explaining a power's existence. Understanding the priorities of *Records of the Historian* and *History of the Han* is valuable for grasping their strong influence in literature and historiography, respectively.

Structure of the Book

It is a great fortune that, with the remarkable increase in the number of excavated manuscripts and the substantial number of historical works transmitted from early China, we have enough materials to place *Records of the Historian* in the evolution of historiography and, more broadly, the development of textual history. To illuminate the characteristics of *Records of the Historian*, I compare it with many other historical texts in the pages that follow. The two most frequently cited in this volume are *Zuo Commentary* and *History of the Han*. *Zuo Commentary* was compiled about two hundred years earlier than *Records of the Historian*, in the fourth century BCE.[36] As the lengthiest text extant from this era, it is the most significant source for events during the period it covers. As the fountainhead of the Chinese historiographical tradition, it has been transmitted as a commentary to *Chunqiu*, which gave its name to this period. (Unlike *Chunqiu*, *Zuo Commentary* does not stop at 481 BCE but carries the narrative to 468 BCE.) *Records of the Historian* refers to many events in the extant *Zuo Commentary*. *History of the Han* was compiled approximately 150 years after *Records of the Historian* by Ban Gu (and others).[37] *Records of the Historian* provided a large amount of material for *History of the Han*, which narrates the Western Han dynasty from its founding in 202 BCE to the death of the usurper Wang Mang 王莽 (45 BCE–23 CE). Because of the overlapping of time periods and sequences of compilation, parallel accounts between *Records of the Historian* and *Zuo Commentary* and between *Records of the Historian* and *History of the Han* allow for a comparative study of these histories.

This study consists of four chapters. Chapter 1 analyzes the transformation of reading sequence and its influence on the textual structure of *Records of the Historian*. Manuscripts from before and during Sima's time were largely open, loose, and fragmented passages, which did not impose a fixed reading order. Narrative units, as a category of these texts, tended to be short and self-contained passages that did not rely on a larger context of the book to convey meaning. Readers could thus pick one passage and move on to any other passage. *Records of* the Historian is the earliest extant text that shows an effort to connect individual anecdotes into a full and interrelated account of a historical person or subject. Despite the disintegration of certain chapters, many accounts demonstrate a strong effort to build coherent storylines, which are a precondition for foreshadowing, correspondence, twists, suspense, and character development. In the most successful chapters, the textual coherency empowered by the well-designed structure is so forceful that the reader must follow the events in their presented order. This revolutionary practice enormously extended the length of narratives, strengthened the overall textual stability, and enabled Sima Qian to put a representation of meaningful historical process at the center. This textual form established biographical writing as a genre in Chinese literary studies and provided a model of highlighting a coherent plotline for later novels and fiction.

Chapter 2 explores the temporal order of events in the *Records of the Historian*. Historians set up direct or indirect connections between earlier and later events in various ways, inspiring their readers to contemplate the causes of historical direction. I discuss four types of temporal sequence in narratology: the chronological type, the simultaneous type, prolepsis (anticipation), and analepsis (flashback), all of which are employed in *Records of the Historian*. Respectively, these types highlight cumulative causes, situational stimuli, the essential inner quality of character, and specific actions. By using these types of temporal sequences, Sima Qian built an unprecedentedly complicated causality. In contrast to *Zuo Commentary*, *Records of the Historian* presents multiple factors across time rather than identifying one cause for each outcome; in contrast to *History of the Han*, *Records of the Historian* highlights the overall logical chain rather than assembling facts under the name of a historical figure.

Chapter 3 examines the narrative speed of *Records of the Historian*—that is, where the text slows down or speeds up, and where it zooms in and out. The book shows a pattern in manifesting a continuous and accumulated process of power struggles. Two examples of usurpation—the Tian lineage's usurpation of Qi (eighth–fifth century BCE) and Empress Dowager Lü's (241–180 BCE) administration in Han—show that the text devotes more space to explain the rise and decline of powers. The narratives often slow down to provide substantial details regarding a historical figure's key strategies and their cumulative effects in the appropriation of power. The painstaking portrayals of a string of well-connected actions in *Records of the Historian* would be redundant for the purpose of teaching morality but display how the big changes took place. An ambitious reader in the political realm could even copy the process. In contrast, the parallel narratives of these two examples in *Zuo Commentary* and *History of the Han* highlight isolated facts for didactic purposes. The recurrent pattern of *Records of the Historian* reveals that the text is more concerned with the complexity of the historical process that occurred than with judging the morality of individual actions.

Chapter 4 switches to how *Records of the Historian* offers blended points of view in narration. Characters' direct speeches, intentions, and actions in *Records of the Historian* advance a convergent point of view. In particular, *Records of the Historian* goes further than its predecessors in presenting the characters' own perspectives. It is the earliest history to include numerous inner thoughts of the characters through descriptions of their speeches and intentions. Works such as *Zuo Commentary* and *Guoyu* 國語 (Discourses of the States) contain detailed descriptions of battles and discussions, but they do not often include individual characters' emotions, desires, and mental process. Unlike the characters in these earlier works, who speak for the authors behind the text as the authors try to convey moral lessons, *Records of the Historian* gives more freedom to its protagonists, antagonists, and supporting roles. Through multiple points of view that well match with characters' identities, readers of *Records of the Historian* understand the same events from multiple characters' motivations and pursuits in two important relationships in early China: that between ruler and minister and that between husband and wife. The dynamics—traced from submerged intentions to observable behavior—define boundaries of representative relationships in political realms.

For my textual analysis of stories, I have relied heavily on the extant *Zuo Commentary*, *Records of the Historian*, and *History of the Han* and have selected the representations of events dated to a wide range of historical periods. Although a complete understanding of all three voluminous books is unrealistic, this study attempts to capture a glimpse of their narrative characteristics. By presenting a useful narratological tool, this text-focused model expands our perspective on the premodern hermeneutic tradition and the evolution process of Chinese texts. In addition to offering specialists a new perspective for approaching historiographical texts, this study also contributes to our knowledge of Chinese narrative tradition.

Chapter 1

The Turn to Textual Unity

Today when we read fiction we open a book and naturally follow the passages according to the order in which they are presented. Rarely does one randomly pick a middle page, or skip the beginning, or jump to the end. This is because we know that doing any of these would cost substantial reading pleasure that can only be gained by following the unfolding of the plot, which has a beginning, middle, climax, and ending. Knowing the ending of a story differs significantly from being able to appreciate the aesthetic effects that accumulate as the narrative advances from beginning to end. One must read *Records of the Historian*'s accounts in exactly the same manner in order to fully understand its stories and appreciate its literary merits, despite the early date of the collection. Having picked an account, one must start with the first line and read the following text to the end. Randomly picking a few episodes from a narrative account would not only obscure the meaning of individual scenes but also cause difficulty in understanding the entire account.

Such a level of obedience to reading order, which is a precondition of literary unity, is naturally taken for granted in the contemporary world and thus easily slips the modern reader's mind, but the question of whether ancient readers had the same reading practice is critically important for us to fully understand the place of *Records of the Historian* among early Chinese texts. Yet this issue has received rare attention in text studies, narrative studies, and the entire field of early China studies. On the one hand, the text is not a completely single-authored work that was written from raw material, but a complicated symposium of composite and composed texts. Scholars across generations have noticed many contradictions and inconsistencies within related chapters and even within the same account.¹ On the other hand, the high level of obedience to the textual order required by the text has caused the widely accepted but problematic view that *Records of the Historian* is a masterpiece that is completely controlled by Sima Qian and that thus every word or sentence reflects the historian's resentment after the castration. The textual unity seen in many accounts, then, leads many scholars to go to the opposite pole, treating *Records of the Historian* as if it were just as unified and coherent as works dated to a much later era, when authors had greater control over their works.

What kind of text, then, is *Records of the Historian*? In particular, how should we understand the coexistence of the many contradictions and the high level of textual unity? The hybrid nature of *Records of the Historian* alerts us that we must restore the text to its historical context, in which "open" texts were becoming "closed" during the Western Han. The repositioning of the text within the ongoing textual transformation reveals *Records of the Historian*'s revolutionary significance in the textual development in early China and illuminates the formation of its literary characteristics. These two aspects together explain the validity of narratological method for such a complicated text.

Historical Context: Fragmentation and Fluidity of Early Texts

In the last few decades, a large number of tombs from the preimperial period to the first few decades of the Western Han were excavated, and in them were found manuscripts written on bamboo or wood slips. These early manuscripts mostly exist as independent textual units (*pian* 篇 bundles), a textual form distinctive from their received counterparts, the complete and large texts that circulate as whole books with ordered passages. These excavated texts are mostly fragmentary and fluid, forming a public reservoir of intellectual knowledge, including history, rhetoric, philosophy, politics, and so forth. The geographic breadth of the tombs and the diversity of textual topics verify that before these short units were compiled into books, they circulated independently for easier memorization and flexible insertion into teaching and persuasive political speech.²

Stand-alone passages of a similar nature or related to the same figures were often grouped together,³ but they formed a textual collection that differed drastically from a modern book in two aspects: their complicated authorship and their lack of interrelation between accounts. Instead of being associated with any particular authors, these texts commonly went through the hands of several authors, editors, or compilers, who (re)assembled and (re)ordered these passages when needed;[4] as William G. Boltz points out, "The practice of compiling texts from a reservoir of preexisting materials, combined with whatever newly composed material was called for, was not just widespread but perhaps the norm."[5] In this sense, the excavated texts show us the form and content of the accounts at the time that the texts were buried in tombs, a moment that stopped an ongoing editing process. Otherwise, they would have been edited again, because they were not yet closed.[6]

Such a text-making process and fluid textual structure unavoidably led to the detachment of one textual segment from another, which means that, although the author or editor has arranged the materials in a certain sequence, the reader does not have to follow their prescribed order at all. Since any given unit is typically unrelated to either the previous or the following entries, it does not matter which chapter or even entry the reader starts with. Moreover, over an entire book, readers should not expect a logical order that strings the individual chapters together to a conclusion. They can proceed to any chapter. Even within the same chapter, when the entries were grouped together under the same theme, two neighboring entries could be completely unrelated in content. In these cases, a reader should not worry about missing any important clues or failing to fully understand any other entry. The reading order of these texts completely depends on the reader's will.

Within this early Chinese textual tradition, narrative texts that record fictional and historical events are no exception. In the aforementioned public intellectual reservoir, one prevailing category of knowledge revolves around history and mainly consists of short, freestanding stories. In fact, it is also the largest category.[7] Most of them are short passages focusing on single events to illustrate a principle, to make an argument, or to teach certain rhetorical skills. Some examples are conversations attributed to kings and their consultants, anecdotes regarding famous historical figures, or past events illustrating philosophical principles. Factual differences between records of the same story in different texts are easy to find, because variations are deliberately made to enable the various transmitters to highlight different aspects of a core story for their own purposes. By the late Warring States period (third century BCE), these stories were expansively spread and employed in historical and philosophical writings.⁸ Texts such as *Lüshi Chunqiu* 呂氏春秋 (Master Lü's Annals of Spring and Autumn), *Yanzi Chunqiu* 晏子春秋 (Master Yan's Annals of Spring and Autumn), *Hanfei zi* 韓非子 (Master Han Fei), and *Guanzi* 管子 (Master Guan) imply the existence of an immense anecdotal pool.⁹ The functions of these "Chunqiu" anecdotes determine that their meaning did not depend on their transmission, nor vice versa.

Meanwhile, a large collection of stories is preserved in the historiographical works. The court historians take advantage of both the anecdotes from the public intellectual reservoir and their own records. One distinction of the historical writings is that their records only focus on historical events and political speeches, although their contents overlap to some degree with those preserved in the "Chunqiu" texts mentioned earlier. The other distinction is that historians systematically aggregated entries to form vast historical writings. Regardless of the two differences, most entries in historical writings remain self-contained narratives.

Three common organizing styles dominated early historical texts. *Zuo Commentary* and *Discourses of the States*, both dated to around the fourth century BCE, represent the two most important styles: *biannian ti* (the annal style) and *guobie ti* (the state-centered style), respectively. Although the ancient and the received *Zuo Commentary* are not completely the same, the ancient *Zuo Commentary* did follow a year-by-year framework, like its current form,¹⁰ and most of its entries were self-contained stories. The latter text, *Discourses of the States*, recounts some of the same events as *Zuo Commentary*, with or without significant differences.¹¹ But *Discourses of the States* groups its entries according to geographical locations, that is, eight competing states, each in one or more chapters. While entries in every chapter follow a chronological order, they are disjointed units with lengthy speeches framed by a minimum of historical context. Another text organized in this style is *Zhanguo ce* 戰國策 (Stratagems of the Warring States), a book that is filled with pre-Qin materials and was collated by the Han bibliographer 劉向 Liu Xiang (79–8 BCE).¹² The third way to frame a narrative text during the Warring States period that is rarely seen today is genealogy. Many texts that Sima Qian referred to fall into this category. Two of them are *Shiben* 世本 (Roots of the Generations) and *Pudie* 譜諜 (Records of the Families), both of which record the royal genealogy of ancient rulers.¹³ These texts were lost, and it is unclear to what degree they were narrative, or whether they simply consisted of family trees; but some preserved fragments of *Shiben* show that it probably comprises brief entries, one for each emperor or king.[14] This structure might have inspired Sima Qian's creation of three of *Records of the Historian*'s divisions, *benji* (Basic Annals), *shijia* (Hereditary Houses), and *liezhuan* (Arrayed Traditions), which all organize materials in a linear fashion.

The fluid and disconnected textual features from the Warring States continued into the early Western Han. Some excavated texts dated to the Warring States period do show the compilers' preliminary efforts to connect a handful of *pian*, but the scale of these texts is rather limited, and connections are weak.[15] In 1973, archaeologists discovered the early Han manuscript *Zhangguo zonghengjia shu* 戰國縱橫家書 (A Text of the Strategists in the Warring States) in Mawangdui tomb no. 3 (sealed in 168 BCE). This well-preserved silk scroll contains twenty-seven self-contained anecdotal passages, each depicting a single scene.[16]

Another narrative text dated slightly later than the silk scroll is Lu Jia's 陸賈 (ca. 228–ca. 140 BCE) *Chu-Han Chunqiu* 楚漢春秋 (Annals of the Chu-Han Period), an important source for *Records of the Historian*'s narration of events during the Qin-Han transition. Records in *Records of the Historian*, *History of the Han*, and later official histories imply that Lu Jia's *Annals* was probably organized thematically, a structure that was adopted by many other philosophical works produced in the early Western Han.[17] Thus, one generation earlier than Sima Qian, it was still common for editors and compilers of narrative texts to structure them loosely. The tradition even continued toward the end of the Western Han.

Regardless of their organizing principles, all of the aforementioned texts, such as the various *Annals*, *Zuo Commentary*, *Discourses of the States*, or *A Text of the Strategists in the Warring States*, are composed of separate and independent units. Even though two or more consecutive entries focus on the same subject, readers still have a great deal of freedom in reading practice. What does the loose structure mean for narrative texts? It prevents accounts in the aforementioned texts from producing meaning as a unity. I take *Zuo Commentary* as an example to illustrate this point in four respects. First, the text recounts unrelated events occurring in the same year and splits apart single events that transpire over several years, making it extremely hard to trace the rise and fall of a state or family. As Hayden White suggests, annals have "no central subject, no well-marked beginning, middle, and end, no peripeteia, and no conclusion."[18] Similarly, events that transpire over several years are separated into several so-called single events defined by the editors, obscuring the events' possible causal relationships and far-reaching effects. Precisely for this reason, historians such as Gao Shiqi 高士奇 (1645–1703 CE) rearranged *Zuo Commentary* in a new style called the *jishi benmo* 紀事本末, which literally means to examine the roots and branches of recorded events in order to discern the interrelation between events and evaluate an event from the perspective of the big picture.[19]

Second, the lack of textual unity is also manifested in the scattered descriptions of the same characters. Although *Zuo Commentary* does depict a number of vivid characters, the structure of their descriptions prevents highly developed characterization on a larger scale. *Zuo Commentary* focuses on events with didactic codes rather than specific figures, leading to two outcomes: without any cross-references or a good grasp of the text, it is extremely hard to locate all the events in which a character appears; and regardless of the significance of characters, the text mentions them only to complete the narration of an event in which they participate. The fragmented descriptions of the same character distributed in multiple entries diminish the possibility of collectively understanding the motivation and deeds of a character with coherence. The long-ruling Lord Zhuang of Zheng 鄭莊公 (r. 743–701 BCE) is a typical example. *Zuo Commentary* begins with the power struggle between his brother and him in 722 BCE and continues, in dozens of entries appended over twenty-two years, to report events involving him until his death. He appears in multiple entries, but few entries focus on him, making it unlikely for readers to grasp a logical chain that explains his deeds.

Third, the self-contained episodes are very likely to raise conflicts between traits of the same character. As Gerald Prince has pointed out, "What we usually call a character is a topic (or 'logical participant') common to a set of propositions predicating of it at least some characteristics generally associated with human beings."[20] Thus, a character is a *logical* whole consisting of multiple propositions. When a proposition is successfully attached to a character in an entry, if the character is an important figure in several entries, it means that two or more propositions would coexist in the same character, and their compatibility becomes a key issue. Regardless of the organizing principles at work (e.g., chronology or geography), the fragmental and fluid self-contained accounts lack connections between two neighboring entries, obscuring any overarching coherence in the character's overall personality, let alone their character arc over their life span. Entries in *Zuo Commentary* stand on their own to convey meaning. The possibility that it was composed by multiple authors further decreases the likelihood of any unity in this text.[21] Little care was given to the conflicting propositions attached to the same personage in different entries. Lord Mu of Qin 秦穆公 (r. 659–621 BCE) is first portrayed as a paragon of a ruler, who wisely heeds his advisers and exhibits virtues when dealing with a neighboring state in the Battle of Han. Eighteen years later, however, despite pointed remonstration from his advisers, Lord Mu greedily launches the Battle of Yao, at which he is severely defeated.[22] King Zhuang of Chu 楚莊王 (r. 613–591 BCE) is presented as an exemplary ruler in some entries and an aggressive figure in others.[23] Applying Prince's definition of character, we can say that the representations of historical personages in *Zuo Commentary* and other pre-Han texts are characters; yet the propositions predicated of these particular characters lack interconnections between episodes, preventing the establishment of believable characters as seen in *Records of the Historian*.

Finally, the emphasis on morality, causality, or other messages may decrease the validity of a character's traits, as readers are not necessarily convinced by the similarities that a text strives to present between written versions of people and their real-world counterparts. If we agree with Prince that to report an event is to attach certain propositions to a "topic," then the attachment can fail in many occasions. The successful attachment only happens when the propositions are valid, in the sense that they help to illustrate the character's persona, not expound the author's doctrine. *Zuo Commentary* elaborates with striking details on the bare bones of events recorded in *Annals of the Spring and Autumn*, characterizing a handful of vivid historical personages such as Lord Wen of Jin and Lord Mu of Qin. But in many other cases, the propositions attributed to characters turn out to be invalid. For instance, it is not uncommon for a long conversation—filling dozens of lines or even several pages—to consist solely of didactic discourse that is simply placed in the mouth of a character. Promoting the author's teachings, these speeches morph from evaluations of a specific event or action into commentary on contemporary rituals and morality. Many speeches in *Zuo Commentary* do not provide readers with more information about a character. While the deeds of characters could sometimes supplement this lack, readers are still unable to attach traits to a character to perceive them as fully human.

Narratives organized according to themes and geographic locations, such as those in *Discourses of the States* and *Stratagems of the States*, reflect some or all of the aforementioned issues. In sum, authors of these texts emphasize specific knowledge that they have embedded into their accounts. These individual accounts are only readable on their own; when related entries are connected together, they bring varying and even mutually contradictory perspectives. Although some text makers showed preliminary concern for connection between textual segments, major pre-Han texts that we have access to are still open and fluid, in order to teach moral lessons and rhetorical skills in separate settings. It was from such a historical context that *Records of the Historian* later emerged.

Records of the Historian: The Turning Point

With the enormous social changes brought by the founding of the Qin and Han empires, early texts were structurally transformed from short, fluid, open passages to expanded, firmly established texts. The most well-known effort to finalize and "close" texts was that of Liu Xiang, followed by that of his son, Liu Xin, under Emperor Cheng's (r. 32–7 BCE) command in 26 BCE.[24] The Lius assembled and collated texts from across the empire to compile the imperial catalog, which was a large-scale effort involving numerous decisions regarding the contents, sequence, and authorship of earlier texts in various categories.[25] Nonetheless, decades earlier, Sima Qian and his father, Sima Tan, had already done some similar work to "lock" texts. According to the postface of *Records of the Historian*, "not a single text or historical event was left out by the grand historian" (天下遺文古事靡不畢集太史公).[26] *History of the Han* records that Emperor Wu established a policy of collecting writings, which was the beginning of official textual recovery.[27] Sima Qian's composition of *Records of the Historian* played a key role in stabilizing and finalizing texts, being the turning point from "open" to "closed" texts. *Records of the Historian* does so in two respects: first, it attributes hundreds of poems and prose texts to individuals by either preserving a literary work in an account devoted to a protagonist or connecting the literary production of a work to an individual's life experiences;[28] second, and most important to the current study, *Records of the Historian* imposes a revolutionary linear structure on self-contained passages to bring textual unity within extended accounts.

As discussed in the introduction, the tight association between Sima Qian's trauma of castration and the composition of *Records of the Historian*, established since the Six Dynasties (220–589), has caused the text to be studied as a whole for centuries. It seems that there are no differences between accounts in terms of the nature of composition and textual control. In fact, the degrees to which they were edited and their internal coherence vary significantly, from the most well-crafted accounts to the most meager chapters. Thus, according to the composition process, I divide all the narratives into two large categories: those compiled on the basis of preexisting materials—such as classics, genealogical records, and so on—and those composed from firsthand sources, such as archives and in-person experiences. When approaching *Records of the Historian*, we must make this distinction, since disclosing the complex nature of the text enables us to reveal the text's actual place in early Chinese textual history.

The compiled chapters tend to be accounts narrating the more distant eras before the Qin-Han era. First, the scarcity of the preexisting materials causes difficulty in achieving textual unity. Second, when sources have contradictions regarding the same event, *Records of the Historian* shows an inclination to preserve the contradictions rather than align them. On some occasions, inconsistencies and incoherence even happen within the same accounts. "The Hereditary House of Confucius" and the account devoted to Qu Yuan are two patchy accounts that remind us of these compiled narratives.[29] Although these passages generally follow a chronological order, they lack logical connections in between and need further integration.

On the other hand, the composed accounts in *Records of the Historian* recount the historical events in the Qin-Han era. These chapters streamline individual episodes into entities that tend to be highly unified, forming the new literary form *zhuan* 傳 (traditions). In the postface of *Records of the Historian*, Sima Qian summarizes his work as 整齊其世傳, which literally means to "put what has been transmitted about them [i.e., the subjects] over the generations into a neat order."[30] As a new way to organize materials, *zhuan* is a great departure from the earlier, annalistic form and thus has exclusively been debated as the rival form to annals within the historiographical tradition;[31] however, the linear unity seen in the most integrated chapters of *Records of the Historian* has been overlooked. By linear unity I mean that this new form provides a precondition to ensure a beginning, middle, climax, and logical end point.[32] This form is revolutionary in that, no matter who or what the subject is, the narrative framework often imposes on the account a pattern from birth to death, from rise to fall, from prosperity to decline, or from waxing to waning. Linear unity is critical for understanding the development of Chinese literature, because it is the premise for achieving textual unity.

The connotation of *zhuan* is noteworthy for two reasons. First, the largest section of *Records of the Historian* is titled *liezhuan* (Arrayed Traditions),³³ and the overall structure of *Records of the Historian* is called *ji-zhuan ti* 紀傳體 (annal-tradition style). Understanding this new form helps us study the narrative structure of *Records of the Historian*'s chapters, not only the *liezhuan* section but also the *benji* (Basic Annals) and the *shijia* (Hereditary Houses) sections. Second, this form has profoundly shaped the subsequent narrative literature. By the third century, the connotation of *zhuan* seemed to have narrowed down in meaning to indicate a genre that centers on the narration of a person's life from their birth to death. In the history of Chinese literature, biography (*zhuanji* 傳記) as a genre focusing on characters rather than events developed various subgenres such as autobiography, epitaph, biographical fiction, and so on.³⁴

In *Records of the Historian*, a well-integrated *liezhuan* account presents a protagonist's entire life, which typically begins with a formulaic profile including name(s), hometown (ancestral temple location), genealogy (if the person is connected to a promising figure in the same lineage), profession, and other introductory information, followed by episodes from the protagonist's childhood or early career, through the prime of life, to death.³⁵ Among the seventy chapters in the *liezhuan* division, sixty-four report the life experiences of one or more historical individuals by following the formulaic structure of *liezhuan*. The most well-crafted narratives pay particular attention to events with decisive and far-reaching effects and skillfully interweave them as early as in the opening of an account, which often includes the aforementioned formulaic profile and a few lines sketching the early years of the protagonist. Such an opening before the first full episode unfolds may seem insignificant or even trivial, but it is dexterously narrated and effectively prepares the reader to approach the account. In particular, it has one or all of the following three functions: (1) it introduces the family background of the hero, offering a clue to help readers understand the hero's rise, influence, or even the obstacles they will face during their era; (2) it sets up the historical context, so that readers can quickly grasp the environment in which the hero lived; (3) most importantly, it efficiently informs readers of the account's theme and thus its main direction. In sum, although such an opening is usually short, it plays a critical role in bonding the whole account together and illuminating its theme.

The opening passage of the "Traditions of the Noble Scion of Wei" (ch. 77) is typical:

魏公子無忌者，魏昭王少子而魏安釐王異母弟也。昭王薨，安釐王即位，封公子為信陵君。是時，范睢亡魏而相秦，以怨魏齊故，秦兵圍大梁，破魏華陽下軍，走芒卯。魏王及公子患之。公子為人仁而下士，士無賢不肖者皆謙而禮交之，不敢以其富貴驕士。士以此方數千里往歸之，至食客三千人。當是時，諸侯以公子賢，多客，不敢加兵謀魏十餘年。 36

The noble scion of Wei, Wuji, was the youngest son of King Zhao of Wei and the younger brother of Lord Anxi. After King Zhao passed away, King Anxi ascended to the throne and enfeoffed Wuji as Lord Xinling. At this time, Fan Sui had fled from Wei to serve Qin. Since he resented Wei and Qi, [he made] the Qin army besiege the Wei capital, Daliang, and defeated Wei's troops at Huayang, causing General Mang Mao to flee. The king of Wei and Lord Xinling were worried. Lord Xinling's personality was humane, and he humbled himself in front of the guest-retainers. He was modest and got along with all of them according to propriety, [whether they were] worthy or unworthy. He never dared to take pride in front of these guest-retainers because of his wealth and nobility. Therefore, the guest-retainers went to serve him from places that were thousands of *li* away, up to thousands of people. At that time, since the noble scion was worthy and had many guests, the regional lords did not dare for more than ten years to use their armies or to scheme against Wei.

This passage covers all the basic elements of a formulaic "profile" mentioned earlier. All of these elements are important and connected, jointly paving the way for the upcoming episodes. First, readers who are familiar with early Chinese texts would absolutely notice that the hero and the contemporary ruler of Wei, King Anxi, are half-brothers, a relationship that almost certainly leads to problems. This fact prepares readers for the first and last episodes in this account, which are both about the ruler's wariness of the hero's potential threat. The first episode narrates that the scion's guests make him so informative that the king does not dare to let him help with state affairs; the last episode recounts that, even though the king relies on the scion to save his state, he soon believes in the enemy's slandering of his half-brother and deposed him from the position of commander-in-chief in the army. Second, the passage highlights that, although the scion is born in the royal family, he is always humble and polite, showing respect to the guest-retainers in his residence and thus drawing thousands more to serve him. The close relationship between the scion and his guest-retainers is a key component that appears frequently in several other episodes. Third, the excerpt suggests that the scion has a strong influence upon interstate politics. Indeed, the entire account centers on how his virtues save his neighboring state and his own state. All of these elements contribute to the king's distrust of the protagonist and eventually lead to the latter's desperate death. The opening passage skillfully introduces the major themes that are also interconnected factors driving a series of events in the ensuing plot. In this way, the entire chapter is a tightly woven masterpiece.

In addition to the chapter-length *zhuan*, at other times *Records of the Historian* embeds "lesser" *zhuan* into the "greater" ones. A lesser *zhuan* often briefly introduces one or more supporting figures related to the subject. Such an introduction sketches part of the life experiences of the supporting figures (often from their birth or rise up to a certain historical moment linked to the protagonist), helping to smooth the plot or provide enough context on the subject. Although these "lesser" *zhuan* are usually shorter, they bear the same major characteristics listed earlier and are easy to find across sections of *Records of the Historian*. A splendid example is "The Arrayed Traditions of the Marquis of Weiji and Marquis of Wu'an" (ch. 107), which, after a banquet scene, inserts a short biography of Guan Ying, a key figure who inflames and intensifies the conflicts between the two marquises.[37] Even though it is just a few lines, the inserted account not only introduces all the aforementioned basic elements of a formulaic profile but also reveals what Prince, as previously noted, would call Guan Ying's key propositions: he earns a position in the court because of his brave fighting in pacifying the Wu-Chu rebellion and is removed from the position for violent behavior after drinking. More importantly, these propositions are connected later in the main storyline, serving to drive the conflicts between the two marquises forward. Despite the limit in length, the "lesser" *zhuan* accounts share many commonalities with the "greater" ones.

The *zhuan* form centering on a person is applied not only to the biographical section but also to other divisions of *Records of the Historian*.

For example, among the twelve chapters in the *benji* (Basic Annals) segment, eight are fully devoted to rulers, including emperors, or executives without the title of emperor but who are actually in charge of the empire.[38] The structure of these chapters is as the same as that of the *zhuan* accounts in the *liezhuan* section; the only difference is the social status of the protagonists. The most adept chapters on rulers contain juicy episodes recounting events from long before the rulers' ascent to the throne to their last moment in life.

On other occasions, the *zhuan* structure is extended to chapters centering on a dynasty, a lineage, or a regional regime. While the subjects of these chapters are not historical individuals, these chapters adopt the same form as person-focused traditions. As Lu Yaodong noticed, Sima Qian uses characters as a way to collect a series of related events within one account, just as the annals use chronologies to do so.[39] Each of the remaining four chapters in the *benji* division narrates a pre-Han dynasty; the *shijia* (Hereditary Houses) chapters recount the influential families, generation by generation; and six chapters in the *liezhuan* section introduce six regional powers, reporting their origin, development, and decline.[40] Despite their varying subjects and varied degrees of textual unity, these chapters are composed of a string of human-focused units, together making up a large *zhuan* chapter that also follows the cycle of rise and decline for their subjects. In this sense, all of the narrative chapters in *Records of the Historian* are structured in the same fashion, with no fundamental difference in nature.

In comparison to entries in *Zuo Commentary*, *Master Lü's Annals of Spring and Autumn*, *A Text of the Strategists in the Warring States*, and probably *Annals of the Chu-Han Period* as well, accounts in *Records of the Historian* are distinct in three respects. First, the *Records of the Historian* accounts are extended to a significant degree. Most entries in these earlier writings range from several dozens to hundreds of characters; but in *Records of the Historian*, accounts written in several thousand or even tens of thousands of characters are not uncommon. Second, although a historical figure may appear in other chapters, he is definitely the center in his own account, rather than serving the narration of an event. For example, while many officials appear as supporting characters in their rulers' accounts, they are undeniably the protagonists in their own chapters, which revolve around their development and decline. The third and most radical difference is that the *zhuan* form brings linearity to *Records of the Historian*'s narratives. These three qualities prioritize the linear structure, even at the cost of intensive labor—recording the same events multiple times in related chapters. The same historical events, especially the big ones, have different impacts upon different historical figures. In many meticulously composed chapters, the careful selection of episodes pertaining to the protagonist even ensures that each event is presented as a factor impacting his rise or decline. For example, "The Arrayed Traditions of Wu Zixu" (ch. 66) recounts the entire life of the hero, a filial son and witty political figure who avenges the deaths of his father and older brother. The protagonist eventually defeats the Chu by using the Wu armies. Although *Records of the Historian* narrates the battles between the two states in "The Hereditary House of Tai Bo of Wu" (ch. 31) and "The Hereditary House of Chu" (ch. 40), Sima Qian took pains to renarrate them in Wu Zixu's chapter to relate the battles to the hero's personal resentment and pursuit of revenge. Besides, events such as his flight to Wu, the power struggle within Wu's court, his relationship with the two Wu kings, and so on are presented as factors contributing to his seizing of power and helpless suicide.

Similarly, the technique of arranging all the components of a story along a common thematic thread is used in some of the dynasty-focused *benji* (Basic Annals) chapters. The composition of these *benji* chapters may be constrained by the scarcity of sources and the limited length of accounts representing long spans of time, but Sima Qian still embeds a thread to organize all the events whenever possible. For instance, "The Basic Annals of Zhou" (ch. 4) begins with the virtuous ancestors of Zhou, followed by stories of every Zhou king from the dynasty's official founder King Wen (d. 1050 BCE) to the last ruler's death in 256 BCE, either briefly or in great detail. From time to time, the text marks the significance of individual events by telling the reader to what extent the dynasty rose or declined, reminding the readers of the overall picture. Although the chief threads of these chapters are less tight than those of the *liezhuan* chapters, at least the subthread within a king's reign is evident. The accounts of two notorious rulers, King Li (r. 857/53–842/28 BCE) and King You (r. 781–771 BCE), take up much more space. Particularly, the text carefully depicts the latter, the last ruler of the Western Zhou. His misconduct follows a logical thread in his *zhuan*, which strings together the events that eventually lead to the king's death and also the dynastic downfall.[41]

The same principle is applied to the "Hereditary House" section, whose chapters are mostly devoted to promising families. Many chapters in this section are not evenly edited; even within the same account, some rulers have a more unified subaccount; others have a disjointed one. But the author's attempt to impose a linear structure is clear. For example, Lord Xian's (r. 676–651 BCE) *zhuan* in "The Hereditary House of Jin" (ch. 39) is more carefully crafted than those of other rulers in the chapter, as we will see in my analysis in chapter 4. This complete image of Lord Xian as an unwise ruler contrasts markedly with his fragmented and sketchy persona in *Zuo Commentary*. Despite the varied levels of unification seen in "Basic Annals" and "Hereditary House" chapters, multiple rulers' subaccounts together outline the general picture of the rise and fall of a dynasty or state.

The linear framework built into these chapters not only extends a thread from beginning to end but also provides a structural foundation to strengthen the mortar between the bricks—interconnections between episodes. When compiling the accounts, Sima Qian did not simply aggregate scattered records from their sources but strove to tightly knit them together, turning each chapter into an integrated whole. Unlike the fragmented entries in earlier narrative works, many episodes in *Records of the Historian* are interlocked components depending on each other for meaning. In a given account, a previous episode relates to and paves the way for the next, which removes the autonomy that characterized the texts of pre-Han authors. In Sima's narration, an earlier episode might even be suspended for a while and resumed after a few episodes. For example, in "The Traditions of the Noble Scion of Wei," the disrespectful reactions of two supporting characters, Hou Sheng and Zhu Hai, to the protagonist are left off in the middle. The author does not explain until several passages later,[42] effectively stimulating readers' interest in finding an answer in the subsequent narration and reinforcing the hero's humble attitude toward his guests. *Records of the Historian* secures a reading order that readers must follow to take away the utmost meaning of an account. Having picked an integrated chapter, if one randomly picks an individual episode from it, the text is still readable or even entertaining to some degree; but this one glimpse into the protagonist's life hardly empowers a full understanding of the episode's significance in the unceasing cord of rise and fall; one can reap the fruit of such understanding only by following the exact order set up by Sima Qian.

Records of the Historian has numerous examples of tightly knit episodes. As discussed earlier, "The Arrayed Traditions of the Marquis of Weiji and Marquis of Wu'an" includes Guan Ying's "lesser traditions" to introduce his reckless personality and foreshadow his acts in the later plot. The short account of Guan Ying is an indispensable component of the entire chapter because it presages a series of Guan Ying's impetuous behaviors. One is in the subsequent episode at the Marquis of Wu'an's wedding banquet, which is the direct (but not the only) fuse leading to the irreconcilable rupture between the two marquises. They both insist on their respective standing and quickly expand the debate to the court, in front of the emperor and other ministers. The account also introduces the firm friendship between the Marquis of Weiji and Guan Ying, which paves the way for the two's alliance in confronting Wu'an. Another example is the "Hereditary House of Chen She" (ch. 48), which revolves around the uprising leader who subverted the Qin dynasty. From the very beginning, the account reveals that the hero is ambitious when he is still a hired laborer working in fields, which accounts for his extraordinary leadership in overthrowing the Qin. Even though he was no more than a commoner during the early years, the very first episode in the chapter recounts that when another workhand laughs at his aspiration to become prominent in the future, Chen She analogizes that man as a little sparrow who does not understand the ambitions of a swan.[43] This episode not only completes the hero's account by including his early years but also vividly reveals his ambition to prepare readers for his initial uprising. Thus, readers would not be surprised that a lowly peasant could shock the world.

Returning to my division of compiled chapters and composed accounts in *Records of the Historian*, their coexistence demonstrates that *Records of the Historian* was at the tip of the new literary era of "closed texts." Although some chapters are not as skillful as others, Sima Qian's efforts to adopt a linear framework are evident. This framework stabilizes text composition and secures the reading sequence to an unprecedented degree. The next two sections in this chapter illustrate the strong textual unification best embodied in *Records of the Historian*'s characters.

Consistency in Character

Due to the relatively shorter life span of individuals in comparison to other subjects, such as influential lineages and dynasties, the most unified accounts in the text are those focusing on a protagonist. As introduced in the first section in this chapter, Gerald Prince defines character as "topic."⁴⁴ Accepting this definition, I deconstruct characters in *Records of the Historian* into series of episodes to show how Sima Qian develops consistent threads throughout the narration. I pick characters within chapters rather than other subjects in *Records of the Historian* because their life span is the shortest, and thus they best illustrate the unification of the accounts. Chapters accounting for multiple generations of families and dynasties do not. The goal of my discussion is not to show *Records of the Historian*'s excellent characterization skills, but how the linear structure enabled the authors to lay out historical processes.

Previous scholarship has devoted much attention to the text's diverse categories of character descriptions, such as appearance, personality, emotion, motivation, speech, and logic, which are exceptionally individualized and well matched to each character's temperament, education level, and even region of origin.⁴⁵ Nonetheless, the large number of impressive characters in the text does not owe much to the variety of these categories of descriptions. Instead, when all of the propositions are valid, the decisive elements are interrelations and correspondences between these seemingly cross-category descriptions. The linear structure of *Records of the Historian*'s accounts allows the author to repeatedly attach the main and essential propositions to a protagonist throughout an account. These propositions together create his consistent personality and coherent behavior, which real people possess in life. Several cross-category descriptions may attach the same trait to a character; it is the continuity of the same embedded traits that causes readers to perceive the protagonist as behaving consistently and logically. Indeed, an account is thus a textual layout of character traits through a series of episodes, relying heavily on a controlled and linear textual structure.

This calculated consistency is widely seen in *Records of the Historian*'s characters.⁴⁶ No earlier narrative texts show such a feature. The best example of a consistent character is in "The Basic Annals of Xiang Yu" (ch. 7), a masterpiece that stands on its own. The hero, Xiang Yu 項羽 (232–202 BCE; also known as the King of Xiang), was a noble warrior who rose at the end of the Qin dynasty and became a dictator followed by a group of major warlords. Although he led a coalition force to subvert the Qin dynasty in merely three years, his rival, Liu Bang 劉邦 (r. 202–195 BCE), eventually defeated him and founded the Han dynasty. Since *Records of the Historian* devotes an entire chapter to each of the rivals—each beginning the narration from the protagonist's early years, long before the starting point of his political career—it has been a tradition to read the rivals' chapters side by side. Whereas this "horizontal" (comparative) reading highlights the parallel episodes in these two chapters and thereby emphasizes the rivals' contrasting personalities,[47] my examination of Xiang Yu as the most vivid character in *Records of the Historian* reveals the effects of "vertical" (linear) textual arrangement within his chapter as a unity.

Arranged in the *liezhuan* form, "The Basic Annals of Xiang Yu" depicts many aspects of a courageous and tragic warrior, including his ambition, physical strength, individual heroism, honor of nobility, and so on; but four qualifications, consisting of two rival pairs, are most essential—namely, (1) agility and recklessness and (2) candidness and simplemindedness—the two traits in each pair are compatible with each other but can produce completely opposite effects on different occasions. For example, agility and recklessness are two sides of one personality. The same goes for the second pair. The chapter also demonstrates other propositions, but they are extended from these four basic ones to reveal both the rise and fall of Xiang Yu. Immediately after the routine profile introduction to Xiang Yu and the Xiang family's military history, the narrative repeatedly attaches the four aforementioned traits to the hero throughout the literary presentations of his life experiences, from the first episode to the last scene. The first two episodes preview the protagonist's personality and philosophy, setting up the fundamental color of the character and establishing a coherent logical chain that guides the entire chapter.

Although Xiang Yu's chapter is in the "Basic Annals" division, it begins with the sort of well-crafted opening typical of many "Arrayed Traditions" accounts. It describes the hero's teenage period, before his military career began. Immediately following the formulaic profile are two brief episodes that efficiently pave the way for the rest of the plot. In the first, Xiang Yu's uncle arranges for him to study first writing and later swordsmanship, but this young man quits both before mastering either. He rationalizes the latter decision by declaring that, while swordsmanship assumes just a single man as one's opponent, he himself yearns to take on ten thousand men. Although his uncle later teaches him the art of warfare at his request, Xiang Yu again fails to learn the craft thoroughly. The other episode depicts a scene in which the uncle and nephew witness the First Emperor's imperial processions in 210 BCE. At the age of twenty-three, Xiang Yu dares to say: "That man can be taken and replaced!" His uncle quickly covers Xiang Yu's mouth, anxiously telling him, "Don't speak recklessly! The entire class will be executed!"[48] Thereafter, the uncle treats his nephew with peculiar respect. The opening then ends with a sketch of Xiang Yu's extraordinary height, physical strength, and competence, closing with the comment that all of the local young people were afraid him. Both of the episodes skillfully attach one of the main traits to the topic "Xiang Yu": the first portrays his recklessness (lack of discipline), and the second illustrates his straightforwardness or simple-mindedness (lack of sophistication). These two traits both contribute to the hero's rise and fall as an important political figure.

These characteristics that are embedded in the protagonist's early years continue to impact his behavior after he embarks on a military career, when the Qin Empire is shocked by uprisings from the six states previously unified by the Qin. On his journey to power, one episode of particular importance is Xiang Yu's assassination of his superior, the general-in-chief Song Yi. In comparison to the famous scenes such as the banquet at Hongmen, this critical step upward in the power hierarchy has rarely been discussed in previous scholarship; indeed, this assassination episode is a backstory for the hero's first battle—later known as the "Battle at Julu"—which establishes his leadership and power in the Chu army. Earlier, when Xiang Yu's uncle initially launches Chu's uprising against Qin, Xiang Yu is merely one of many generals in the camp. Xiang Yu follows Song Yi on a mission to rescue the uprising troops in Zhao that are surrounded by the Qin troops, but the two generals think differently. Song Yi deliberately halts his army in order to arrive only when the Qin and Zhao have weakened each other so that he can thoroughly defeat Qin. Song says to Xiang, "In wearing armor and holding weapons [on the battlefield], I am inferior to you; [but speaking of] sitting down and making strategies, you are not as good as I." Xiang Yu argues against this idea, holding that (1) Chu and Zhao plan to defeat Qin together, and halting would hurt the common mission, and (2) Chu soldiers are suffering from a shortage of supplies in rainy weather. Enraged by Song's "slow" decision, Xiang Yu goes into Song's tent and kills him the next morning. The murder shocks all the fellow generals, and Xiang Yu immediately claims to be the new general-in-chief. Thereafter, as Song Yi rightly predicts, Xiang Yu has no patience to sit down and make a thoughtful plan for the rescue. He hurriedly leads the army to Zhao and beats the Qin forces, which far outnumber his own. The great victory enables him to stand out from other leaders in the rescue expedition and go on to become the commander-in-chief of all the rebel lords' troops, a key step closer to his peak.

In this episode, despite their common goal of defeating Qin, Song Yi's and Xiang Yu's approaches differ remarkably. The former's strategy, based on careful planning, is calculative and requires substantial patience. If Chu were to take advantage of the Qin's tiredness, Chu would have a bigger chance of winning the battle and lowering the cost. In contrast, Xiang Yu's approach is impatient and direct. For him, to delay offering help means to fail the mission and break the promise. Even more straightforward is his way of solving the disagreement about decision making by killing Song Yi. Moreover, this episode sheds light on the hero's political immaturity. In comparison to Song Yi, Xiang Yu is much less calculative, believing in the so-called common mission of rescuing Zhao. In this episode, Xiang Yu's two main propositions are presented in a more positive way: his direct and fast approach sometimes can solve problems efficiently. While the episode alerts readers through the mouth of Song Yi that Xiang Yu's use of the army is problematic, it mainly serves to explain that the reason Xiang Yu is able to take this initial step toward military power is precisely his swiftness of action and unsophistication.

As the narrative proceeds, despite Xiang Yu's elevation in the army, his personality does not change. But, as we shall see, the same propositions contributing to his rise cause trouble on other occasions. Before the formidable hero enters the Qin capital, a man named Cao Wushang, a subordinate of Xiang Yu's potential rival Liu Bang, discloses to Xiang Yu that Liu has already arrived in the city and plans to make himself the king of the region. Xiang therefore decides to follow his adviser's plan to kill Liu Bang by inviting Liu Bang to a banquet at Hongmen. Liu Bang foils the plot by tricking Xiang into believing that he has no desire to become a king and that he has entered the capital earlier only to prepare for Xiang Yu's arrival. Hearing this, Xiang not only completely believes Liu but also frankly tells him that it is Cao Wushang who causes the "misunderstanding." Therefore, Liu Bang leaves the banquet early and executes the traitor Cao Wushang upon returning to his camp. Although candidness may be a positive personality trait for a commoner, in a qualified politician it is merely simplemindedness.

After missing the best opportunity to eliminate Liu Bang, Xiang Yu demonstrates his lack of sophistication to the extreme in Guangwu, where his sudden decline commences and eventually causes his suicide. When the rivals' troops have been contained for months, the protagonist naïvely proposes a duel with Liu Bang to resolve their conflict. But Liu Bang merely responds with a laugh. Finally, the two sides agree to divide the territory, and each promises to return to his base. However, when Xiang Yu heads back, Liu Bang attacks Xiang by surprise and encircles him at Gaixia. By this time, although the hero has attempted to swiftly fight across regions to solve the crises, there are too many to pacify all at once. The associated troops led by Liu Bang surround him several layers deep. Being aware that he is approaching the tragic end of his life, right before Xiang Yu leads several hundred horsemen to break through the siege, he accuses Heaven: "Never once did I suffer defeat, until at last I became dictator of the world. But now suddenly I am driven to this desperate position! It is because Heaven would destroy me, not because I have committed any fault in battle. I have resolved to die today. Before I die, I yearn to fight bravely and win for you three victories."[49] After a final demonstration of his military competence, the hero commits suicide. His comments on his own rise and fall echo the opening of this chapter—where he fails to learn the art of warfare thoroughly—and correspond with Song Yi's comment that Xiang Yu is not good at strategy. Although the hero's agility is well displayed at the last moment of his life, his swift actions fail to save him from decline.

From Xiang Yu's youth at the beginning to his suicide in the end, the chapter proceeds through episodes carefully arranged to illustrate consistent personalities. In particular, the two seemingly insignificant incidents before he joins the army shed light on his traits that significantly affect the development of the later storyline. What the character says and what he does during his political career in a total of eight years are forged to correspond neatly with the opening and ending. Each episode is an indispensable segment of the entire thread of the storyline, and none contradicts the character's overall image. The repeated attribution of the same propositions creates a consistent overall picture of the hero's character and makes him believable, just like a real person, whose personality is largely stable and steadily directs their behavior.

Character Development

In addition to presenting characters with consistent and stable traits, *Records of the Historian* builds characters who transform as their environment or political power changes. This kind of growth or development in a character across stages of life is known as a character arc or character development and is commonly seen in *Records of the Historian*. Like character consistency, character development also depends on a linear textual structure. Chapters that develop character, like chapters that present character consistency, follow the logical chain from rise to fall or from prosperity to decline to frame the storyline. Over the course of such an account, the intrinsic narrative pattern allows *Records of the Historian* to logically attach new propositions while removing old ones throughout periods of a protagonist's life, forging character development. This is an unprecedented feature that is precluded by the fragmented and fluid structural features of earlier texts. To discern the arc of character development, readers must not miss any part and must read strictly from the beginning to the end of an account; otherwise, the arc will be broken and the interpretation of an episode may completely diverge from the arc. Because the order is secure, readers cannot diverge from it, but must follow it.

The best example is "The Arrayed Traditions of Li Si" (ch. 87), which portrays the protagonist Li Si 李斯 (ca. 280–208) as a political opportunist who grows regretful. The protagonist is merely a lowly official at the beginning, reaches an extremely high position in the middle, and eventually realizes his mistake by the end of his life. Born to a commoner family in the state of Chu, Li became the chancellor of the state of Qin and, later, of the Qin Empire after the First Emperor's unification of China in 221 BCE. This peak in his life divides the account into two segments, the first being the stage from his service as a minor official in Chu to his dramatic rise to the peak of his power in Qin and the second being his radical decline and tragic end, marked by his being executed with his son. Focusing on his pursuit of power and wealth, this chapter narrates all the radical ups and downs in Li Si's entire life.

The first episode is a monologue on Li Si's philosophy of life when he was young. The episode recounts that Li Si saw rats at his workplace and commented on them. It reads:

見吏舍廁中鼠食不絜，近人犬，數驚恐之。斯入倉，觀倉中鼠，食積粟，居大廡之下，不見人犬之憂。於是李斯乃嘆曰：「人之賢不肖譬如鼠矣，在所自處耳！」[50]

He saw that the rats in the latrines and the functionaries' quarters ate refuse and would be terrified whenever people or dogs approached. When [Li] Si entered the granary, he observed that the rats in the granary ate mounds of grain and, living under a great portico, were not bothered by people or dogs. Then, Si sighed and said: "People are worthy or ignoble just like rats: [one's fate] depends on where one is located!"

This episode at the beginning of the chapter, through Li Si's observation of the contrasting living environment of rats, reveals his insight that one's placement of oneself in a given circumstance determines what one can attain. The protagonist's reflection on the rats soon leads him to study *diwang zhi shu* 帝王之術 (techniques of an emperor or king) with Master Xunzi 荀子 (313?–238? BCE). His goal is obvious: to change his current humble status. Li Si's perception of a cause-and-effect sequence is reinforced by the conjunction *nai* 乃 (then), which is put right after the first episode to connect with Li Si's study with Xunzi: 乃從荀卿學帝王之術.⁵¹

After he completes his studies, the protagonist decides to go to Qin rather than staying in his native state, Chu. This is the first application of his theory of the decisive role of one's circumstances. Before he leaves his master, he explains why he chooses Qin and what his ambitions are:

> 斯聞得時無怠，今萬乘方爭時，游者主事。今秦王欲吞天下，稱帝而治，此布衣馳騖之時而游說者之秋也。處卑賤之位而計不為者，此禽鹿視肉，人面而能閒行者耳。故詬莫大於卑賤，而悲莫甚於窮困。久處卑賤之位，困苦之地，非世而惡利，自託於無為，此非士之情也。故斯將西說秦王矣。⁵²

> I have heard that if one gets the opportunity, one should not be idle. Now is the time when [the states] of ten thousand chariots are vying for power, when the wandering schoolman can take command of affairs. Currently, the king of Qin wants to swallow up the world, to call himself emperor and rule it. [Therefore,] this is the moment for commoners to gallop toward him and [is] good timing for the lobbyists to [achieve their goals]. [If] one occupies a lowly and humble position but does not plan for advancement [at this moment], one is like a bird or beast that spies a piece of meat but can only force itself to walk away because there are people around. Therefore, there is no greater disgrace than being lowly and humble, and no greater sorrow than failing [to achieve] one's ambition and [being] restrained [by surroundings]. Being in a

lowly and humble position and in a situation of hardship and trial for a long time, but condemning the age, speaking ill of gain, and trusting in inaction—this is not the disposition of a gentleman. Therefore, I will go to the west and speak to the king of Qin.

The farewell speech, in which Li Si frankly expresses his urge to chase after power and wealth, serves as the motto of the protagonist. Those who fail to take advantage of the opportunity to advance themselves he finds incompetent, and those who claim no interest in profit he judges disingenuous; these critiques rationalize his own materialistic path of life. Li Si enters Qin, a state aspiring to unify other states. This decision not only aligns with his own ambition but also allows him to change his circumstances.

After arriving in Qin, Li Si not only applies these principles but also sells them to the king, who will become the First Emperor of Qin. When anxiety about all the foreigners living in Qin is aroused in 237 BCE, the king decrees that foreigners must be expelled. Li Si, as a native of Chu, is one of those to be banished. In order to persuade the king to revoke the irrational decree, he writes a famous memorial, "Jian zhuke shu" 諫逐客書 (A Memorial to Remonstrate against the Expelling of Foreigners), reminding the king that none of the wonders and treasures that he favors—such as the shining gems, luxury clothing, sultry women—comes from Qin. By the same token, as long as the officials work for Qin's unification, where they come from should not be of concern. Li's argument is so powerful that the king finally removes the decree, and foreigners in Qin are allowed to stay. While these perspectives may have been chosen to serve the author's rhetorical purpose, they are in accordance with Li Si's own materialistic desire. Sima Qian's preservation of the entire memorial in Li Si's account is probably another example of using the protagonist's own writing to reveal his personality in *Records of the Historian*.

With the First Emperor's unification of China in 221 BCE, Li Si reaches the peak of his life, becoming the chancellor of the Qin Empire. All his children marry those of the emperor. In the preceding twenty years, Li Si has not only assisted the king with the ambitious plans they have made together but has also fulfilled his own goals of achieving power and wealth, rising from a minor official of Chu to the most powerful official under Heaven. Seeing thousands of chariots carrying enormous numbers of officials come to his drinking party, Li expresses his anxiety about losing his fortunes:

嗟乎！吾聞之荀卿曰「物禁大盛」。夫斯乃上蔡布衣，閭巷之黔首，上不知其駑下，遂擢至此。當今人臣之位無居臣上者，可謂富貴極矣。物極則衰，吾未知所稅駕也！ 53

Alas! I have heard Xunzi say, "Do not let things flourish too greatly." I wore a commoner's clothes at Shangcai; I was an ordinary subject from the lanes and alleyways. The emperor did not realize that his nag was inferior, so he raised me to this [position]. No one with a ministerial position occupies a post higher than mine; one could call this the pinnacle of wealth and honor. When things reach their pinnacle, they decline. I do not yet know where my carriage will be halted.54

This premonition scene is the turning point of the chapter, signaling to the reader that the characterization of Li Si in the chapter will go in a different direction. The reference to Li's great wealth invokes a new trait that is attached to the second part of Li Si's life: his goal is no longer to obtain more fame and profit, but to maintain the prosperity that he has enjoyed, even at the cost of treachery. In 211 BC, the First Emperor made his fifth circuit through the empire, accompanied by his younger son Huhai 胡亥 (230–207 BCE), Chancellor Li Si, and the eunuch Zhao Gao 趙高 (d. 208 BCE), who was the superintendent of the imperial carriage house and also acted as the superintendent for imperial seals.55 According to Li Si's account, when the First Emperor falls deathly ill on the way, he dictates a letter to his oldest son, Fusu 扶蘇 (?–210 BCE), implying that Fusu will be his successor; but the emperor expires before the sealed letter is given to a messenger. Thus, the letter is in the hands of Zhao Gao, who plans to fabricate a letter and designate Huhai as the successor.56

In order to implement this plan, Zhao Gao comes to Li Si to seek his cooperation. Their conversation occupies a large portion of the account, serving as a crucial piece of *Records of the Historian*'s characterization of Li. Although Li Si argues against Zhao several times, the most powerful man eventually gives up his original stance and accepts the eunuch's plan; but, among the seven exchanges, what deserves particular attention is which points raised by Zhao Gao cause Li Si to betray the

First Emperor. At the beginning, when Zhao proposes to replace the successor, Li instantly stops and firmly rebukes him, stating that Zhao's words are *wangguo zhi yan* 亡國之言 (state-destroying speech) and that this issue is inappropriate for a ruler's subject to discuss. However, when Zhao asks Li to compare himself with Meng Tian, a capable general and close associate of Fusu, Li becomes much less assertive. Zhao then goes further by connecting the issue of succession with Li's personal welfare. He bluntly reminds Li that all previous chancellors of Qin were executed and that if Fusu ascends the throne, he will undoubtedly appoint Meng to replace Li, and that Li will not even be able to safely return home. Zhao then importunes Li by relating the succession issue to Li's own gains and losses, with an emphasis that safety could turn into danger, or vice versa. In this round, Li's irresolution is obvious when he says, "I beg you to say no more of this, or you will force me to commit a crime!" Zhao then takes advantage of this moment to point out the remarkable difference that Li's decision could make for himself and his family: he and his descendants could be kings for generations if he cooperates with Zhao, or he could bring calamities upon not only himself but also his offspring. Hearing this, Li stops resisting.

In this process, the topic, Li Si, logically takes on a new proposition: the protagonist is no longer the ambitious chancellor but a humiliated traitor. He attempts to be a loyal minister to repay the emperor. He is fully aware of the fatal consequence that the empire might collapse if he follows Zhao to enthrone Huhai as the new emperor. But, as we discussed previously, Li Si has already shown anxiety about losing material prosperity. Zhao's repeated lobbying precisely addresses Li's weakness: his potential loss of the chancellor's position and his desire to maintain prosperity for his descendants, both of which resonate well with the premonition scene analyzed earlier.

Despite the successful conspiracy, the situation after Huhai's ascension as the second emperor quickly destroys Li Si's expectation. Zhao Gao swiftly seizes exclusive power by encouraging the puerile emperor to indulge in his excessive desires. As Li Si loses the emperor's favor, he loses his hope of maintaining his position and his entire family's prosperity. Even though he once again gives up his determination, which is to present a fawning memorial to the second emperor, Zhao Gao is determined to eliminate Li Si. Being falsely accused of rebelling against Qin, Li Si and his son are sentenced to death.

After recounting the ups and downs in Li Si's political life, the account ends with Li Si's reflection before the execution. He says to his son: "I wish you and I could take our brown dog and go out through the eastern gate of Shangcai to chase the crafty hare. But how would we be able to do it!" (吾欲與若復牽黃犬俱出上蔡東門逐狡兔，豈可得乎！).[57] In this final scene, the once ambitious, avaricious protagonist expresses regret and misses the old days as a commoner. His pathos indicates that he finally gives up his pursuit of power and material prosperity. From the determined and cunning opportunist to the lowly prisoner who would like to relinquish fame and power, the character arc of Li Si is achieved.[58] When readers start with Li Si's comments on the rats, go through episodes delineating his promotion and decline, and finally come to Li Si's reflection, they understand that the person who destroyed Li Si was not Zhao Gao, but Li Si himself: the fame and wealth that he took pains to pursue and maintain ironically destroyed him.

Conclusion

So far, I hope I have demonstrated that *Records of the Historian* is neither a collection of only fragmental and fluid accounts nor a collection of completely unified chapters. The spectrum of editing degrees among *Records of the Historian*'s accounts shows that the text was at a turning point in the textual transformation from the preimperial period to the late Western Han. Sima Qian and his father took great efforts to impose a linear structure, both on the large body of textual fragments in earlier historical works and on the carefully composed accounts based on raw materials. Thus, we cannot assume that every word choice discloses Sima Qian's intention—nor was searching for the intention the only way to interpret *Records of the Historian*. But the close relationship between *Records of the Historian* and other extant narratives enables us to compare them and examine what the historians have done to arrange and connect the materials; and the strong textual coherence embodied in characters' consistency and development allows us to find how the historians frame their own narratives. The narratological theories, approaching from a structural perspective, accommodate different editing degrees in both categories and illuminate the recurring patterns in *Records of the Historian*. We need not identify the author of individual chapters—which are from the father and which by the son—the text speaks for itself.

Chapter 2

Temporal Order
Weaving a Synthesized Causality

To compile a history is to arrange events. Historians must discern the causality of an incident based on the data they possess and how they personally perceive the development of historical direction. This complicated process is both selective and constrained. On the one hand, since a historical work has no way to contain all the elements related to a subject, historians must choose the essential ones and correlate them into a meaningful narration of the past. Through this process, historians establish direct or indirect connections between earlier and later events, which guide readers to contemplate the triggering of history. On the other hand, historians can only choose from what is available to them. Their sources regarding different historical periods must vary in quantity and quality, and this variation limits compilation to a certain degree.[1] Thus, to narrate historical events is more than to lay out their dates: it is, as well, to explain why they happened. By building a framework of causality, historians endow history with meaning.[2]

Records of the Historian builds a synthesized causal network whose level of sophistication is not seen in its predecessors. The current chapter explores this feature by comparing the temporal order of the succession of events in the story and the pseudo-temporal order of their arrangement in the text. Recounting the rise and decline of a ruler, an empire, a state, or an individual, the main exposition in the "Basic Annals," "Hereditary Houses," and "Arrayed Traditions" chapters is arranged in chronological order; but, at the same time, this principle has many exceptions. Scholars have not adequately studied the issue of how Sima Qian—author of *Records of the Historian*—and other early Chinese historians have built causalities through temporal sequences. In light of Gérard Genette's narratological method, we will not only notice the dual orders coexisting within narratives but also penetrate *Records of the Historian*'s structure to see how Sima linked the events. My scope of examination substantially extends from the traditional focus on divinations, prognostications, and flashbacks to all chronological and nonchronological knitting within the text.

I shall first define two significant terms related to temporal orders in narrative analysis: story order and narrative order. Their consonance and discrepancy give rise to four types of narrative orders—chronological order, simultaneous order, prolepsis, and analepsis—each of which will be discussed in one of the four main sections of this chapter following the first section. I then use specific examples of each of these categories in *Records of the Historian* to show how the temporal order of the narratives impacts the building of the causes and effects within a given account. The parallel accounts that are narrated in both *Zuo Commentary* and *Records of the Historian* or in both *Records of the Historian* and *History of the Han* illustrate *Records of the Historian*'s new model of causality, a remarkably intricate causal network that interweaves cumulative effects, circumstantial elements, human agency, and immediate causes in driving history forward. Through its particular structure, this model obscures any simple historical pattern and provokes the reader to view historical changes as a result of synthesized factors.

Temporal Orders

The media that are used to recount a story are diverse—including, for example, the moving images in a film or the still images of a comic strip as well as oral or written words—but all narratives must present the events in a certain order. As Gérard Genette points out, "One can run a film backwards, image by image, but one cannot read a text backwards, letter by letter, or even word by word, or even sentence by sentence, without its ceasing to be a text."[3] Some may argue that we may skip text or may read a page or paragraph repeatedly. But we still read forward, word by word, because we go back only to reread a part, and then move forward. This constrained reading order is due to the *linearity* of the linguistic signifier.

At the same time, our reading order is not necessarily the order of a story or a series of stories. Genette cites the French film theorist Christian Metz's (1931–1993) point that narrative has a doubly temporal sequence, the time of the signified (story time) and the time of the signifier (narrative time), which invites us to consider that one of the functions of narrative is to invent one time scheme in terms of another time scheme.[4] Based on this feature, Genette further articulates that "to study the temporal order of a narrative is to compare the order in which events or temporal sections are arranged in the narrative discourse with the order of succession these same events or temporal segments have in the story, to the extent that story order is explicitly indicated by the narrative itself or inferable from one or another indirect clue."[5] This kind of comparison between the two orders is applicable for two reasons. One is that a narrative discourse never inverts the order of events without saying so, as authors always notify the reader with temporal signals, such as "three months earlier" or "two years later." The other reason is that, technically speaking, a perfect temporal correspondence between narrative and story would never occur.[6]

The duality of temporal orders existing in narratives dictates two major possibilities: if the narrative follows the actual story order (the order of the actual sequence of events), the narrative order is chronological; if the two diverge, then the narrative order is a distorted one, which is anachrony. Note that although events in chronological order seem to be free from distortion, they are results of active selection. They appear with a chronological sequence in a text only because the historian arranges the text in this way. Meanwhile, anachrony is different from anachronism, which means that the historical figures and events are placed where they do not belong. *Anachrony* refers to a presented sequence of events that does not follow the natural succession from early to late events. Anachrony can be further divided into three subtypes: the simultaneous type, prolepsis, and analepsis.

The *simultaneous type* occurs in a situation in which at least two events happen at the same time or have durations that overlap. When all characters are in the same space, several characters may act or speak at the same time; or, more complicatedly, in a cross-space scene, different events or situations may happen in more than one place at the same time. In both situations, the narrator has no ability to simultaneously recount multiple characters' actions or speeches that take place simultaneously. In practice, the narrator must describe one character's actions first and then go back in the timeline where he left off, to describe the actions of another figure, starting at the same time that the already-reported actions of the first character were occurring.[7] In so doing, the narrator creates a narrative order that differs from the story order. The simultaneous type is very common in ambitious military tales, in which the narrator communicates the effects of complicated circumstances by describing at least two armies acting at the same time but in different places. *Records of the Historian* includes many examples of this type, since it depicts political decisions and situational changes in battles, which often involve simultaneous actions of several parties.

Genette designates *prolepsis* as any narrative maneuver that consists of narrating or evoking in advance an event that will take place later, and he designates *analepsis* as any evocation after the fact of an event that took place earlier than the point in the story where we are at any given moment. This order is not due to the historian's inability to represent the simultaneous actions of characters or to represent scenes happening in another, different space, but rather (1) due to some purpose that the narrator has for presenting an episode through analepsis and (2) the narrator's ability to do so without doing harm to the reader's understanding. A good narrative always gives clues about the development of the storyline to its readers or audience at the right time.[8] For historians, representing events in a certain order—chronology, simultaneity, prolepsis, and analepsis—is a way to set up logical connections among events distributed in various stages of a narrative. *Records of the Historian* manipulates temporal order in all four forms, each of which will be discussed in one of the remaining sections of the chapter.

Chronological Order Establishing Cumulative Causes

In *Records of the Historian*, most chapters follow a chronological order to organize a primary storyline at the account level. As discussed earlier, this indicates that the narrative order is the same as the story order; but since the neighboring episodes always focus on the same subject, chronological textual order not only indicates the sequence of events but also implicitly suggests their correlation—a later event relates to or depends on the completion of an earlier one. This noticeable feature of *Records of the Historian* distinguishes the text from its predecessors. For example, while entries in *Zuo Commentary* are also arranged in chronological order, since its neighboring entries normally depict different subjects across several competing states, the correlation between consecutive entries can be vague or even enigmatic. This chronological organization that prevents the text from presenting a sound logical chain between events is also used in *Discourses of the States* and *Stratagems of the Warring States*. For these texts, even though their entries within the same chapter all concern the same state and even though two neighboring episodes may involve the same character, their self-contained feature allows little chance of building logical connections across entries. For example, among the total of twenty-one chapters in *Discourses of the States*, nine are devoted to the state of Jin. In the first chapter about Jin, all seven entries are related to Jin's attack on the Rong tribe. Despite their richness and relation, these entries are separate units of complete narrative. They neither have textual coherency as a whole nor depend on each other in conveying meanings.

Records of the Historian demonstrates an attempt to strengthen the logical connection between components within the same account or chapter to an unprecedented degree, although the level of this effort varies from one chapter to another. In many cases, there are no specific words to signal the relationship between two neighboring episodes, because readers can just follow with common sense. Of course, this is not to say that the later event is exclusively caused by the earlier one. In fact, the text frequently integrates several causes to lead to one consequence (though one cause may be the proximate or the most important), as I will demonstrate in the rest of the chapter. The special effect that chronological order brings to *Records of the Historian* is that the consequences (such as the loss of a battle, the decline of a family, or the collapse of a dynasty) are always presented as resulting from an accumulation of a series of related events, rather than from a single cause at one certain point. This exhibition of a gradual and developing process turns every single event into a contributing factor in the logical chain.

In terms of literary quality, chapters in the "Hereditary Houses" division do not represent the best of *Records of the Historian*. Since a large portion of this section deals with the Spring and Autumn period, *Records of the Historian* heavily depends on earlier sources such as *Zuo Commentary* and *Discourses of the States*. As a result, the "Hereditary Houses" accounts are primarily composed of combined entries in predated texts and of analepses restored into a general chronological order. But for this exact reason, chapters in this section leave us some hints of how the author reorganized old entries from earlier sources to build a new narrative frame. This is best illustrated in the bloody power struggle between the two branches of Jin's ruling house, an incident narrated by both *Zuo Commentary* and *Records of the Historian* (ch. 39, "The Hereditary House of Jin"). While the latter was probably compiled on the basis of the former,[9] *Records of the Historian* structures a different causality for the chaotic period from 785 to 678 BCE. Whereas *Zuo Commentary* constructs the correspondence between two time points as a seemingly trivial cause and its severe consequence, *Records of the Historian* manifests the cumulative effects of a string of events leading toward a single outcome. Both texts trace the initial cause of the chaos to Lord Mu's inappropriate naming of his two sons, an episode that is recounted in more or less the same manner in the two texts, save for minor differences in wording.[10] As the story goes, the lord names his crown prince Chou 仇 (enemy), as he is born during a battle in which the lord is defeated. Years later, the lord names his younger son, who is born after Jin's victory, Chengshi 成師 (successful troops). Noticing that the lord violates ritual propriety, a minister of Jin, Shifu, rightly predicts that turmoil will arise—Chengshi's branch will replace Chou's and rule Jin.[11]

The difference between *Zuo Commentary* and *Records of the Historian* lies in the aftermath. In the same entry in *Zuo Commentary*, immediately following are three scattered instances of turbulence that fulfill Shifu's prophecy made earlier, when Chengshi was born. First, Jin falls into disorder in 745 BCE, which leads to Chengshi's enfeoffment in Quwo, an area larger than the territory of the legitimate ruler. Second, six years later (739 BCE), another minister of Jin, Panfu, assassinates the legitimate ruler, the son of Chou, to enthrone Chengshi. Third, another fifteen years later, in 724 BCE, Chengshi's son attacks the lord's domain and assassinates the ruler of Jin, Chou's grandson Lord Xiao. *Zuo Commentary* explains this attack as a result of Jin's invasion of Jingting. While each incident is individually presented as a consequence of Lord Mu's inappropriate naming, the causal logic between these events is vague, as they are three fragmented time points retrospectively selected from over decades. As Wai-yee Li argues, this full entry triggered by the troublesome naming shows how the chronological frame brings together an omen and its fulfillment, which highlights small beginnings and great consequences, thereby creating a sense of inevitability.[12]

In *Records of the Historian*, the same storyline strings together a series of subsequent events that are skipped in the *Zuo Commentary* entry, making the auxiliary line's eventual control of Jin less of a consequence of naming and much more of a highly hybrid result. The forward movement of the story is not driven by the naming omen; instead, eleven events (summarized as follows), including ones that occur in Jin, Quwo, and Zhou, are woven together, whose time sequence naturally forms an accrued force leading to the collapse of the legitimate line. Almost all of the events added to *Records of the Historian*'s storyline are reported elsewhere in *Zuo Commentary*; despite their relation to the power struggle, *Zuo Commentary* disperses them under various years without a clear logical frame. *Records of the Historian* incorporates them and sets up a fused causal chain by following the chronological sequence of nine lords of Jin (corresponding to three contemporary rulers from Quwo). From the naming tale to the unification of Jin, *Records of the Historian* associates Quwo's final control of Jin with three major causes: the accelerating weakening of Jin, the increasing strength of Quwo, and the declining political authority of the central court of the Zhou state, the foundation of the social order at that time.[13] No cause is demonstrated explicitly; instead, all causes are shown indirectly, through the sequence of the eleven following events.

> Event 1: After Lord Mu of Jin died in 785, his brother usurped the throne. The crown prince, Chou, fled. Four years later, Chou returned to Jin and restored his legitimate succession to his father as the new ruler.
>
> Event 2: In 771, King You of Zhou was killed in a rebellion. Lord Xiang of Qin was first recognized as a regional lord.
>
> Event 3: In 745, Chou passed away; his son succeeded him as Lord Zhao. The new ruler enfeoffed his uncle Chengshi in Quwo, an area larger than his own capital of Jin, providing the auxiliary branch (Chengshi's line) with a base to outcompete Jin. Chengshi's virtuous administration in Quwo attracted people to come there to join him.
>
> Event 4: In 739, Panfu, a minister of Jin, assassinated Lord Zhao in order to get Chengshi into Jin; but the Jin people defeated Chengshi, expelling him back to Quwo. In the same year, Lord Zhao's son was installed as Lord Xiao.

Event 5: In 731, Chengshi died; his son, Zhuangbo (Liege Zhuang), succeeded him. Seven years later, Zhuangbo killed Lord Xiao in the Jin capital. The Jin people attacked Zhuangbo, forcing him to retreat to Quwo. In that same year, 724, Lord Xiao's son, Lord E, became the new ruler.

Event 6: In 718, hearing that Lord E passed away, Zhuangbo attacked Jin. King Ping of Zhou[14] sent an army to save Jin. Zhuangbo retreated to Quwo. In 717, Lord E's son succeeded to the throne as Lord Ai.

Event 7: In 716, Zhuangbo died; his son, Wugong (Lord Wu), inherited his title. Four years later, Lord Yin of Lu was killed by the Lu people. In 710, Jin invaded Xingting. One year later, Wugong conspired with Xingting and captured Lord Ai. Lord Ai's son was enthroned by the Jin people as Lord Xiaozi.

Event 8: In 709, Wugong had Lord Ai killed. Quwo became even stronger. Jin was no longer able to resist the power of Quwo.

Event 9: In 704, Wugong lured Lord Xiaozi and killed him. King Huan of Zhou sent a troop to attack Wugong. In 703, Jin installed the younger brother of Lord Ai, Min, to be the new ruler.

Event 10: In 701, a minister of Zheng installed a younger brother of the legitimate ruler Lord Zhao as the new ruler, causing Lord Zhao of Zheng's exile.[15] Fifteen years later, a minister of Qi killed Lord Xiang of Qi.

Event 11: In 678, Lord Huan of Qi first became a hegemon. Wugong conquered Jin and sent its treasures to bribe King Li of Zhou. The king thus appointed Wugong to rule both Jin and Quwo and officially recognized him as one of the regional lords.

Summation: Chengshi's offspring, through three generations in sixty-seven years,[16] eventually replaced Chou's branch to rule Jin as a regional lord.[17]

Records of the Historian assembles these events, filling them into the storyline between the naming omen and its three fulfillments seen in *Zuo Commentary*. First, *Records of the Historian* presents a much fuller logical chain to pin down the direction of the historical development. The inserted events turn the three individual symptoms of the naming omen—the problematic enfeoffment of Chengshi in Quwo (event 3), Panfu's killing of Lord Zhao of Jin (event 4), and the confrontation between the two branches at Xingting (event 7)—into correlated time points that indicate the growth of Quwo on its path to power. Both texts highlight the profound effect of Lord Zhao's assigning Quwo to Chengshi, but the difference is that this episode in *Records of the Historian* paves the way for the relentless confrontation in the subsequent plot rather than merely proving the danger of having "a weak trunk but a strong branch," a point emphasized in *Zuo Commentary*. In event 3, *Records of the Historian* also supplements the account by describing Chengshi's virtuous administration in Quwo, a factor that never appears in *Zuo Commentary*. In *Records of the Historian*, a nobleman's comment that follows, "the branch is larger than the trunk and has won the heart of its people, what chaos would wait for" (君子曰：「晉之亂其在曲沃矣。末大於本而得民心，不亂何待！」),[18] summarizes two key factors—territory and popular support—that spark Quwo's repeated attacks against Jin. In *Records of the Historian*, the connection between event 3 and the following events thus turns it into a cause rather than the omen's fulfillment.

From event 4 onward, *Records of the Historian* depicts Quwo's deleterious attack on Jin. At the beginning, as seen in event 4, it is Jin's minister Panfu who kills Lord Zhao in order to get Chengshi into Jin (and install him as the new ruler). At this initial stage, the Jin people defeat Quwo, not only designating Lord Zhao's son as Lord Xiao but also killing the rebellious murderer. In event 5, Quwo's Zhuangbo successfully assassinates Lord Xiao, a further step toward destroying Jin. This is also the last time that Jin is able to defend itself alone. From this point on, Jin has no way to constrain Quwo other than by repeatedly enthroning a new ruler. In event 8, we read that "Quwo becomes increasingly stronger; Jin does not know how to deal with it." Quwo's killing of the Jin rulers never stops until Jin's downfall in event 11, in which Quwo's Wugong is officially recognized as a territorial lord. During this long-term process, neither Jin nor Quwo makes hasty changes; instead, an earlier event often paves the way for the next (or for a few subsequent events). Despite the absence of logical conjunctions indicating explicit linking between events, the chronological order implies that Quwo's annexing of Jin in event 11 is a blended result rather than a neat outcome merely associated with any singular reason. The joint causation knitted between eleven events across generations blurs the seemingly decisive importance of Lord Mu's problematic naming of his sons. Although, in *Records of the Historian*, the final outcome does comply with Shifu's prognostication, the inevitability established in *Zuo Commentary* is greatly reduced by human agency in the eleven events.

Moreover, the bloody competition does not only involve the two rivaling branches of Jin. The multiple interventions of the Zhou kings are particularly noteworthy. The descriptions of these interventions delineate the collapse of the old social order that was established by the Western Zhou.[19] In *Records of the Historian*, the decay of the hierarchy based on noble kinship serves as much more than historical context; it is a direct cause interwoven into the long turmoil of Jin. As early as in event 2, we are told that the last king of the Western Zhou is killed by the Quanrong people; two consequences of this are that Zhou relocates its capital eastward and that the head of a minor group, Qin, is recognized by the Zhou court as one of the territorial lords. Any reader who is familiar with early Chinese history would understand that the two incidents indicate the decline of Zhou's authority in maintaining the social order. In events 6 and 9, the central court sends troops to attack Quwo twice but only temporarily delays Quwo's invasion of Jin.[20] At the same time, events 7 and 10 report the repeated assassinations of territorial lords outside of Jin, a gradually developing symptom of the way that Zhou is no longer capable of mediating violations of hierarchical order within the territorial lords' domains. The last event recounts Lord Huan of Qi's hegemonic status, marking Zhou's decline to an even greater extent. The Zhou king's final official recognition of the Quwo branch is a result of bribery, which defies the order Zhou itself strives to hold. With the chronological frame, *Records of the Historian* naturally knits side effects into the course of the main plot.

It is noteworthy that the power struggle between Jin and Quwo does not represent the best quality of causality that *Records of the Historian* builds, but it is a good example to show the structural effects in establishing a causal chain through textual comparison. This account, as an example from *Records of the Historian*, lacks the explicit logical chain and the stronger causation as seen in *Records of the Historian*'s chapters devoted to the Han dynasty. It is very likely that the compilation of this account was to some extent limited by the lack of clear correlations in

Zuo Commentary, which is the only received text that includes the major events among the aforementioned eleven.[21] One piece of evidence for this limitation is that Records of the Historian does not include all the military actions taken by Quwo, Jin, and Zhou as recorded in Zuo Commentary.[22] In examining those entries in Zuo Commentary that were skipped by Records of the Historian, one sees that their causal force in the struggle is vague.

In summation, the Records of the Historian account shows a distinctive effort in building a new model to manifest correlations among events. Whereas Zuo Commentary presents the inappropriate naming as the only reason for Quwo's eventual replacement of Jin, Records of the Historian only expounds it as a symbolic cause, which is intertwined with many other elements in the later storyline. The Records of the Historian model emphasizes the combining and cumulative effects of various causes over a period, rather than the decisive effect of any single cause. This characteristic has two impacts. First, one can hardly interpret a major historical change in Records of the Historian as a simple outcome of a cause. Each episode is bound to both earlier and later events. Second, the momentum of inevitability and symbolic signs created by omens, divinations, and even moral injunctions in some Zuo Commentary narratives has been decreased. While both texts pay attention to small beginnings, Records of the Historian rarely bonds an outcome exclusively with a small beginning in its narrations. The text demonstrates a preference toward exhibiting how a small beginning develops into a great crisis in the long term, creating a sense that the historical development is a result of spontaneously occurring accretion. Records of the Historian thus obscures the overwhelming symbolic quotient of small actions that violate ritual propriety and moral code, but it highlights the practical and consequential danger of losing control of issues in the political realm. This pattern frequently recurs in Records of the Historian's recounting of the rises and falls of dynasties, states, families, and individuals.

Simultaneous Events Incorporating Situational Stimuli

Records of the Historian has many descriptions of simultaneous events, which is a distinguishing feature of the text. This is the first time that synchrony was highlighted in Chinese historiography. Narratives with simultaneous scenes are usually related to military operations involving several parties and major political events that require a full understanding of international circumstances. Presenting these scenes in writing requires masterful historical knowledge of specific events and careful planning of sequence of events.

This emphasis on simultaneous events in *Records of the Historian* is best embodied in its description of events dated to the Spring and Autumn period and the Warring States period, when interstate tensions were so important that domestic tactics or maneuvers were heavily impacted. The clearest presentation of simultaneous events lies in chapters within the "Tables" section. "The Table by Years of the Twelve Regional Lords" demonstrates important events of the twelve states from 841 to 477 BCE. With a total of 14 columns and 365 rows, it lists events in the Zhou, Lu, and 12 regional territories, making it easy to see what events happened in the same year.[23] "The Yearly Table of the Six States" lays out events from 476 to 207 BCE. In addition to the six columns for the six states, which were eventually unified by the Qin, the columns for Zhou and Qin serve as good references for grasping the full picture of the chaotic period. The most intense table is "The Table by Months of the Times of Qin and Chu" 秦楚之際月表, which displays the quickly shifting circumstances from 209 to 202 BCE, the ending point of the Chu regime and the start of the Han Empire. Reading the grids across in a row, one distinctly sees the simultaneous movements of all the competing powers of this period. Technically speaking, these rows form true simultaneous narratives, which suggest indefinite relations between the grids.

Sima Qian builds more explicit causal relationships between events within some chapters devoted to later periods (from the late Warring States to the Han era) in the divisions of "Basic Annals," "Hereditary Houses," and "Arrayed Traditions." These chapters bring in rich details, such as the ascent of a new ruler, the court politics of a state, the contemporary military strength of a state, and so on. The text clearly represents the actions of each party or the tensions of the circumstances by using conjunctions and adverbial expressions that signal events that happened simultaneously. Examples of temporal phrases include *shishi* 是時, *dangcishi* 當此時, or *dangshishi* 當是時, all of which mean "at this time," to introduce momentous concurrent information to the readers. Logical conjunctions such as *gu* 故 (thus), *yigu* 以故 (therefore), *sui* 遂 (then; thus), and *nai* 乃 (then; therefore) usually follow the temporal words in the next sentence to explain the immediately following movement. It is not easy to sketch the complicated and simultaneous military movements because of the constantly changing circumstances involving several powers. These chapters differ from the tables, as they cannot literally present the simultaneous events across the rows. As discussed earlier, the narrative order is different from the story order because the narrator has to introduce the moves of all parties one by one, although they did happen simultaneously. In these intensive narratives, the clause directed by the temporal words provides situational factors for a protagonist's next movement, accounting for his or her political success and failure.

Echoing the intense simultaneous events in "The Table by Months of the Times of Qin and Chu," "The Basic Annals of Xiang Yu" (ch. 7) and "The Basic Annals of Emperor Gaozu" (ch. 8) have many more temporal phrases than the average in *Records of the Historian*. Xiang Yu's chapter, through a total of seventeen temporal phrases, delineates a string of synchronous events in constantly changing circumstances during the period of the rivalry between Xiang Yu (i.e., the king of Chu; King Xiang) and Liu Bang (i.e., the king of Han; Emperor Gaozu of Han). One battle that is depicted in great detail is known as the Battle of Chenggao 成皋之戰. The narration primarily depicts four powerful parties. In addition to the rivals, the other two parties involved are Han Xin 韓信 (230–196 BCE) and Peng Yue 彭越 (?–196 BCE), who together play a decisive role: if they side with Xiang, then Xiang will win; if they side with Liu, then Liu will win. The following episode recounts the simultaneous movements of Liu, Xiang, and Peng over roughly seven months.[24] I divide it into three sections, with the second and the third beginning with underlined temporal words, which introduce external factors and link them as immediate causes that drive Xiang Yu's responsive movements.

> 漢之四年，項王進兵圍成皋。漢王逃，獨與滕公出成皋北門，渡河走修武，從張耳、韓信軍。諸將稍稍得出成皋，從漢王。楚遂拔成皋，欲西。漢使兵距之鞏，令其不得西。

In the fourth year of Han [204 BCE], King Xiang advanced his army to surround Chenggao. The king of Han escaped. He went out through the north gate of Chenggao merely with Lord Teng. [They] crossed the Yellow River to flee to Xiuwu and joined the armies of Zhang Er and Han Xin. [The king of Han's] generals were gradually able to get out of Chenggao and follow the king of Han. The Chu therefore captured Chenggao and wished to move westward. Han sent troops to resist at Gong and prevented Chu from going westward.

是時，彭越渡河擊楚東阿，殺楚將軍薛公。項王乃自東擊彭越。漢王得淮陰侯兵，欲渡河南。鄭忠說漢王，乃止壁河內。使劉賈將兵佐彭越，燒楚積聚。項王東擊破之，走彭越。漢王則引兵渡河，復取成皋，軍廣武，就敖倉食。項王已定東海來，西，與漢俱臨廣武而軍，相守數月。

At the same time, Peng Yue crossed the Yellow River to attack Chu's army at Dong'e. [He] killed the Chu general, Lord Xue. King Xiang, therefore, marched to the east in person to attack Peng Yue. The king of Han obtained the army of the Marquis of Huaiyin and wished to cross the Yellow River to be on the south [bank]. Zheng Zhong persuaded the king of Han [not to do so]; the king of Han then stopped and built a walled camp at Henei.[25] [He] sent Liu Jia to lead an army to assist Peng Yue and burn Chu's stores and provisions. King Xiang attacked to the east, defeated them, and put Peng Yue to flight. The king of Han then led his troops across the Yellow River, retook Chenggao, and camped at Guangwu to be closer to the provisions at Ao Granary. King Xiang came after he pacified the Donghai county, proceeded west, and camped at Guangwu with Han. [They] both defended for several months.

當此時，彭越數反梁地，絕楚糧食，項王患之。為高俎，置太公其上，告漢王曰：「今不急下，吾烹太公。」[26]

Meanwhile, Peng Yue returned several times to the region of Liang and cut off the supply line of Chu. King Xiang was anxious about it. [He] constructed a high sacrificial altar, placing Liu Bang's father on it, and announced to the king of Han, "If you do not surrender to me at once, I shall boil your father alive!"

The first passage begins with the confrontation between the two rivals by outlining that Liu escapes from Chenggao. Xiang prevails over Liu at this stage. The second passage, starting with *shishi* 是時 (at the same time), quickly shifts to the third party, Peng Yue, who follows Liu Bang's tactic to attack Dong'e, which is located to the northeast of Chenggao. This attack drives Xiang Yu away from his confrontation with Liu, who takes advantage of this time to supplement his military strength with

Han Xin's troops. Xiang Yu's fighting against Peng Yue is linked to the latter's attack at Dong'e with *shishi* and emphasized by *nai* (therefore), as underlined in the passage. When Xiang Yu successfully repels Peng Yue and returns, Liu has recaptured Chenggao and lays out his troop at Guangwu, which allows him to conveniently obtain supplies.

The third passage describes Xiang's response to Peng's disruption of Chu's food supply, which happens while Xiang Yu returns to Guangwu and camps there with his rival. The phrase *dangshishi* 當是時 (meanwhile) indicates that these operations take place at the same time. Xiang's anxiety about the threat from Peng drives him to use Liu's father to coerce Liu to head west. The collaboration between Liu Bang, Peng Yue, and other generals largely keeps Xiang Yu busy reacting to each of them. When the Chu and Han confront each other in Guangwu, Liu Bang's power has finally become comparable with Xiang Yu's, making this episode a key element of the Chu-Han contention. Later in the plot, additional temporal words link more simultaneous events. We are told that while Han Xin takes over Qi, Peng Yue successfully cuts Xiang Yu's supply. Thus, Xiang Yu falls into a difficult position and eventually reaches an agreement with Liu Bang.

By using the temporal phrases, the text builds a causal network between the simultaneous actions of all four parties on the battlefield and presents highly complicated, fierce, and constantly changing tensions. External factors are thus integrated into the narration. Although the battle at Chenggao is also recounted in Liu Bang's basic annals, the account there uses fewer simultaneous temporal phrases. Xiang Yu's confrontation of several enemies at the same time in his own chapter demonstrates that his actions are always led by Liu Bang's tactics. This fact suggests Xiang Yu's failure to be a true leader, a key issue that contributes to Xiang Yu's collapse in the end.

On other occasions, simultaneous actions are often seen in ephemeral and urgent scenes. Temporal words are supplemented with the natural change of subject, from one character to another. Readers understand that, even though multiple characters act at the same time in the same location, the text has to move its focus from one to another, arranging the leading and supporting characters so that they act or speak in a certain environment. But this does not mean that the temporal words are not essential; indeed, they are often associated with logical conjunctions and serve to invoke elements brought about by specific environments in the narrative. A good example is the famous assassination attempt by Jing Ke

荊軻 (?–227 BCE), a swordsman who aims to save the Yan from being annexed by Qin.²⁷ His account in "The Arrayed Traditions of Assassins" narrates that he and his thirteen-year-old assistant, Qin Wuyang 秦舞陽, go to Qin to assassinate the king of Qin, who eventually unified China and became the First Emperor of Qin (259–210 BCE). Unlike the previous example of the Battle at Chenggao, this scene happens in a special, enclosed space, Xianyang Palace. Claiming to have brought the map of Yan and the head of a Qin traitor to the king, Jing Ke and Qin Wuyang successfully tempt the king to meet them in person, creating an opportunity to stand close enough to the king and implement their plan. The following excerpt depicts a short and urgent period, from the moment when Jing Ke presents the map to the fight between Jing and the king. The three temporal words underlined are used in the episode to explain four circumstantial causes. It reads:

秦王謂軻曰：「取舞陽所持地圖。」軻既取圖奏之，秦王發圖，圖窮而匕首見。因左手把秦王之袖，而右手持匕首揕之。未至身，秦王驚，自引而起，袖絕。拔劍，劍長，操其室。<u>時</u>惶急，劍堅，故不可立拔。荊軻逐秦王，秦王環柱而走。²⁸

The king of Qin said to Jing Ke, "Bring the map that Wuyang is carrying." Ke took the map [from the case] and presented it [to the king]. The king of Qin opened the map. When he came to the end of the map, a dagger appeared. Taking advantage of that moment, [Jing Ke] seized the king's sleeve with his left hand while he held the dagger to stab the king. Before the dagger reached his body, the king was alarmed and leapt from his seat; his sleeve was torn. [The king] tried to draw his sword, but it was long and clung to the scabbard. <u>At that time</u>, [the king] was scared and in crisis, and the sword was firm [in the scabbard]; he thus could not get it out immediately. Jing Ke pursued the king of Qin and the king of Qin ran around a pillar.

群臣皆愕，卒起不意，盡失其度。而秦法，群臣侍殿上者不得持尺寸之兵；諸郎中執兵皆陳殿下，非有詔召不得上。<u>方急時</u>，不及召下兵，以故荊軻乃逐秦王。而卒惶急，無以擊軻，而以手共搏之。

All the ministers were astonished. Since it happened unexpectedly, they all failed to consider the problem. But according to the law of Qin, all the ministers serving in the throne room were not allowed to bring a weapon of any size. Various palace guards stood at the bottom of the hall. They were not permitted to ascend to the hall without a command from the king. <u>At that urgent moment</u>, [the king] did not have the time to summon the soldiers from the bottom. For this reason, Jing Ke was then able to pursue him. [The king] was in a panic and rushed about. [Since] he had nothing to attack Ke with, he clenched his hands together to flail at Ke.

<u>是時</u>侍醫夏無且以其所奉藥囊提荊軻也。秦王方環柱走，卒惶急，不知所為，左右乃曰：「王負劍！」負劍，遂拔以擊荊軻，斷其左股。荊軻廢，乃引其匕首以擿秦王，不中，中桐柱。秦王復擊軻，軻被八創。[29]

<u>At the same time</u>, the attending physician, Xia Wuju, used the medicine bag he was carrying to batter Jing Ke. When the king of Qin was running around the pillar, he did not know what to do since he was in a panic and rushing about. His attendants therefore said, "Your majesty, put the sword [on your back]." Putting the sword on his back, [the king] finally drew it and attacked Jing Ke, slicing his left thigh. Jing Ke, staggering to the ground, thus raised the dagger and hurled it at the king. It struck not [the king] but the bronze pillar. The king of Qin attacked Jing Ke again. Ke was wounded in eight places.

Each of the preceding passages uses a temporal phrase to introduce a concrete factor that directly affects the result of the attempted assassination. In the first passage, the text presents these factors in order, which indicates the internal logic of the plot. Immediately following the king's failure to draw his sword is the short sentence beginning with "at that time." It introduces two external factors that contribute to this failure: the king is in a panic and the sword is secured in the scabbard. Having its two parts connected by the conjunction *gu* (thus), this sentence explains why the king has no choice but to run around the pillar.

64 | Narrative Devices in the *Shiji*

In the next passage, the focus shifts to the ministers, who are too anxious to help the king. In the middle, we are told the Qin rules regarding bringing weapons into the hall. Then, the underlined phrase "at that urgent moment" initiates a sentence explaining that there is no time to order the guards in the hallway, the third cause that benefits Jing Ke's implementation. Through *yigu* (for this reason), this reason is connected with the fact that Jing Ke runs after the king without hindrance and that the king has nothing but hands to flail at Ke.

In the third passage, the temporal phrase *shishi* (at the same time), directs the readers to the doctor, the fourth element that affects the final result. The doctor's medicine box hits Jing Ke, which buys the king precious time. The ministers then get a chance to remind the king to put the sword on his back, so that the king finally takes out his sword. The doctor, as an environmental factor, turns the scene around. Near the end of the episode, we are directed back to the king's counterattack. Thereafter, the narration restores the flow of time and ends with the outcome. Eventually, Jing Ke is wounded so seriously that this mission ends with his heroic death.

In this episode, three temporal words assist in depicting the complicated and imperative factors in the assassination process. Advancing and thwarting Jing Ke's attempt to assassinate the king, the four factors substantially improve the rationality of this incident, one of the most important scenes in Chinese history.

So far, I have discussed the practice of presenting simultaneous actions and events in *Records of the Historian*. The Battle of Chenggao and the assassination attempt by Jing Ke demonstrate the text's enormous concern with multiple factors involved in historical events. The outcomes of the two examples are subject not only to the protagonists' actions but also their situations, and thus the text builds a complicated causal network within the narratives. *Records of the Historian* shows a tendency to embrace the comprehensiveness of history rather than simplifying it.

Prolepses Highlighting Essential Inner Qualities

Records of the Historian employs numerous prolepses in various forms. Genette's definition of this narrative technique encompasses any advance notice of what happens later, including omens, divinations, predictions of battle outcome, anticipation of the rise or the collapse of a regime, and so on. In this sense, prolepses in *Records of the Historian* are so common that they appear in accounts devoted to all periods from the legendary beginning to Sima Qian's own time. Nonetheless, these prolepses differ in origin and cannot be discussed without classifications. In order to illustrate the characteristics of prolepses in *Records of the Historian*, I divide prolepsis in this text into two categories: (1) the stories edited on the basis of earlier texts produced in the Warring States period; and (2) accounts composed by Sima Qian with raw materials such as archives, interviews, and oral transmission of episodes dated to the Qin-Han era. The later the dates of narratives are, the more autonomy *Records of the Historian* has in compilation. When we follow this chronology of sources, the way *Records of the Historian* uses prolepses gradually becomes apparent: the text seldom places prolepses themselves at the center of the narrative; it tends instead to make them part of an episode to reveal important qualities or principles of the protagonist, which are integrated as key factors in the later development of the account.

This is not to say that personal qualities are not seen in *Records of the Historian*'s narration of the Spring and Autumn period. Indeed, these narratives do exhibit this new style of *Records of the Historian* to some degree. But the major chapters of this period, including several in the "Basic Annals" section and many in the "Hereditary Houses" section, are based on *Zuo Commentary* and *Discourses of the States*, whose own prolepses heavily affect those in *Records of the Historian*. A large number of their narratives revolve around the fulfillment of predictions. This is their most evident feature. Some of their entries start with a prophecy and end with its fulfillment; others contain a prophecy, but its fulfillment is in another entry listed years later. As Wai-yee Li rightly argues, prolepses in *Zuo Commentary* are signs that direct the plot of an entry and dictate its ending. The prolepses are the causes as well as the outcomes.[30] At the level of entries, *Zuo Commentary* builds a direct causal relationship between ritual propriety, moral sense, and the destiny of a battle, a person, a family, or a state. While the text's other entries may interpret the same outcomes from a different perspective, this tight and corresponding causal relationship highlights the determinative power of Heaven's will, a ruler's moral standing, or his attitudes toward remonstrating advice. Although a character's behavior and speech may reveal some aspects of his or her personality, motivation, capability, and principles, none of these personal qualities is built as a direct cause for the outcome of the same or another related entry. Since *Records of the*

66 | Narrative Devices in the *Shiji*

Historian heavily relies on the two sources when recounting the Spring and Autumn period, the Han text to some extent preserves this feature.

When *Records of the Historian* recounts events dated to the Warring States and consequent periods, its better access to sources, particularly the historical narrative pool that I discussed in chapter 1, enables the text to reveal personal qualities of characters more easily. Of course, the primary goal of these narrative passages is not to portray the characters, as in later fiction, but to teach important qualities of ministers and rulers in the political realm. For example, many passages in *Stratagems of the Warring States* are believed to be samples of ministers' rhetorical techniques, statesmen's diplomatic strategies, and rulers' qualities.[31] However, these passages provide *Records of the Historian* with a foundation to integrate the character's personal qualities as an important cause for historical explanation. The prolepses in *Records of the Historian* play a critical role in building such causal chains, which are hardly seen in previous historical narratives.

A good example is the account of Shang Yang (商鞅; ?395–338 BCE), an agile reformist also known as Wei Yang 衛鞅 and Gongsun Yang 公孫鞅. In "The Arrayed Traditions of Lord Shang," a full chapter devoted to him, *Records of the Historian* uses multiple layers of prolepses to illustrate the protagonist's extraordinary competence, and these prolepses seamlessly converge with the development of later episodes. It remains unclear how much elaboration comes from Sima Qian. The added levels of prolepses are probably Sima Qian's modifications based on a widely transmitted episode, because *Records of the Historian* is the only received text that preserves this full version. Even if it had been well developed by the Han and was simply copied into *Records of the Historian*, the way it is preserved in *Records of the Historian* and its connection with the following episodes in Shang Yang's account still deserve our attention. The popular, preliminary episode appears in the extant *Stratagems of the Warring States* and *Master Lü's Annals of Spring and Autumn* with a minor difference in wording. It is a conversation between the prime minister of Wei, Gongshu Cuo 公叔座 (痤) (?–360 BCE), and his ruler, King Hui of Wei (r. 369–319 BCE). Shang Yang is merely a minor subordinate of Gongshu Cuo. My comparison between the *Stratagems of the Warring States* and *Records of the Historian* versions demonstrates how *Records of the Historian* uses prolepsis to advance its portrayal of Shang Yang, rather than highlighting the importance of heeding right advice. The passage in *Stratagems of the Warring States* reads:

魏公叔痤病，惠王往問之。曰：「公叔病，即不可諱，將奈社稷何？」公叔痤對曰：「痤有御庶子公孫鞅，願王以國事聽之也。為弗能聽，勿使出竟。」王弗應，出而謂左右曰：「豈不悲哉！以公叔之賢，而謂寡人必以國事聽鞅，不亦悖乎！」公孫痤死，公孫鞅聞之，已葬，西之秦，孝公受而用之。秦果日以強，魏日以削。此非公叔之悖也，惠王之悖也。悖者之患，固以不悖者為悖。³²

Gongshu Cuo of Wei was sick. King Hui went to ask and said, "If your sickness cannot be avoided, what shall I do with our altars of the soil and grain?" Gongshu Cuo responded: "I have a *yushu zi*, Gongsun Yang. I hope Your Majesty will listen to him in all state [affairs]; if not, do not let him cross the border." The king did not respond. He exited [the house of Gongshu] and said to his attendants: "Isn't it sad! Gongshu Cuo is worthy, but he told me to entrust Gongsun Yang with the state. Isn't it absurd?!" After Gongshu died, Gongsun Yang heard what happened. After the burial, Gongsun Yang went to the Qin in the west. King Xiao of Qin received and employed him. Unsurprisingly, Qin became stronger while the Wei declined day by day. It is not that Gongshu is absurd, but that King Hui is absurd. The problem of absurd people is that they take reasonable things as absurd.

Despite Shang Yang's central position in the dialogue, as the ending comment suggests, the primary goal of the episode is to reveal the king's problem. As Gongshu Cuo implicitly predicts at the beginning, Shang Yang is so capable that he alone would affect the strength of a state. Qin's rise and Wei's decline testify to Gongshu Cuo's penetrating insight, which highlights the king's failure to heed reasonable advice. In *Master Lü's Annals of Spring and Autumn*, the episode is listed under "Changjian" (farsighted envisioning) to emphasize a similar point.³³

In the account of Shang Yang, *Records of the Historian* embellishes the same episode with more details, adding an exchange between Shang Yang and Gongshu. The revised episode then becomes Shang Yang's prediction of the king's reaction to Gongshu's prediction about Shang Yang. With only minor changes to the basic storyline, the *Records of the Historian* version refocuses on Shang Yang rather than the prime minister or the king:

鞅少好刑名之學，事魏相公叔座為中庶子。公叔座知其賢，未及進。會座病，魏惠王親往問病，曰：「公叔病有如不可諱，將奈社稷何？」公叔曰：「座之中庶子公孫鞅，年雖少，有奇才，願王舉國而聽之。」王嘿然。王且去，座屏人言曰：「王即不聽用鞅，必殺之，無令出境。」王許諾而去。公叔座召鞅謝曰：「今者王問可以為相者，我言若，王色不許我。我方先君後臣，因謂王即弗用鞅，當殺之。王許我。汝可疾去矣，且見禽。」鞅曰：「彼王不能用君之言任臣，又安能用君之言殺臣乎？」卒不去。惠王既去，而謂左右曰：「公叔病甚，悲乎，欲令寡人以國聽公孫鞅也，豈不悖哉！」公叔既死，公孫鞅聞秦孝公下令國中求賢者，將修繆公之業，東復侵地，乃遂西入秦。[34]

Yang was fond of the teachings of performance and title.[35] He served as *zhongshu zi* to the prime minister of Wei, Gongshu Cuo. Gongshu Cuo recognized his talent but had not yet recommended him for advancement. When Cuo was ill, King Hui of Wei went in person to inquire about his sickness and said, "If Gongshu's sickness cannot be avoided, what can I do with our altars of the soil and grain?"

Gongshu said, "Cuo's *zhongshu zi*, Gongsun Yang, has rare talent, although he is young. I hope Your Majesty will listen to him in all state [affairs]." The king remained silent. When the king was about to leave, Cuo dismissed other people and said, "If you do not heed me and make use of Yang, then be sure to kill him. Do not allow him to cross the border [of Wei]." The king agreed and left.

Gongshu Cuo summoned Yang and apologized, "Just now, when the king asked for a person who can be the prime minister, I mentioned you, but his expression suggested that [he] did not agree with me. I take the ruler as primary and the minister as secondary. Therefore, I told the king, 'If you do not make use of Yang, [you] should kill him.' The king used his expression to agree with me. You can depart quickly. You are about to be captured."

Yang said, "At that time, the king was not able to make use of your words to appoint me; [now] how can he use your words to kill me?" [He] did not leave after all. The king left [the house of Gongshu] and said to his attendants: "Gongshu is seriously ill. It is sad, but he wanted me to entrust Gongsun Yang with the entire state. Isn't it absurd?!" After Gongshu died, Gongsun Yang heard that King Xiao of Qin issued a command in his state to seek talented people, hoping to continue the achievement of Lord Mu [of Qin] and recover the lost lands in the east. Yang, therefore, went west and entered Qin.

With added levels of predictions, the embellished version in *Records of the Historian* pushes Shang Yang's talents above Gongshu Cuo's. The experienced chancellor's extremely polarized proposals—that the king either entrusts the entire state to Shang Yang or kills him before he flees to Wei—imply the first level: Shang Yang will, or would, be an excellent prime minister. The second level of prediction is also from Gongshu Cuo. He believes that the king will partially follow his advice, at least killing Shang Yang, if not appointing the young man to be the next prime minister. Immediately following is the third level, Shang Yang's prediction of Gongshu Cuo's failure in estimating the king's decision. At the end of the episode, the king's disbelief in the dying patient's vision fulfills Shang Yang's judgment about the king. Apparently, Gongshu Cuo is an intelligent statesman; but the last level of prophecy, by Shang Yang, denies the second level, highlighting Shang Yang's rare talent, which in turn echoes Gongshu Cuo's recognition of the young man at the beginning.

The three tightly knit and aptly structured prolepses not only effectively portray the protagonist's extreme intelligence but also pave the way for all of his astonishing achievements that unfold later in the chapter. Gongshu Cuo's worry that Shang Yang will empower a foreign state and pose a threat to the Wei comes true. On the one hand, after arriving in Qin, Shang Yang carries out a series of reforms in economics, military incentives, and law enforcement, which effectively and significantly improve Qin's strength. On the other hand, he actively helps Qin expand territory, which impairs Wei. The tricky surprise attack that he launches against Wei results in Wei's ceding land and relocating the capital. *Records of the Historian* then immediately evokes Gongshu Cuo's prediction by citing King Hui of Wei's words of regret that he had not heeded Gongshu Cuo's advice. References to Shang Yang's *qicai* 奇才 (rare talents)—a keyword used by the prime minister—string the entire account together as an organic whole. It is the three-level prolepsis that directly identifies Shang Yang's extraordinary capability as an indispensable factor for understanding the protagonist's success.

This episode represents *Records of the Historian*'s typical use of prolepses to account for historical changes. When the text recounts the Warring States and early imperial periods, more prolepses tend to reveal certain qualities of characters, such as their personalities, talents, abilities, and other traits. These prolepses are embedded into the speeches, analyses, or judgments of a supporting character and point to these qualities of characters as root causes or important elements for later plot development. Although entries of *Zuo Commentary*, *Discourses of the States*, and other earlier texts also exhibit characters' traits, their qualifications are rarely connected to the causal chain to explain the outcome of events.

When *Records of the Historian* narrates the Qin-Han era, the text has more freedom to structure the overall accounts. In these stories, prolepsis is not limited within one single episode but can buttress a primary storyline across several episodes. In this way, the storyline highlights the effects of personal choices that can completely change one's life track. This category of prolepses is often set up in a strategist's analysis of military or political situations; and the fulfillment is usually conveyed through the repetition of key phrases or a brief recapitulation of the prediction in a later episode in the same account, which strongly verifies the rationality and accuracy of a profound insight. "The Arrayed Traditions of Marquis of Huaiyin" (ch. 92) recounts the entire life of Han Xin 韓信, who refuses to listen to proper advice and is eventually executed for plotting a revolt. In the form of prolepsis, the advice frames the second half of the chapter. *History of the Han* narrates the same story under a varying structure. A close comparison between the *Records of the Historian* and *History of the Han* versions demonstrates how prolepsis impacts the reception of the same facts.

As introduced earlier, Han Xin was a brilliant general who played a substantial role in the power struggle between Xiang Yu and Liu Bang (the future Emperor Gaozu). Originally, the general serves Xiang Yu, but soon he switches to Liu Bang because of Xiang Yu's failure to recognize the wisdom of Han Xin's military advice. In a remarkable contrast, Liu entrusts all the troops to Han Xin when the latter has not established any reputation at all. This newly appointed commander-in-chief soon validates his extraordinary military talent in a series of battles that will become well known. After the Battle of Chenggao, which is discussed in the previous section, Han Xin hastily increases his prominence and power.[36] By 202 BCE, when the Chu and Han were locked in a stalemate in the central plain, Han Xin had just occupied the Qi in the north and thus became the third important power. His personal decision had the full potential to change the balance of the contention—even the overall picture of China.

At this critical moment, two schemers come to Han Xin with exactly the same strategy. One is Wu She 武涉, who is sent by Xiang Yu. He points out that Han Xin's safety depends on Xiang Yu's presence and protection. If Xiang Yu were to be defeated, Liu Bang would respond immediately to prevent Han Xin from threatening him; thus, claiming independence from Liu Bang and becoming the third regional warlord would benefit Han Xin the most. Recalling Liu Bang's good treatment of him, Han Xin immediately refuses Xiang Yu. Soon afterward, the other strategist, Kuai Tong, warns Han Xin of the fatal risk from Liu Bang if Han Xin misses this precise timing. Relating neither to Xiang nor Liu, Kuai Tong objectively analyzes Han Xin's two choices and their two contrasting upcoming paths: preserving the rivals and basing himself in Qi would enable Han Xin to further develop the area into the third major power, probably the strongest among the three; in contrast, the relationship between Han Xin and Liu Bang is constantly changing and actually has deteriorated, and Liu Bang, if given the chance, will inevitably eliminate Han Xin. Nonetheless, Han Xin again refuses to betray Liu Bang. Then, Kuai Tong appeals to historical and contemporary examples to refute the commander's illusion of his safety. The following passage is Kuai Tong's accurate prediction that Liu Bang will endanger Han Xin once Xiang Yu is vanquished. Underlined is the key phrase that Han Xin will evoke in a later plot.

> 臣以為足下必漢王之不危己，亦誤矣。大夫種、范蠡存亡越，霸句踐，立功成名而身死亡。<u>野獸已盡而獵狗亨（烹）</u>。夫以交友言之，則不如張耳之與成安君者也；以忠信言之，則不過大夫種、范蠡之於句踐也。此二人者，足以觀矣。願足下深慮之。且臣聞勇略震主者身危，而功蓋天下者不賞。臣請言大王功略：足下涉西河，虜魏王，禽夏說，引兵下井陘，誅成安君，徇趙，脅燕，定齊，南摧楚人之兵二十萬，東殺龍且，西鄉以報，此所謂功無二於天下，而略不世出者也。今足下戴震主之威，挾不賞之功，歸楚，楚人不信；歸漢，漢人震恐：足下欲持是安歸乎？夫勢在人臣之位而有震主之威，名高天下，竊為足下危之。[37]

I believe that you are mistaken in being certain that the King of Han [i.e., Liu Bang] will not endanger you. Grandee

72 | Narrative Devices in the *Shiji*

> Zhong and Fan Li saved the doomed state of Yue and made [King] Goujian a hegemon. [They] established their merits and completed their fame, but they themselves perished. "<u>When there are no more wild beasts, the hunting dog will be boiled.</u>" You talk of friendship, but yours is not comparable to that of Zhang Er and Lord Cheng'an (i.e., Chen Yu); you speak of loyalty, but yours does not exceed that of the Grandee officials, Zhong and Fan Li, to Goujian. These two cases are enough to perceive. I beg you to consider them deeply. Furthermore, I have heard that people whose bravery and strategy make their ruler tremble will endanger themselves; people whose merit overshadows all under Heaven are not rewarded. I beg to speak of your merits and cunning: you crossed the western reaches of the Yellow River, captured the king of Wei, apprehended Xia Yue, led the troops to conquer Jingxing, killed Lord Cheng'an, subdued Zhao, terrified Yan, pacified Qi, destroyed two hundred thousand men of Chu in the south, killed Long Ju in the east, and turned west to repay [the King of Han]. This is what is meant by "merit that is not inferior to anyone under Heaven and cunnings that no one can exceed for generations." Now you wield enough might to make a sovereign tremble and have won more merit than can be rewarded. If you return to Chu, the people of Chu will not trust you; if you follow Han, the people of Han will quake with fear. Which side would you follow with such [merit and cunning] in your possession? Your position is that of a subject, but you possess enough power to make a sovereign tremble and a name praised by all under Heaven. I sense danger for you in these matters.

In the speech, Kuai Tong first uses historical examples to illustrate the unstable relationship between capable ministers and a king. Wen Zhong 文種 and Fan Li 范蠡 assisted Goujian 勾踐 (?520–465 BCE), the king of Yue, in successfully restoring his state. But as soon as the mission was achieved, the king forced Wen Zhong to commit suicide; Fan Li, fearing Goujian's distrust, had to flee the state. After recounting this episode to Han Xin, the strategist appeals to the contemporary example of Zhang Er 張耳 (264–202 BCE) and Chen Yu 陳餘 (?–204 BCE) to demonstrate the capriciousness of friendship in the political realm. Although they "would have died for each other" 刎頸之交, the brothers cannot avoid competing for power and finally becoming enemies who want to slaughter each other.[38] Accordingly, if the relationship between Liu Bang and Han Xin is defined as that between a ruler and his minister, then it cannot be compared to that between Goujian and his counselors; if defined as friendship, then it is hardly as good as that between Zhang Er and Chen Yu. Not to mention that Han Xin has achieved numerous significant military successes that will arouse Liu Bang's anxiety and distrust. Kuai Tong's expression, "野獸已盡而獵狗烹" (When there are no more wild beasts, the hunting dog will be boiled), probably comes from the story of Wen Zhong and Fan Li with minor editing.[39] This analogy reveals the ruthlessness of rulers and repeatedly appears in the rest of the plot.

Despite some hesitation, Han Xin eventually chooses to side with Liu Bang. Following his quick turndown of Wu She, this is the second time that the commander refuses to claim independence. Unfortunately, Kuai Tong's prediction soon comes true after Liu Bang founds the Han Empire. The subsequent plot is filled with Liu Bang's suspicion and investigation of two reported rebellions attributed to Han Xin. In the narration of both cases, the analogy of the hunting dogs is evoked, corresponding to Kuai Tong's speech. When charged for the first time, Han Xin expresses his innocence with anger upon his capture: "It is just as people say, 'When the wily hares are dead, the good dog is fried; when the soaring birds are no more, the good bow is hidden; when the enemy states are defeated, the artful minister is doomed.' All under Heaven has been pacified. I should certainly be boiled" (果若人言，狡兔死，良狗亨(烹)；高鳥盡，良弓藏；敵國破，謀臣亡。天下已定，我固當亨！).[40]

After being released, Han Xin is so bitter that he participates in a conspiracy. Liu Bang's primary wife, Empress Lü, lures Han Xin to meet in the palace and arrests him. Right before the execution, Han Xin laments: "I regret that I did not make use of Kuai Tong's scheme. Hence, I have been tricked by a woman and her lackey. Is it not [because of] Heaven?" (吾悔不用蒯通之計，乃為兒女子所詐，豈非天哉！).[41] These final words explicitly recall Kuai Tong's proposal, which envisions a promising future rather than the tragic ending. This deep regret at not having heeded Kuai Tong's advice reiterates the importance of the protagonist's personal decision. Despite Han Xin's mistaken attribution of his own defeat to

Heaven, readers surely remember his repeated renunciations of Wu She's and Kuai Tong's advice in prolepses. The two evocations of a completely different political path substantially reinforce the importance of personal choice as a key causal factor in Han Xin's death.

History of the Han preserves the entire storyline, but it redistributes the materials into two separate accounts, one devoted to Han Xin and the other to Kuai Tong.[42] In *Records of the Historian*, Kuai Tong is a supporting character in Han Xin's chapter and does not have a full account of his own, despite the long speeches and detailed descriptions of the character. His accurate forecasting of Han Xin's tragedy certainly contributes to the character's own image as an outstanding strategist and probably even a master of rhetoric; but the two fulfillments of his predictions in *Records of the Historian*, illustrated through Han Xin's repentant speeches, generate a primary focus on Han Xin. In contrast, Ban Gu (or anyone else who edited this account) cuts the speeches and descriptions of Kuai Tong from Han Xin's chapter in *Records of the Historian* and organizes them into an independent biographical account for Kuai Tong in *History of the Han*. This rearrangement of materials within *History of the Han*, despite its nearly verbatim preservation at the sentence level, breaks the correspondence between prolepses and their fulfillments in *Records of the Historian* within the account. The following passage from Han Xin's account in *History of the Han* turns the two prolepses and their two fulfillments into a terse summary, leaving the strategist's vision summarized in merely four graphs that I have underlined.

> 武涉已去，蒯通知天下權在於信，深說以<u>三分天下</u>（之計）。語在通傳。信不忍背漢，又自以功大，漢王不奪我齊，遂不聽。...高祖令武士縛信，載後車。信曰：「果若人言，『狡兔死，良狗亨。』」上曰：「人告公反。」遂械信。...信方斬，曰：「吾不用蒯通計，反為女子所詐，豈非天哉！」」[43]

Wu She had already left. Kuai Tong knew that the weight of all under Heaven was placed on Han Xin. [Kuai Tong] tried hard to persuade [Han Xin] of the scheme of <u>dividing all under Heaven into three</u>, as recorded in the biography of Tong. Han Xin could not bear to betray the Han. He also thought that, because he had great merit, the king of Han would not take Qi from him. Therefore, he did not listen to [Kuai Tong]. . . .

Emperor Gaozu ordered warriors to bind Xin and put him into the rear carriage. Xin said, "It is really as people say: 'When the cunning hares are dead, the good dog will be boiled.'"

The emperor said, "Someone reported that you revolted." Therefore, [the emperor] had him put into fetters. . . .

When Xin was about to be beheaded, he said, "I regret that I did not make use of Kuai Tong's scheme, but have, on the contrary, been tricked by a woman and her lackey. Is it not [because of] Heaven?"

The episodes in *Records of the Historian* are heavily diminished in this excerpt, resulting in the deemphasis of Han Xin's personal decision in *History of the Han*. Although Han Xin's words in the first arresting scene are fully preserved, the analogy of hares and dogs is much less powerful, as it has never appeared earlier in the text. Moreover, while Han Xin's final words remain unchanged, they lose the literary effects they have in *Records of the Historian*, where they stir the reader's emotions. Since Kuai Tong's detailed analysis of the relationship between Liu Bang and Han Xin is not laid out, the causality of Han Xin's decline is obscured. Because the thread is broken, Han Xin's lack of ambition, lack of determination, and even his final, desperate regret at not having heeded Kuai Tong's words are lost. Even though the compiler of *History of the Han* may have never intended to characterize these two personages in the same way that Sima Qian did, regardless of his intentions, his approaches to building causal relations regarding Han Xin and Kuai Tong lead to very different aesthetic effects. The separation of one chapter into two independent accounts omits much information about the circumstances in which Han Xin refuses to betray Liu Bang, although in some sense this new structure increases objectivity by presenting more absolute facts about both protagonists and less interpretation of causality.[44] In sum, whereas *Records of the Historian* pays attention to the interactions among various episodes by distorting the narrative order, constructing a theme, or establishing a thread in a chapter, *History of the Han* cares about "facts" much more than about the connections among them.

Analepses Connecting Specific Actions

Analepses are another way of manipulating narrative order. An analepsis is any delayed report of an earlier event, exactly the opposite of prolepsis.

Since *Records of the Historian*'s narration generally follows a chronological order, analepses are not often used to recount the main storyline. Often, they are an efficient technique to bring in a subsidiary event of which the reader must be informed. For this reason, most analepses in *Records of the Historian* are rather short, inserted as an immediate cause to support the proceeding of the main storyline. As with prolepses, temporal words are essential to alert readers to the beginning of the inserted or supplemented information from an earlier point. These signals include *chu* 初 (previously), *chang* 嘗 (once, like Latin *olim*), *shi* 始 (once upon a time, at first), *xi* 昔 (in the past), and so on. Sometimes, a temporal adverbial phrase ending with the word *shi* 時 (at the time of . . .) is used to suggest a retrospection defined by a more specific time. After the insertion, the narration reverts to the main storyline. In this way, the analepsis is added to the main plot, assisting in the narration right before or after the recalled episode.

On many occasions, a logical conjunction is associated with the time phrase, which further strengthens the analepsis as the direct cause of a foregoing outcome. In "The Hereditary House of Zheng" (ch. 42), as shown in the following example, Lord Xiang of Qi organizes regional lords to meet at Shouzhi. The ruler of Zheng, Lord Wei (i.e., Ziwei), joins the meeting, but his two prominent ministers, Gao Qumi and Zhai Zhong, make different decisions: whereas the former goes with the ruler, the latter does not. I have underlined the time phrases and logical conjunctions of this episode. It reads:

> 子亹元年七月，齊襄公會諸侯於首止，鄭子亹往會，高渠彌相，從，祭仲稱疾不行。<u>所以然者</u>，子亹自齊襄公為公子<u>之時</u>，嘗會鬥，相仇。及會諸侯，祭仲請子亹無行。子亹曰：「齊彊，而厲公居櫟，即不往，是率諸侯伐我，內厲公。我不如往，往何遽必辱，且又何至是！」卒行。於是祭仲恐齊并殺之，<u>故稱疾</u>。⁴⁵

In the seventh month of Lord Wei's first year, Lord Xiang of Qi met the regional lords at Shouzhi. Lord Wei of Zheng went to the meeting. Gao Qumi served as the prime minister and followed [Lord Wei]. Zhai Zhong claimed to be sick and did not go. <u>The reason for this situation</u> was that, <u>when</u> Ziwei of Zheng and Lord Xiang of Qi were still noble scions, they once fought and came to regard each other as enemies. When it was time to meet the regional lords, Zhai Zhong requested that Lord Wei not go. Ziwei said, "The state of Qi is strong and Lord Li [Ziwei's older brother] is in Yue. If I do not go, [Qi] will lead the regional lords to attack me and let Lord Li in. I'd rather go [to the meeting]. Going will not necessarily lead to disgrace. It also would not be like this [what Zhai Zhong predicted]." Finally, [Lord Wei] went to [the meeting]. At that time, Zhai Zhong was afraid that Qi would kill him too. He <u>therefore</u> said that he was sick.

In this excerpt, the narrator first tells the reader that Zhai Zhong refuses to go with his ruler, claiming to be sick. In order to explain this decision, the narrator inserts an analepsis. The time phrase starting with "when" brings in the earlier, hostile relationship between the lords of Qi and Zheng. Then, this inserted timeline continues and connects with an alerting request from Zhai Zhong that Lord Wei not go, because going would put the lord in danger; unfortunately, Lord Wei does not listen to him. Then the narrative goes back to the main storyline and informs the reader that, fearing that he may be killed in Qi, this practical minister does not join the trip. Also note that the insertion begins with *suo yi ran zhe* 所以然者 (the reason for this situation was) and ends with *gu* 故 (therefore), which consolidates the previous conflicts between the rulers and the unheeded advice as the direct reason for Zhai Zhong's cautious decision. In this way, events that are chronologically distant are connected in the logical chain. The chapter later tells us that the ruler of Qi is enraged by Lord Wei and assassinates him.

Another example is "The Hereditary Houses of the Families Related to the Emperors by Marriage" (ch. 49), which contains accounts of the Han emperors' empresses. The account of Wei Zifu, the second empress of Emperor Wu, relates her rise to the downfall of the emperor's first empress, Empress Chen. The two women differ remarkably in social status and fertility: Wei Zifu was born in a commoner's family and gives birth to four children; in contrast, Empress Chen, whose mother is Emperor Wu's aunt, the grand princess, has never borne the emperor any children. Eventually, despite Chen's continuous attempts, she fails to restore her position before she dies. In the narrative, the emperor's sister comments that Chen's demotion is due to her sterility; however, the following excerpt actually attributes it to her terrible personality. I have underlined the markers of the beginning and ending of the analepsis.

衛子夫得見，涕泣請出。上憐之，復幸，遂有身，尊寵日隆。召其兄衛長君弟青為侍中。而子夫後大幸，有寵，凡生三女一男。男名據。初，上為太子時，娶長公主女為妃。立為帝，妃立為皇后，姓陳氏，無子。上之得為嗣，大長公主有力焉，以故陳皇后驕貴。聞衛子夫大幸，恚，幾死者數矣。上愈怒。陳皇后挾婦人媚道，其事頗覺，於是廢陳皇后，而立衛子夫為皇后。[46]

When Wei Zifu obtained the chance to meet [the emperor], she wept and begged to exit [the palace]. The emperor pitied her and favored her once more. Thereupon, she became pregnant, and her honor and the emperor's favor increased day by day. [The emperor] summoned her older brother, Changjun, and younger brother, Wei Qing, to be palace attendants. Thereafter, Zifu enjoyed extraordinary favor with the emperor. She bore him three daughters and a son. The son's name was Ju. Sometime earlier, when Emperor Wu was crown prince, he had married the daughter of the grand princess as the consort. [The crown prince] ascended the throne, and the consort ascended as empress, with Chen as her last name. [She] had no children. The grand princess contributed to the emperor's becoming the successor. For this reason, Empress Chen was haughty and gave herself airs of grandeur. When she heard that Wei Zifu had won great favor [from the emperor], she was furious and was several times on the verge of death. The emperor became even more enraged. Empress Chen resorted to the way of female sorcery. The affair was detected. Therefore, [the emperor] dismissed Empress Chen and installed Wei Zifu as the empress.

The narrative begins with Wei Zifu's notable fertility. Then it uses *chu* (sometime earlier) to go back to the earlier time when Emperor Wu was still the crown prince. This insertion reveals the cooperating relationship between the emperor and his wife's family: the grand princess supported Emperor Wu in his bid to be selected as the crown prince, and the text directly correlates this support with Empress Chen's excessive pride. With the end of this analepsis marked with *gu*, the narrative goes back to the normal, primary, chronological storyline. The analepsis serves as an immediate cause for Empress Chen's reaction to the emperor's favor in Wei Zifu. This brief insertion paves the way for the following plot, wherein Empress Chen behaves insanely, finally causing the emperor to demote her. Thus, the primary reason for Chen's demotion is not her sterility but her prideful personality, which the emperor no longer wants to endure.

Conclusion

By employing chronological order, simultaneous order, prolepses, and analepses in the narratives, *Records of the Historian* creates an unprecedented, complicated causal network. Through these four types of orders, the text correlates individual episodes at the account (or chapter) level and represents the past in a meaningful evolution. In this text, one finds it impossible to isolate one incident from others; the text does not provide a simple explanation of the past; rather, it strives to present an interrelated causal network. The success and failure of a historical person, a family, and a state are not attributed to one incident, nor are rewards and punishments neatly correlated to one's morality, proprietary rules, or behavior codes. Despite the constraints of early sources, the text's narration of the Spring and Autumn era and following periods depicts the ending of a subject's life or existence as a collective result, which has been impacted by historical events, simultaneous stimuli, a historical figure's capability, personal choice, and individual personality. It is these practical factors that string the chapters into a meaningful whole, which illuminates the causes of prosperity and failure.

Chapter 3

Narrative Speed

Elaborating Stairs Ascending to Power

While the temporal order of events displayed through a manipulated sequence in a history suggests how historians build logic between past events, the concept of narrative speed is used to qualify historians' regulation of information on various levels. When historians compile or compose an account, they must constantly decide how much information to offer. While editing, they have the options of curtailing the sources to concisely report an event, retaining all the details provided by the sources, or elaborating the event with more descriptions. This speeding up or slowing down in narration determines how much information readers have access to. Through this device, historians redefine the reader's focus on past events, thereby shifting the text's emphases and rhetorical functions.

To measure the density of information within a narrative unit, I bring in Gérard Genette's concept of narrative speed, a quantitative tool that allows us to closely examine what is emphasized and deemphasized in a historical work. With the advantage of the extensive linear structure of the accounts in *Records of the Historian*, the text demonstrates a pattern of slowing down to describe *how* small beginnings accumulate over time and ultimately lead to major historical changes. By manifesting the interrelations between actions in a series, *Records of the Historian* prioritizes the unbroken, internal chain that holds multiple episodes together. Thus, rather than emphasizing any single event or any single cause of an event, Sima Qian elevated the importance of the overall historical processes to an unparalleled level in early China. In comparison to earlier and later historical works, such emphasis inevitably undermines *Records of the Historian*'s didactic function while increasing its multiplicity of meanings.

Narrative Speed

When not constrained by the scarcity of sources, the limit of textual length, and other factors, narrators can indicate the relative importance of events by providing more information about some and less about others. Consequently, it is common to see narratives devote much of their space to an event lasting a few hours or, conversely, use one or two sentences to describe a period of many years. In this model, a good way to measure the importance of events is narrative speed, or, according to Gérard Genette, "the relationship between a duration (that of the story, measured in seconds, minutes, hours, days, months, and years) and a length (that of the text, measured in lines and in pages)."[1] The faster the narrative speed, the greater the ratio between the story duration and the information. A "fast" narrative, for example, would relate a period of decades in only a few sentences. This allows us to distinguish the more important events or episodes from the less important ones in *Zuo Commentary*, *Records of the Historian*, and *History of the Han*.

Yet, in contrast to fiction, the amount of information in historical texts is not purely a question of craft but is also determined by the limits of the authors' sources. In terms of the entire *Records of the Historian*, the narration follows the compiling principle of *yuanlüe jinxiang* 遠略近詳, meaning that sections on ancient times are briefer than those on recent times. This principle is absolutely true in terms of the number of chapters devoted to pre-Han and Han periods, which is largely a result of the availability of sources.[2] Sima Qian repeatedly mentions the dearth of relevant documents and historical records, particularly for the preimperial states other than Qin. By Sima's time, the few extant sources for this era were cursory and undated.

> 秦既得意，燒天下詩書，諸侯史記尤甚，為其有所刺譏也。詩書所以復見者，多藏人家，而史記獨藏周室，以故滅。惜哉，惜哉！獨有秦記，又不載日月，其文略不具。[3]

After Qin had achieved its goal [of unification], it burned [all the copies of] the *Odes* and *Documents* under Heaven.

[Its government targeted] in particular the historical records of the various rulers, because they satirized and ridiculed [the Qin]. The reason why the *Odes* and *Documents* have reappeared is that most of them were stored by private families, whereas the historical records were stored only by the house of Zhou, and therefore were all destroyed. How regrettable! How regrettable! The only historical records that have survived are those of Qin, and they did not record dates. Their texts are abbreviated and incomplete.

Another factor affecting the speed of a narrative is historians' perception of the past. This is particularly true at the account level in *Records of the Historian*. In order to narrate a subject's active period, which lasted at least for several decades and may have endured for several generations, Sima Qian must decide where to invest his ink and space. When he had ample sources for an account and limited space, such a decision became even more unavoidable. For example, the power struggle between Lord Zhuang of Zheng 鄭莊公 (r. 743–701 BCE) and his younger brother Duan 段 (fl. 722 BCE) is narrated in both *Zuo Commentary* and *Records of the Historian*.[4] For the years from the time when Lord Zhuang ascended the throne in 743 to Duan's final defeat in 722, *Zuo Commentary* uses 270 characters, whereas *Records of the Historian* employs 89.[5] Considering that some version of *Zuo Commentary* that was very similar to the received version was available to Sima Qian, his compression of the narrative is not the result of a lack of sources, but it is a choice on his part.

To describe the level of narrative speed, Genette develops a spectrum, with *ellipsis* at one extreme and descriptive *pause* at the other. Theoretically, the former refers to occasions when an event is simply not narrated, whereas the latter refers to the opposite, when the narration pauses as the narrator provides many details. Historians may be said to *pause* when they suspend the progress of the story to offer descriptions. Between the two extremes are two intermediate points: *scene* and *summary*. When the narrator presents the story roughly in real time, with neither acceleration nor slowdown, usually in the form of dialogue, it is said to be told in "scene." Summary, which lies between scene and ellipsis on this spectrum, covers a wide range of narrative speeds, depending on the degree to which the author condenses the story.[6]

A slow narrative offers more details, from the characters' physical appearances to psychological descriptions and thought processes, from depictions of direct or indirect speech to discrete acts, from the arrangement of seats to the food served at a banquet. Within a textual representation, these elaborate descriptions can be imitative of real or fictional events.[7] Vivid narrative is characterized by extraordinary richness of detail. For example, the narrative speed of *Zuo Commentary* varies from entry to entry, but when the narrative slows down, it is often to quote the direct speech of important characters. This slowing down is evident in scenes related to diplomacy, in which the kings or high officials of two states meet and discuss important political issues. This occurs particularly at banquets, as we shall see in the analysis regarding the Tian family.

Nonetheless, this does not mean that heavy intrusions by the narrator fail to create a feeling of imitation, or mimesis in other words. For nonverbal events, the narrator can provide a tremendous amount of information to mimetically represent even the briefest actions. In "The Arrayed Traditions of General Li" (i.e., Li Guang 李廣; d. 119 BCE), Sima Qian describes Li Guang's escape from the Xiongnu 匈奴 in vivid detail:

> 胡騎得廣，廣時傷病，置廣兩馬閒，絡而盛臥廣。行十餘里，廣詳死，睨其旁有一胡兒騎善馬，廣暫騰而上胡兒馬，因推墮兒，取其弓，鞭馬南馳數十里，復得其餘軍，因引而入塞。[8]

> The barbarian horsemen captured Li Guang. Li Guang at that time was wounded. [Therefore, the horsemen] put Li Guang between two horses and strung a hammock for Li Guang to rest in. After they had traveled more than ten *li*, Li Guang pretended to be dead. [He] peered around and saw a young Xiongnu boy right beside him mounted on a fine horse. Li Guang suddenly leapt out of the hammock and onto the boy's horse. Pushing the boy off, he seized his bow, whipped the horse, and galloped dozens of *li* southwards. [There, Li Guang] joined the remnants of his army, leading it into a camp.

In relating this episode, the narrative provides a detailed description of a series of actions by Li Guang—his capture, his secret observation of his surroundings, and his abrupt and successful escape—which makes the episode easier to envision. It is worth noting that the escape of Li Guang is also narrated almost identically in *History of the Han*.[9] In this sense, not all parallel narratives in *Records of the Historian* and *History of* the Han show such a remarkable difference of narrative speed. In sum, narrative speed gives us a metric, a quantitative tool, for measuring the variability of narrative speed, which will more visibly manifest the relative emphasis placed on an event in a narrative.

Two examples from *Records of the Historian*, set in different time periods but sharing the same theme of seizing power, represent the principle that the same event can be narrated for different purposes. The first is the Tian lineage's takeover of the state of Qi 田氏代齊 (Tianshi dai Qi), a story that starts during the eighth century and ends in the fifth century BCE. *Zuo Commentary* reports individual events related to this transformative power transfer in its self-contained entries. On the basis of entries in *Zuo Commentary*, *Records of the Historian*, covering the same historical period, follows a linear structure to recount the Tian lineage's rise in Qi and ultimate control of Qi. Although this is a compiled account, Sima Qian did not struggle with a scarcity of materials. The other instance concerns Empress Lü's (241–180 BCE) usurpation during the early Han (202 BCE–220 CE). This story ended with the empress's death, merely three decades earlier than Sima Qian's birth. Sima recounts this story in the "Basic Annals of Empress Dowager Lü." Ban Gu revised this chapter to retell the same story when compiling *History of the Han*.

These examples illustrate the effects of narrative pace. First, *Records of the Historian*'s accounts of the two examples represent two major categories of the work's accounts: those compiled on the bases of predated texts and those composed with raw materials, which I have discussed in previous chapters. Meanwhile, the datings of the two stories are centuries apart, showing how Sima Qian handled his narration of events from the preimperial period and the Han dynasty. Second, in both cases, Sima didn't suffer from a lack of sources, meaning the *Records of the Historian* versions of both stories are the outcome of his personal editorial decision. The basic facts of the two examples in different versions are more or less the same. Neither Sima Qian nor Ban Gu heavily altered the facts from his sources in his own retellings. Thus, the divergence in narrative effects is rooted in the narrative pace. Third, the two examples share the common theme of power struggle, a sensitive topic that can be interpreted from opposite standpoints. Thus, by comparing the parallel versions of the two examples we can see more clearly how the narrative pace as a device reinforces or undermines the moral codes of the same story.

Prophecy versus Process: The Tian Lineage's Usurpation in *Zuo Commentary* and *Records of the Historian*

It is easy to find similar, sometimes even verbatim, narrations of the same events in *Zuo Commentary* and *Records of the Historian*.[10] Yet despite their similarities, *Zuo Commentary* and *Records of the Historian* differ in narrative speed when recounting the same stories. The representations of Tian's usurpation in the two texts illustrate this difference. The basic facts regarding the Tian family are as follows. The ancestor of the Tian lineage was Chen Wan 陳完 (b. 706 BCE), a member of the ruling house of Chen. Because of continual factional strife at court, in 672 BCE he fled to Qi, where he was welcomed by Lord Huan of Qi 齊桓公 (r. 685–643 BCE). Chen Wan thus settled in Qi and changed his family name to Tian. In 386 BCE, Lord Huan's offspring Lord Kang of Qi 齊康公, the last of the Jiang 姜 to govern Qi, was dethroned by Tian He 田和 (r. 404–384 BCE), the tenth-generation descendant of Chen Wan (hereafter Tian Wan). The Zhou court then officially recognized the Tian as the new ruling house of Qi.[11] *Records of the Historian* devotes a full chapter to the Tian family in "The Tian Jingzhong Wan Shijia" 田敬仲完世家 (The Hereditary House of Tian Jingzhong Wan), starting with Tian Wan's flight to Qi, through the family's takeover of Qi, and ending with Qi's annexation by Qin in 221 BCE. Whereas *Records of the Historian* recounts the usurpation process—from Tian Wan's arrival in Qi to the enthronement of Tian He—in this chapter, *Zuo Commentary* reports only three events in this process in three disjointed narratives, each using remarkably different narrative speed.

Three factors prevent *Zuo Commentary* from reporting a historical process. The first is the text's ellipses of tangible actions of historical figures and great emphasis on the predictions of scribes and statesmen by connecting forewarning with eventual fulfillment.[12] As a result, even though banquets and divinations are narrated slowly, either in scene or in pause, the plot does not include concrete actions that push the time-line forward. Instead, readers usually get access only to knowledge of a character's good (or bad) qualities that are exhibited at a banquet or in a divination, and to the eventual fulfillment of the prediction years later. What actually connects the two parts is the close correspondence between divinations and their fulfillments, rather than the coherence among the characters' motivations, deeds, and outcome of events. Narratologically, the text slows down at certain causes, predictions, and outcomes. Yet many of the small changes that accumulate and lead to outcomes, and thus constitute the historical process, are skipped. The speeches that take the most space in an entry serve to teach the everlasting principle that the good are rewarded and the bad punished.[13]

Take the first entry regarding the Tian lineage's rise in *Zuo Commentary* as an example. It is placed under the twenty-second year of Lord Zhuang of Lu's reign (672 BCE), when the ancestor, Tian Wan, has settled in Qi. This entry recounts two scenes to which are appended two divinations, which are also narrated in *Records of the Historian*. The first scene reports that Lord Huan of Qi proposes to appoint Tian Wan to be a high official at his court, but Tian, as an appropriate guest seeking Qi's sheltering, politely declines it by citing the *Book of Odes*. In the second, Tian hosts Lord Huan at a banquet during the day. It is so joyful that Lord Huan wants to continue it into the night. Again, Tian Wan behaves properly by indirectly remonstrating with the lord, urging him not to indulge in drinking. The two scenes portray Tian Wan's respectful self-restraint and sense of responsibility in a foreign domain.

These scenes are then directly connected, in detail, to two auspicious divinations, both predicting the future greatness of the Tian lineage before Tian fled to Qi. The first was probably done when Tian married. The head of the Yi clan, a high official of Tian's home state, divined whether he should marry his daughter to Tian Wan. The divination assured the official not only that the marriage would be harmonious but also that in five generations Tian's descendants would flourish, and that after eight generations they would reach unparalleled heights. The second divination was conducted during Tian Wan's childhood by the grand scribe (*taishi* 太史) of Zhou. *Zuo Commentary* pauses the narrative to quote the long interpretations of both divinations, which directly hint at the Tian lineage's prosperity in Qi. Then, the text skips generations ahead and ends the entry by simply confirming what was predicted: the seizure of power by Tian Qi 田乞 (the head of Tian Wan's sixth-generation descendants, with Tian Wan being the first generation; d. 485 BCE) and his heir Tian Chang 田常 (the head of Tian Wan's seventh-generation descendants, sometimes called Tian Chengzi; fl. fifth century BCE).[14]

The fast narrative speed of *Zuo Commentary* reveals that Tian Wan's appropriate actions, which are in line with rituals and morality, dictate the future prosperity of his descendants. Whether members of the Tian lineage have a goal of seizing power, and if so, how they realize it through generations, is not important to *Zuo Commentary* editors. The two divinations are attested, and their fulfillment reinforces the power of the behavior code. While *Records of the Historian* includes both scenes and both divinations, it abbreviates them into summaries and relates both divinations to a gradual realization of this process, as we will see in this chapter.

The second factor that prevents *Zuo Commentary* from reporting historical processes is its slow analytical speech. Many narratives in *Zuo Commentary* do not depict the characters' actions directly but instead let these actions be evaluated by wise ministers or historians, who often didactically explain the outcome of contemporary events by judging the characters' deeds. Narrated in scene, these entries highlight the teaching embedded in the characters' mouths. Their moral judgments turn movable plot into static scenes, causing the narrative timeline to move too little to present a progression in storyline. The *Zuo Commentary* account of the Tian lineage's manipulation of the standards for units of volume is a good example. In the third year of Lord Zhao of Lu (r. 542–510 BCE), the Qi official Yan Ying 晏嬰 (ca. 580–510) goes to Jin on a diplomatic mission and meets the Jin official Shu Xiang 叔向 (fl. 539–536). They exchange ideas about politics in Qi and Jin and predict the futures of the two states respectively. In his speech, Yan Ying comments on the contrastive policies in Qi, that is, the harsh economic policies of the lord and the benevolent administration of the Tian family, who uses larger pecks to lend grain to the people, and smaller pecks to collect repayment:

> 叔向曰：「齊其何如？」
> 　　晏子曰：「此季世也。吾弗知，齊其為陳氏矣。公棄其民，而歸於陳氏。齊舊四量，豆、區、釜、鍾。四升為豆，各自其四，以登於釜。釜十則鍾。陳氏三量皆登一焉，鍾乃大矣。以家量貸，而以公量收之。山木如市，弗加於山，魚、鹽、蜃、蛤，弗加於海。民參其力，二入於公，而衣食其一。公聚朽蠹，而三老凍餒，國之諸市，屨賤踴貴。民人痛疾，而或燠休之。其愛之如父母，而歸之如流水。欲無獲民，將焉辟之？」[15]

Shu Xiang said, "How are [the state affairs] in Qi?"

Master Yan said, "These are the last ruling house's generations. I do not know but that Qi will go to the Chen lineage [i.e., Tian]. The lord has abandoned his people, and they are shifting their allegiance to the Chen lineage. Qi's old four units of measure are the *dou*, the *qu*, the *fu*, and the *zhong*. Four *sheng* make a *dou*, and four of each successive measure make one of the next, up to *fu*. Ten *fu* is one *zhong*. The Chens make each of the [first] three measures once again greater, so that the *zhong* is larger. When they lend [grain], they use their household measures, but when they collect on their loans, they use the lord's measure. For wood in the markets, they charge the same price as when it is on their hills, not adding to the value of the wood on the hills. For their fish, salt, mussels, and clams, they keep the price no higher than it is at the seashore. If the strength of the people is divided into three parts, two parts go to the lord and only one part goes to clothing and feeding the people themselves. The lord's grain stores are rotten and infested with vermin, while the three classes of elders are freezing and starving. In all the markets of the capital, ordinary shoes are cheap, but the shoes designed for amputees are expensive.[16] The people suffer torments, yet there is someone there to offer them a warm reprieve. The people will love the Chen lineage like parents and will give their allegiance to them like water flowing downhill. Even if the Chen lineage did not want to win the people over, how could they avoid doing so?

By putting this story in the mouth of Yan Ying almost as a treatise, *Zuo Commentary* makes it nonnarrative. This banquet scene employs direct speech, but the exchanges between Shu Xiang and Yan Ying do not contribute to the reader's knowledge of the characters or the development of the plot. Therefore, although the narrative proceeds at a slower speed, the plot is not an imitative process that moves forward, but a static lecture. Yan Ying's speech emphasizes the moral logic behind the rise of the Tian lineage: the lord neglected the people while the Tian lineage opportunistically showed them care. From a moral perspective, the juxtaposition explains the inevitability of the outcome that the readers of *Zuo Commentary* already knew well. Behind the comment is the reinforced correlation between Tian's moral standing and the legitimation of their becoming the new ruling house of Qi. In contrast, *Records of the Historian* turns Yan Ying's analytical comment into a single step in a string of the Tians' actions in seizing power in Qi, depicting it as a tactic rather than a sacrifice.

The third factor that deemphasizes the logical historical process in *Zuo Commentary* is the relatively constant narrative speed of entries. It is difficult to distinguish between the protagonist and supporting characters because they are given more or less equal space in the text, and the focus of the narrative is similarly blurred. As we shall see in the third entry that is related to the Tians' usurpation in *Zuo Commentary*, before Lord Jing of Qi (Qi Jing gong 齊景公; r. 547–490 BCE) died, he designated one of his younger sons, Tu 荼 (fl. 490), as the crown prince; but Tian Qi supported an older son, Yangsheng 陽生, soon-to-be Lord Dao 悼公 (r. 489–485).[17]

Whereas the account of the installation of Yangsheng in *Records of the Historian* slows down whenever Tian Qi speaks and acts, the *Zuo Commentary* version reports the same plot by spilling more ink to describe Yangsheng. In *Records of the Historian*, Tian Qi is undoubtedly the core character who enables Yangsheng to succeed to the throne. He sends a messenger to take Yangsheng back to Qi and arranges for him to appear abruptly in front of the high officials of Qi, forcing them to agree to establish Yangsheng as the new ruler. This scheme implemented by Tian Qi played a critical role in turning these officials' attitude, particularly by causing the minister Bao Mu 鮑牧 to give up his objection and switch his support to Yangsheng.

Unlike *Records of the Historian*, *Zuo Commentary* speeds up Tian Qi's actions and speeches and slows down to report Yangsheng's behavior. The entry (Ai 6.6) first carefully describes Yangsheng's tricky return to Qi from exile in Lu, then reports Yangsheng's long, didactic speech to Bao Mu, which changes Bao Mu's mind so that he supports Yangsheng's installation as the new ruler. Not only that: once enthroned, Yangsheng continues to be an active character in the *Zuo Commentary* version. The last part of the entry records Yangsheng warning Tian Qi that, as the new ruler, he will not allow disloyalty to threaten his throne. Tian Qi's careful response successfully allays Yangsheng's mistrust, and Yangsheng then decides to give Tian Qi responsibility for major affairs of state.[18] In *Zuo Commentary*, the narrative proceeds at a relatively constant pace regardless of who is speaking and acting, and as a result Yangsheng becomes an important character who exhibits political wisdom in grasping the opportunity to change his fate, which minimizes Tian Qi's decisive role in enthroning Yangsheng as seen in *Records of the Historian*.

This chronicle-style organization of discrete narratives in *Zuo Commentary* only intensifies this lack of overt focus. All events that happened in the same year—in different states, to different people, of different types—are recorded in the same entry. While the *Zuo Commen-*

tary entry previously analyzed represents a fragment cut out of a longer historical process, this scattered organization makes it difficult to connect events, let alone to track the long process whereby a person or a family develops. For example, three entries above the entry of Ai 6.6 in *Zuo Commentary*, there is another entry involving Tian Qi, narrating that Tian and Bao Mu engineer a coup and drive the newly installed ruler, Tu, into exile. Despite the close relationship between the two entries, the disconnected format of *Zuo Commentary* obscures the coherent logic behind Tian Qi's acts in these entries. Moreover, the episode in 6.6 has no direct relationship with the event that immediately precedes it or the event narrated immediately after.

In the full chapter revolving around the Tian lineage, "The Tian Jing-zhong Wan Shijia" (The Hereditary House of Tian Jing-zhong Wan),[19] *Records of the Historian* covers six critical steps by which the Tian lineage gradually took control of Qi over the course of sixteen generations. The uneven narrative speed of the text enables it to focus in particular on the actions and lives of Tian Qi, Tian Wan's sixth-generation descendant (otherwise known as Tian Xizi 田釐子), and Tian Chang 田常 (fl. 485 BCE), who was the heir of Tian Qi as well as the seventh-generation lineage head. These two figures are special, as they set the cornerstone for the Tian lineage's rise to influence and power in the Qi court. Narrating their concrete operations at an extremely slow speed is not a random but an active editing choice.

The beginning of the *Records of the Historian* chapter incorporates the two auspicious divinations in *Zuo Commentary* (one by the grand scribe of Zhou and the other by the Yi family) that predict that Tian Wan's descendants will replace the Jiang family as the ruling house of Qi. After the narrative quickly introduces Tian Wan's father, it briefly narrates the genealogy of the Tian lineage over five generations in two lines. When it comes to Tian Qi's father, Tian Xuwu 田須無 (fl. 548 BCE), the narrative slightly slows down. Lord Jing of Qi's favor toward Tian Xuwu gives rise to the first elevation of the Tian family in Qi, marking the beginning of the rise of Tian.

When the chapter reaches Tian Qi, its narrative speed slows down substantially. Tian Qi eventually became Lord Jing's prime minister and, in that role, cemented the dominance of the Tian lineage over affairs of state in Qi. In the *Records of the Historian* account, Tian seizes power first by altering the standard measures described in *Zuo Commentary*.

The first step:

田釐子乞事齊景公為大夫，其收賦稅於民以小斗受之，其（粟）［稟］予民以大斗，行陰德於民，而景公弗禁。由此田氏得齊眾心，宗族益彊，民思田氏。晏子數諫景公，景公弗聽。已而使於晉，與叔向私語曰「齊之政卒歸田氏矣。」[20]

Tian Xizi [i.e., Tian Qi] served Lord Jing of Qi as a grandee. When he collected taxes from the people, he would measure out the taxes due in small pecks, [but] he would distribute [grain] to the people in large pecks. [In doing so], he secretly gained favor among the people, but Lord Jing did not forbid it. <u>From then on, the Tian lineage won the hearts of the people in Qi. The [Tian] lineage and families grew in power, and people grew fond of the Tian lineage.</u> Master Yan [i.e., Yan Ying] remonstrated several times. The lord did not heed [the advice]. Soon when he went on a mission to Jin, Yan Ying privately told Shu Xiang that "the government of Qi will eventually go to the Tian lineage."

Unlike the static reported speech attributed to Yan Ying in *Zuo Commentary*, the *Records of the Historian* episode narrates Tian Qi's implementation of nonstandard measures through his own actions. The preceding episode also skips Yan Ying's windy analysis in *Zuo Commentary* concerning the contrasting outcomes resulting from the lord's and Tian's different measures, only preserving Yan Ying's vision of Qi's future. These editorial changes turn *Zuo Commentary*'s static moral compliment of Tian into a description of pure action. This passage from *Records of the Historian* explains how Tian Qi expanded the Tian's influence outside court, how Lord Jing reacted, and how this action succeeded in building popular support for the Tian lineage. The middle sentence, which I have underlined, highlights the effects of this step by marking this event as the beginning of the rise of the Tian lineage. Sima Qian slows the narrative to lay out the implementation of the concrete actions and their outcome and influence, a pattern repeated throughout the Tian usurpation. Without altering any facts recorded in *Zuo Commentary*, Sima Qian presents the popular support as a practical effect of the first step, rather than as the cause that accounts for Tian's legitimation.

Tian Qi next wanted to set up Yangsheng as the new ruler, a key step in bringing the Tian lineage closer to the throne. In *Records of the Historian*, in order to realize this goal, Tian Qi purposefully sparked factional conflict, which became so severe that the contemporary ruler, Tu, was expelled from the capital. Tian Qi took advantage of Tu's flight to enthrone Yangsheng, who got along well with him. The installation of Yangsheng as the new lord (i.e., Lord Dao of Qi) is presented in the scene at a narrative speed even slower than that of the scheme of manipulating the weight measures. The following passage, based on *Zuo Commentary* but rewritten, describes how Tian Qi directed the event so that it would proceed according to his design. It contains a wealth of information about Yangsheng's installation: the banquet setting, direct speech, and detailed descriptions of the actions and thoughts of the characters involved.

The second step:

> 田乞使人之魯，迎陽生。陽生至齊，匿田乞家。請諸大夫曰：「常之母有魚菽之祭，幸而來會飲。」會飲田氏。田乞盛陽生橐中，置坐中央。發橐，出陽生，曰：「此乃齊君矣。」大夫皆伏謁。將盟立之，田乞誣曰：「吾與鮑牧謀共立陽生也。」鮑牧怒曰：「大夫忘景公之命乎？」諸大夫欲悔，陽生乃頓首曰：「可則立之，不可則已。」鮑牧恐禍及己，乃復曰：「皆景公之子，何為不可！遂立陽生於田乞之家，是為悼公。乃使人遷晏孺子於駘，而殺孺子荼。<u>悼公既立，田乞為相，專齊政</u>。²¹

Tian Qi sent an emissary to Lu to welcome Yangsheng [back to Qi]. When Yangsheng arrived in Qi, he hid himself in Tian Qi's house. [Tian Qi] invited other high officials over, saying, "Although I can offer only a humble repast, how fortunate we would be if you would gather together with us and feast!" [The officials] then got together and drank at Tian's house. Tian Qi had Yangsheng placed in a sack and had the sack placed on a seat in the middle [of the room]. He opened the sack and let Yangsheng out, whereupon he said, "This is the lord of Qi." The high officials all bowed before him, paying their respects. When it was time to make a covenant and establish him as the ruler, Tian Qi lied, saying, "Bao Mu and I schemed together to install Yangsheng." Bao Mu was infuriated [by this] and said, "Did my fellow high officials forget Lord Jing's will?" The officials wanted to renege on the agreement. Yangsheng then kowtowed to the officials and said, "If [you] approve of [me], then place me upon the throne; if [you] do not approve of [me], then put a stop to this." Bao Mu was afraid that misfortune might happen to him, and so he backtracked and said, "Both [of you] are sons of Lord Jing. Why [do I] not approve of [you]?" Therefore, [the ministers] installed Yangsheng at Tian Qi's house. This was Lord Dao. [Tian Qi] then sent someone to escort Yan Ruzi [the legitimate ruler—i.e., Tu] to Tai and kill Ruzi. <u>After Lord Dao was installed, Tian Qi became the prime minister and had absolute power in Qi.</u>

Once again, we have an important scheme described in great detail, from setting its goal to its execution. While supporting characters such as Yangsheng and Bao Mu are presented, the episode still focuses on Tian Qi as the main character, who plans, executes, and benefits from the plot. And once again, the episode ends with an evaluative sentence commenting on how this scheme furthered the ambitions of the Tian lineage, as underlined in the previous passage.

Tian Qi's efforts seen in the two aforementioned steps created a solid foundation, and his son, Tian Chang, built on that foundation to increase the family's power. From the time of Tian Chang onward, the Qi lords were no more than puppets enthroned or deposed depending on the whims of whichever powerful family was then ascendant at court. During Lord Jian's 簡公 reign (484–481 BCE), Tian Chang and Kan Zhi served as prime ministers. To overcome his rival Kan Zhi, Tian Chang again manipulated the measures to win the heart of the people and then established a new ruler, Lord Ping (Ping gong 平公; r. 480–456 BCE). The strategy of measures had been employed by Tian Qi, but rather than omit or summarize Tian Chang's actions, Sima Qian chooses once again to narrate in detail and highlight its effects at the end of this episode. I have underlined in the following passage.

The third step:

田常成子與監止俱為左右相，相簡公。田常心害監止，闞止幸於簡公，權弗能去。於是田常復修釐子之政，以大斗出貸，以小斗收。齊人歌之曰：「嫗乎采芑，<u>歸乎田成子</u>！」[22]

Tian Chang and Kan Zhi served together as left prime minister and right prime minister, assisting Lord Jian. Tian Chang was secretly envious of Kan Zhi. [Since] Kan Zhi was favored by

Lord Jian, he could not be removed from power. Therefore, Tian Chang once again put into practice the policy of Tian Xizi. [He] used big pecks to lend [grain] and small pecks to collect [repayments]. The Qi people sang: "The women gather vegetables, and <u>bring them all to Tian Chengzi</u>!"

The power struggle between Tian Chang and Kan Zhi later developed into a conflict with great consequences for the two families. Since Lord Jian didn't side with either family, when the Tian family broke into the palace to eradicate Kan Zhi's followers, the lord was afraid and escaped to Xuzhou.[23] *Records of the Historian* abbreviates this section—which is described in great detail in *Zuo Commentary*—by focusing on how the Tian sons eliminated their enemy, which contributes to the next step, in which the Tian lineage took Lord Jian into custody and, fearing the repercussions, decided to kill him and establish another member of the Jiang lineage in his place:

The fourth step:

田氏之徒恐簡公復立而誅己，遂殺簡公。簡公立四年而殺。於是田常立簡公弟驁，是為平公。平公即位，<u>田常為相</u>。[24]

The members of the Tian lineage were worried that Lord Jian would be restored and put them all to death. Therefore, [they] assassinated Lord Jian. After Lord Jian had been enthroned for four years, [he] was assassinated. Thereafter, Tian Chang installed the younger brother of Lord Jian, Ao, as Lord Ping. After Lord Ping ascended the throne, <u>Tian Chang became prime minister</u>.

In this way, Tian Chang overcame his rival Kan Zhi. With Lord Ping enthroned, Tian became the sole prime minister. As in earlier *Records of the Historian* steps, the underlined final sentences in the two previous passages state the outcome of these two steps, which indicate the consequences of these incidents.

Next (the fifth step), Tian Chang then asked Lord Ping to hand over penal authority to him, claiming that he would thus be able to serve as political cover for the sovereign. As Sima Qian indicates in the sentence underlined in the next passage, however, Tian Chang's true aim was to trick his lord into giving Tian almost unlimited power, which Tian then used to eliminate all the rival families. With his power uncontested, Tian Chang was able to carve out a domain from the territory of Qi for himself. In the last sentence of the passage that relates this development (the sixth step), the narrator informs us that Tian's fief was even larger than the private landholdings of Lord Ping—by this stage, Tian Chang was the ruler of Qi in all but name.

The fifth step:

田常言於齊平公曰：「德施，人之所欲；君其行之。刑罰，人之所惡；臣請行之。」<u>行之五年，齊國之政皆歸田常</u>。[25]

Tian Chang said to Lord Ping, "Virtue and charity are what people desire, and so my lord should put them into practice. Punishments and penalties are what people hate; so please let your humble minister carry these out." <u>After five years of this practice, all responsibility for governance in Qi had come to reside with Tian Chang.</u>

The sixth step:

田常於是盡誅鮑、晏、監止及公族之彊者，而割齊自安平以東至瑯邪，自為封邑。<u>封邑大於平公之所食</u>。[26]

Tian Chang then killed off all members of the Bao and Yan family, Kan Zhi, and the powerful members of the ruling clan. [He] also sliced off a piece of territory from the east of Anping to Langya in Qi as his own fief. <u>His fief was bigger than the [private] estate from which Lord Ping received his revenue.</u>

Records of the Historian devotes a substantial amount of text to the six steps of the Tian lineage's rise to power: Tian Qi's manipulating the measures to gain the favor of the people; Tian Qi's enthroning Yangsheng (Lord Dao); Tian Chang's manipulating the measures to ensure the favor of the people; Tian Chang's killing of an uncooperative ruler and enthroning Lord Ping; Tian Chang's taking control of the administration of the state; and Tian Chang's carving out a fief even larger than Lord Ping's estate. With each step, Sima Qian summarizes the change in the status of the Tian lineage and underlines its significance.

After narrating the actions of Tian Chang, the narrative enormously speeds up, and *Records of the Historian* uses only a few lines to inform us that, after two generations, the head of the Tian lineage was officially recognized by the Zhou court as the Marquis of Qi. The facts *Records of the Historian* uses in narrating the six steps come almost exclusively from *Zuo Commentary*; but Sima Qian, without distorting the facts, aligned the materials to focus on the Tian family. His control of speed—a quick summary of the Tian lineage's origins, a detailed account of Tian Qi's and Tian Chang's maneuvers, and then back to a quick summary for the legitimating of their power—highlights the pivotal nature of the actions taken by Tian Qi and Tian Chang. The outcome is clearly indicated by the prophecy of the Zhou Grand Scribe at the beginning of the chapter. Yet, by laying out the rise of the Tian lineage step by step, *Records of the Historian* directs the reader's attention to the complicated processes rather than only the outcome.

Moreover, placed between the divinations and the usurpation outcome, these steps decrease the correlation—emphasized in *Zuo Commentary*—between the Tians' success and their moral sense. In *Records of the Historian*, the Tian family's eventual control of Qi is presented as a mixed result of predetermination and careful operations over the long term, rather than as a pure outcome of morally exemplary behavior. On the one hand, *Records of the Historian* follows the divinations' time frame to build the storyline; on the other hand, the text spills much ink describing how Tian Qi and Tian Chang implement schemes to approach the center of power. Despite the coexistence of predetermination and characters' actual exertions, *Records of the Historian*'s efforts to elaborate a major change through a series of coherent steps are clear.

Progress versus "Facts": Empress Dowager Lü in *Records of the Historian* and *History of the Han*

Although *History of the Han* was clearly influenced by *Records of the Historian*—the authors of *History of the Han* employ the kind of consolidated historical narratives introduced by *Records of the Historian* and may even have copied certain passages from it word for word[27]—these authors adapted the model of *Records of the Historian* to suit their own historiographic goals and employed narratives very differently. As a result, unlike *Records of the Historian*, *History of the Han* does not track accumulated changes to present a historical process but instead stresses the preservation of historical facts. One example is their diverging representations of Empress Dowager Lü in their "Basic Annals" sections. The two chapters fully devoted to her, "Lü Taihou benji" 呂太后本紀 (The Basic Annals of Empress Dowager Lü) in *Records of the Historian* and "Gaohou ji" 高后紀 (The Basic Annals of Empress of Gaozu) in *History of the Han*, allow a comparative study illuminating how these texts differ in form and function. In particular, examining where and how these chapters slow down or speed up reveals their divergent emphases. Not all parallel chapters in the two texts differ to the same degree, and the author of "Gaohou ji" might have compiled it according to particular principles, but the author's choice of what *not* to narrate or elaborate and his relocation of *Records of the Historian*'s elements exhibit several characteristics of the "Basic Annals" chapters in *History of the Han*, which in turn bring *Records of the Historian*'s narrative pattern to light.[28]

Empress Dowager Lü (Lü Zhi 呂雉, 241–180 BCE) was the primary wife of Liu Bang 劉邦 (i.e., Emperor Gaozu 高祖; r. 202–195 BCE). Lü married Liu Bang when he was still a village head in Pei County. After Liu Bang founded the Han dynasty in 202 BCE, he appointed Lü as the empress and made her son Liu Ying 劉盈 his crown prince. Ying eventually succeeded Liu Bang, ruling as Emperor Hui 惠 (r. 195–188 BCE). *Records of the Historian* and *History of the Han* refer to Lü as either Lü hou 呂后, Gao hou 高后 (the empress of Gaozu), or Lü taihou 呂太后 (Empress Dowager Lü) after she became a widow.[29]

During the seven years of Emperor Hui's reign, while the emperor performed all the rituals of state, many important policy decisions were made by Lü. After Emperor Hui's death in 188 BCE, his eleven-year-old son, Liu Gong 劉恭 (r. 188–184 BCE), became emperor. During Liu Gong's reign, Empress Dowager Lü was able to "pronounce decrees" (*chengzhi* 稱制)—that is, to administer the empire as the grandmother of the child emperor.[30] In 184 BCE, she deposed Liu Gong and enthroned another son of Liu Ying, Liu Hong 劉弘 (r. 184–180 BCE). Upon Lü's death in 180 BCE, ministers restored the rule of the Liu family by forcing the child emperor Liu Hong to abdicate, installing Liu Heng 劉恆, the adult son of Liu Bang and a concubine, as Emperor Wen 文 (r. 180–157 BCE). Since Lü was officially in charge for eight years in total, both *Records of the Historian* and *History of the Han* report events during these years according to the calendar of her reign.³¹

While both of these texts relate the same basic events summarized earlier, the two "Basic Annals" chapters differ significantly in their use of narrative speed. I divide Lü's life into three stages: (1) from her early days to Liu Bang's death in 195 BCE; (2) Emperor Hui's reign, from 195 to 188 BCE; (3) and her direct rule from 188 until her death in 180 BCE. The speed of each stage in *Records of the Historian* is slower than in *History of the Han*. *Records of the Historian* is thus able to present the rise of Empress Lü to power step by step, as well as to develop the logical connections between these points of time in all three stages. By contrast, *History of the Han* skips the first and second stage entirely, and in treating the third stage, it only summarizes important events and lists policies in chronological order.

Records of the Historian presents the first stage in summary, whereas the *History of the Han* chapter completely omits it. Including earlier events allows us to learn more about the empress dowager, particularly when experiences of her early days shed light on what followed. *Records of the Historian* introduces her: "Empress Dowager Lü was the consort of Gaozu when he was still humble" (呂太后者，高祖微時妃也).³² This foreshadowing of the future implies the account's tendency to trace events long before she became the empress of Liu Bang. The illuminating early episodes in *Records of the Historian* inform the political infighting that filled this woman's later life and explain how she built up political power. The first episode in *Records of the Historian*, for example, is an account of the fierce competition between Liu Ying and Liu Ruyi 劉如意 (208–194 BCE), the son of Lady Qi (Qi furen 戚夫人, 224–194 BCE), a concubine of Liu Bang. This competition, it will be remembered, culminated in Lü's successful defense of Liu Ying's status as crown prince.³³

Two quick summaries then indicate two sources of the Empress Dowager's power before Liu Bang's death in 195 BCE. First, Lü built up her political power as Liu Bang's primary wife and essential partner in his rise to power long before she became the empress dowager. As *Records of the Historian* explains, "The personality of Empress Lü was tough and resolute. [She] assisted Emperor Gaozu in stabilizing all under Heaven" (為人剛毅，佐高祖定天下).³⁴ The account goes on to report that Empress Lü was instrumental in the execution of great ministers who might have threatened Liu Bang's grasp on the throne, probably referring to the deaths of Han Xin 韓信 (d. 196 BCE) and Peng Yue 彭越 (d. 196 BCE), whose significance is discussed in chapter 2 of the present book.[35] Despite their pivotal military support in Liu Bang's campaign against Xiang Yu, the empress decisively eradicated both of them when they were no longer helpful but only risky to the empire. As the *Records of the Historian* account reports, Liu Bang and many of his followers recognized Lü's active role in political affairs. The couple's joint efforts depicted in these aspects suggest a more equal partnership between Lü and her husband than is reflected in *History of the Han*, and this equality certainly helped to secure Lü's status at court and beyond.

The second source of Empress Lü's power, the assistance of her family members, is also depicted in *Records of the Historian* as essential to the founding of the dynasty. For example, Empress Lü's two brothers were important commanders during the wars to establish the dynasty. Her elder brother died in one of the many battles of these conflicts, and his sons and younger brother, who also fought by Liu Bang's side, were all enfeoffed with the title of *hou* 侯 (marquis). By providing these details, *Records of the Historian* presents the foundation of the dynasty as a collaboration between the Lü and Liu families, making Empress Lü's later seizure of power and promotion of her family seem more justified and inviting the reader to understand the contention between the Lü and Liu families through this earlier power dynamic.

In *History of the Han*, Empress Dowager Lü's first stage is presented in ellipsis, which is to say the important events slowly narrated in *Records of the Historian* are completely omitted. The *History of the Han* chapter begins decades later, with Liu Gong's ascension to the throne in 188 BCE, which marks the beginning of official rule by the empress dowager. As a result, the account in *History of the Han* lacks a substantial amount of background information about the protagonist and the relationship between the Liu and Lü families, a key to understanding Lü's rise. The information that is provided in *History of the Han* describes the empress primarily in relation to the imperial family. The chapter begins: "The empress of Gaozu, whose last name is Lü, gave birth to Emperor Hui" (高皇后呂氏，生惠帝).[36] A brief overview of the imperial genealogy immediately follows, with a focus on positions and titles held by members of the Lü family, particularly the number of people who were made marquises and kings. Whereas *Records of the Historian* focuses on Lü's personality, *History of the Han* instead emphasizes her role connecting the Liu and Lü families and the problems of imperial legitimacy.

The second stage of Empress Lü's life—her consolidation of power after Liu Bang's death in 195 BCE—is, like the first stage, recounted in significant detail in *Records of the Historian*, whereas it is completely omitted in *History of the Han*. In addition to naming Liu Ying as crown prince, *Records of the Historian* lists Liu Bang's seven other sons and the titles they held, and then gives a richly detailed account of how the empress dowager eliminated two rival princes, Liu Ruyi and Liu Bang's oldest son, Liu Fei 劉肥 (fl. 201 BCE). Lü summons Ruyi to the palace to put him to death. Although Emperor Hui is warned that his younger brother is in danger, he nevertheless finds himself powerless to prevent his death. Empress Lü's gruesome revenge on her rival Lady Qi is then described in detail: "The empress dowager had Lady Qi's hands and feet cut off, gouged out her eyes, burned off her ears, had her drink a type of decoction to [make her dumb], made her live in a privy, and named her 'human pig'" (太后遂斷戚夫人手足、去眼、煇耳、飲瘖藥、使居廁中, 命曰「人彘」).[37] Emperor Hui is horrified by the inhumane treatment of Lady Qi at the hands of the empress dowager and refuses to rule the empire, abdicating all responsibility for the government to his mother. Liu Fei avoids being assassinated only by surrendering a portion of his fief to the daughter of the empress dowager. The slow speed with which *Records of the Historian* recounts this stage of the empress dowager's life has two advantages: (1) The detailed descriptions enable *Records of the Historian* to present how she consolidated her rule. (2) They demonstrate her toughness and cruelty, establishing the coherence of her personality, and providing a key for understanding the stratagems that she employs in power struggles.

Both *Records of the Historian* and *History of the Han* narrate the third stage of the empress dowager's life, the period of direct rule, which begins in 188 BCE, but the *Records of the Historian* account is far slower than the *History of the Han* account, and, indeed, even slower than the *Records of the Historian*'s own account of the two previous stages. Most of the *Records of the Historian* narrative, in fact, is dedicated to Empress Lü's rule. The divergence is particularly obvious in the case of Lü's elevation of her nephews and other male relatives from lowly positions outside the court, first to the rank of marquis and then to the rank of *wang* 王 (lit., king), second only to the emperor. In *Records of the Historian*, this is a highly complicated, deliberate, multistep process. After the death of Emperor Hui, Zhang Biqiang 張辟彊 (b. 205 BCE), the son of the Marquis of Liu (Liu hou 留侯), Zhang Liang 張良 (251–186 BCE), proposes to comfort the empress dowager by appointing three of her nephews, Lü Tai 呂臺 (d. 187 BCE), Lü Chan 呂產 (d. 180 BCE), and Lü Lu 呂祿 (d. 180 BCE), as generals.[38] The structure of this episode echoes that by which the schemes of the Tian lineage are recounted, with each maneuver concluding with a comment emphasizing its long-term significance:

七年秋八月戊寅，孝惠帝崩。發喪，太后哭，泣不下。留侯子張辟彊為侍中，年十五，謂丞相曰：「太后獨有孝惠，今崩，哭不悲，君知其解乎？」丞相曰：「何解？」辟彊曰：「帝毋壯子，太后畏君等。君今請拜呂臺、呂產、呂祿為將，將兵居南北軍，及諸呂皆入宮，居中用事，如此則太后心安，君等幸得脫禍矣。」丞相乃如辟彊計。太后說，其哭乃哀。<u>呂氏權由此起</u>。[39]

On the *wuyin* day in the eighth month of the seventh year [188 BCE], Emperor Hui passed away. Mourning commenced and the empress dowager wept, but no tears followed.[40] The son of the marquis of Liu, Zhang Biqiang, was a page in the palace; he was in his fifteenth year. [He] said to the prime minister, "The empress dowager has only [this son,] Emperor Hui. Now that he has died, she weeps but is not sorrowful. Do you know why?"

The prime minister asked, "Why?"

Biqiang said, "The emperor does not have a grown son. The Empress Dowager is afraid of you. You should now request that Lü Tai, Lü Chan, and Lü Lu be appointed as generals and be given command over the north and south garrisons, and further request that other members of the Lü clan be allowed to enter the palace and work there. If you make this request, the empress dowager's heart will be at ease. You and your followers will, with luck, escape disaster." The prime minister then followed Biqiang's plan. The empress dowager was pleased, and thereafter, her weeping became mournful. <u>The power of the Lü clan rose from that point on.</u>

This event might seem trivial, yet it attracted Sima Qian's attention. As the underlined sentence makes clear, this scene is the starting point of the Lü family's rise and a crucial step toward abrogating imperial power.

Next comes the slowest section in the *Records of the Historian* account, a section that presents minute details of this process but is completely skipped by *History of the Han*. With the ascendance in 188 BCE of the eleven-year-old Liu Gong, Empress Dowager Lü became the de jure ruler of the empire. From this point on, she had the authority to issue official commands and order personnel changes. *Records of the Historian* presents her actions in great detail, repeatedly using the temporal adverbs *xian* 先 (first, initially) and *nai* 乃 (then, thereafter) to demonstrate the logical connection between the empress dowager's intentions and her actions in the episode that follows.

The *youxiang* 右相 (prime minister of the right), Wang Ling 王陵 (d. 181 BCE), opposed making the Lü family members kings and used an oath by Liu Bang and his ministers, often referred to as the *baima zhi meng* 白馬之盟 (Oath of the White Horse), to justify his opposition. The oath dictated that if anyone who was not a Liu family member ever became a king, all under Heaven should band together and attack him.[41] Because of the obstacle presented by this oath, Empress Dowager Lü took a circuitous approach to elevating her family members. To avoid alarming the court, she began by posthumously conferring the title of king on her deceased elder brother, namely the father of her nephew Lü Tai (marquis of Li). In order to appear impartial, she also gave Feng Wuze 馮無擇 (d. 184 BCE), a minister who had served Liu Bang and was not a member of her family, the title Marquis of Bocheng 博城. She then continued to ennoble members of the Lü family, making Lü Zhong Marquis of Pei 沛 and Lü Ping Marquis of Fuliu 扶柳. As underlined, *Records of the Historian* describes Empress Dowager Lü's thought process for each step in this complicated sequence, highlighting her strategic planning:

> 元年，號令一出太后。太后稱制，議欲立諸呂為王，問右丞相王陵。王陵曰：「高帝刑白馬盟曰『非劉氏而王，天下共擊之』。今王呂氏，非約也。」太后不說。 . . . 十一月，太后欲廢王陵，乃拜為帝太傅，奪之相權。 . . . 乃追尊酈侯父為悼武王，欲以王諸呂為漸。四月，太后欲侯諸呂，乃先封高祖之功臣郎中令無擇為博城侯。 . . . 乃封呂種為沛侯，呂平為扶柳侯，張買為南宮侯。[42]

From the first year [of the empress dowager's reign], all commands and orders were issued by the empress dowager. She started issuing decrees in the name of the emperor (*chengzhi*). She began to discuss her <u>desire</u> to make several Lü family members kings and asked the prime minister of the right [for his opinion].

Wang Ling said, "Emperor Gaozu slaughtered a white horse and swore an oath, 'If someone who is not from the Liu clan is made king, all under Heaven [should] join together to attack him.'" Now making the Lü sons kings is against the oath. The empress dowager was unpleasant. . . . In the eleventh month, the empress dowager <u>wanted to</u> get rid of Wang Ling. She <u>then</u> appointed him grand tutor to the emperor and stripped him of his authority as prime minister. . . . <u>Then</u> [she] honored the father of the marquis of Li by giving him the posthumous title King Daowu, with <u>the intention</u> of eventually making kings of the members of the Lü family. In the fourth month, she <u>wanted to</u> make marquises of members of the Lü family. <u>Then</u> the empress dowager first enfeoffed Wuze, prefect of the palace attendants, and a meritorious official of Emperor Gaozu, as the marquis of Bocheng. . . . [She] <u>then</u> enfeoffed Lü Zhong as marquis of Pei, Lü Ping as marquis of Fuliu, and Zhang Mai as marquis of Nangong.

The empress dowager then used the same tactics to elevate the Lü marquises to the rank of king. She started by elevating the sons of Emperor Hui, who were only little children and posed no immediate threat to the ministers and nobility. She then hinted to the ministers of the state that she wanted them to propose the elevation of members of the Lü family, so the ministers requested the elevation of Lü Tai from the marquis of Li to the rank of king of Lü, which the empress dowager readily approved. These promotions prepared for the empress dowager's subsequent actions—conferring more titles to a much wider scope of relatives.[43]

At the same time she was elevating the members of the Lü family, the empress dowager was demoting the Liu princes who were the kings of various states. *Records of the Historian* goes into detail about how she tortured one after another to death—Liu Bang's son Liu You 劉友 (d. 181 BCE) was starved to death, and another son, Liu Hui 劉恢 (d. 181 BCE), was so despondent that he committed suicide.[44] By demoting the members of the Liu family, she eliminated potential rivals and made their positions available for the Lü sons, transferring at least three kingships from the Liu princes to her relatives:

[七年] 二月，徙梁王恢為趙王。呂王產徙為梁王，梁王不之國，為帝太傅。立皇子平昌侯太為呂王。... (秋)，太傅產、丞相平等言，武信侯呂祿上侯，位次第一，請立為趙王。太后許之，追尊祿父康侯為趙昭王。九月，燕靈王建薨，有美人子，太后使人殺之，無後，國除。八年十月，立呂肅王子東平侯呂通為燕王，封通弟呂莊為東平侯。[45]

In the second month [of the seventh year of the empress dowager's reign], she reassigned the king of Liang to be the king of Zhao. She reassigned the king of Lü, Chan, to be the king of Liang. The king of Liang did not go to his state but instead served as the grand tutor of the emperor. [She] made Emperor Hui's son Liu Tai, Marquis of Pingchang, the king of Lü. . . . (In autumn), Grand Tutor Chan, Prime Minister Chen Ping, and others said, "The marquis of Wuxin, Lü Lu, should be given the highest honors, ranked above the marquises. [Therefore], [we] request that [your majesty] make him the king of Zhao." The empress dowager approved the change, and posthumously made Lü Lu's father, the marquis of Kang, King Zhao of Zhao. In the ninth month, King Ling of Yan died and left a son born to a concubine. The empress dowager sent someone to kill him. [Since the state of Yan then] had no offspring, the kingdom was abolished. In the tenth month of the eighth year of [the empress dowager's reign], she made the son of Lü Tai (who was given the posthumous title of king of Su), Lü Tong, the king of Yan and gave Lü Tong's younger brother Lü Zhuang the title of the marquis of Dongping.

This third stage in the Lü family's ascendancy is described in the richest detail, with each promotion carefully listed. The description of the interactions between Empress Dowager Lü and her family, the Liu princes, and ministers on both sides reveals the tension and collaboration among all the actors involved. Once the position of the Lü family is assured, the narrative speed accelerates. In the end, Empress Dowager Lü successfully does away with her opponents and confers the title of king and marquis on members of the Lü family. Just before her death in 180 BCE, she appoints her nephew Lü Chan as the prime minister, the highest official in the court. By detailing the empress dowager's maneuvers, the *Records of the Historian* account emphasizes how the Lü family's ascendancy was intertwined with the waning of the Liu family.

History of the Han is far less interested than *Records of the Historian* in the schemes and actions that Empress Dowager Lü undertook to achieve her goals. *History of the Han* presents the empress dowager's life in eight brief entries from 188 to 180 BCE in the "Basic Annals" chapter devoted to her reign. This time period covered by *History of the Han* is no more than the final stage of her life seen in the *Records of the Historian* account. Focusing on this shorter period, the *History of the Han* account does not slow down, but proceeds much faster. In this text, the series of actions to get rid of Wang Ling and make Lü sons kings is unnarrated anywhere. The text merely summarizes the empress dowager's promotion of the Lü sons in one sentence: "She then established her elder brother's son Lü Tai, Lü Chan, Lü Lu, and Lü Tai's son Tong as kings, and enfeoffed six other members of the Lü family as marquises" (乃立兄子呂台、產、祿、台子通四人為王，封諸呂六人為列侯).[46] The chapter then directs the readers to "Waiqi zhuan" 外戚傳 (The Arrayed Traditions of Maternal Relatives of the Imperial Family) for more information.[47] This complex process, which takes up about two-thirds of the space of the "Basic Annals" chapter in *Records of the Historian*, is summarized in three sentences in *History of the Han*, at a speed that inevitably omits the details of how the empress dowager builds and wields power:

太后臨朝稱制。復殺高祖子趙幽王友、共王恢及燕靈王建。遂立周呂侯子臺為呂王，臺弟產為梁王，建城侯釋之子祿為趙王，台子通為燕王。又封諸呂凡六人皆為列侯，追尊父呂公為呂宣王，兄周呂侯為悼武王。[48]

The empress dowager attended meetings of the court and ruled in the name of the emperor (*chengzhi*). [She] also killed the sons of Emperor Gaozu, You, King You of Zhao; Hui, King Gong of Zhao; and Jian, King Ling of Yan. Thereafter, [she] appointed Lü Tai, a son of the marquis of Zhoulü, as King of Lü; Tai's younger brother, Chan, as King of Liang; Lu, the son of the marquis of Jiancheng, Lü Shizhi, as King of Zhao; and a son of Tai, Tong, as King of Yan. [She] additionally enfeoffed six members of the Lü family as marquises, gave her father, Lord Lü, the posthumous title King Xuan of Lü, and elevated her older brother, Marquis Zhoulü, to the rank of King Daowu of Lü.

By recounting these events so rapidly, *History of the Han* obscures the process by which the empress dowager first exterminated the Liu princes, then promoted members of the Lü family to the rank of marquis, and finally elevated them to the rank of king. While important facts are reported in this passage, the speed of this summary muddies the connections between the extermination of Liu princes and the elevation of Lü family members. Omitting Empress Dowager Lü's promotion of Lü sons removes the context of her promotion of Emperor Hui's sons, making the latter an isolated event in the "Basic Annals" account in *History of the Han*.[49] In *Records of the Historian*, the initial promotion of the members of the Lü family is presented as a crucial step in her gradual elevation of the Lüs; but in *History of the Han*, it is merely presented as one of several policies issued in the first year of her reign, substantially obscuring the importance of this event.

The more rapid narrative speed of *History of the Han* is due in part to larger structural differences between the two histories. First, *History of the Han* removes many important details that are given in the "Basic Annals" chapter in *Records of the Historian* and disperses them over several chapters, obscuring crucial connections among events that were originally correlated. For example, the rivalry between Empress Dowager Lü and Lady Qi, Empress Dowager Lü's poisoning of Liu Ruyi, and the inhumane treatment of Lady Qi are found in "Waiqi zhuan" (The Arrayed Traditions of Maternal Relatives of the Imperial Family).[50] Empress Dowager Lü's attempted assassination of Liu Fei and the extermination of other Liu princes are separately recounted in "Gao wu wang zhuan" 高五王傳 (The Arrayed Traditions of Gaozu's Five Kings) and "Jing Yan Wu zhuan" 荊燕吳傳 (The Arrayed Traditions of the Kings of Jing, Yan, and Wu).[51] Each of these chapters is centered on the eponymous protagonists and proceeds in chronological order. In the group biographies, these detailed scenes are not well connected to the rest of the account. In the face of this deracination, the reader can do no better than to try to judge each episode singly. The deaths of these innocent Liu princes only facilitate a simplified moral evaluation of Empress Dowager Lü. What is lost is her complex character as limned in *Records of the Historian*, the character of a female ruler who exhibits weakness, toughness, and extraordinary political capability.[52]

A second structural difference affecting narrative speed is that *History of the Han* favors direct citation of relevant edicts over narrating events. *Records of the Historian* seldom contains any direct citation of edicts; when it does refer to edicts, as a rule it briefly paraphrases them, preferring to narrate important events such as the promotion of the Lü family members and the deposition of the Liu princes.[53] By contrast, *History of the Han* recounts the eight years (188–180 BCE) of Empress Dowager Lü's direct rule by alternating between a bare-bones description of political events and lengthy quotation of four edicts issued over the course of four years. In this case, the author(s) of *History of the Han* chose to offer public information, rather than revealing hidden purposes of the protagonist as seen in *Records of the Historian*. This combination of a rapid narrative speed and nondescriptive presentation makes this chapter no more than a list of major policies. The edicts are not necessarily related to the event(s) reported in that year, much less to the Lü family's rise to power. For example, one of the edicts cited in this chapter reads: "In the past, Emperor Hui spoke of wanting to abolish extermination to the third degree and monstrous words. The emperor passed away before deliberations [on these measures] were concluded. Now [the administration] abolishes them" (前日孝惠皇帝言欲除三族罪、妖言令，議未決而崩，今除之).[54] Although this edict narrates the evolution of the law during this period, it has nothing to do with other events that occurred that year and is hardly connected with Empress Dowager Lü's leverage of the Liu and Lü families. Having the *facts* in the form of edicts in the chapter seems to be much more important than tracking the rise of the Lü family.

Furthermore, some of the edicts even misrepresented events because they were public proclamations. In the fourth year of the empress dowager's reign, because the child emperor Liu Gong discovered that the empress dowager had put to death his biological mother, the empress dowager removed Liu Gong from the throne, had him murdered, and established another grandson, Liu Hong, as the new emperor. However, the edict naturally hides this bloody secret, instead attributing ill health to the former emperor as a pretext:

凡有天下治萬民者，蓋之如天，容之如地；上有驩心以使百姓，百姓欣然以事其上，驩欣交通而天下治。今皇帝疾久不已，乃失惑昏亂，不能繼嗣奉宗廟，守祭祀，不可屬天下。其議代之。[55]

He who holds possession of the empire and rules the multitude must shelter them like the heavens and support them like the earth. The ruler governs the people with a joyous heart, and the people gladly serve their ruler, and when this joy and gladness mingle together, the empire will be well governed. Now the emperor's illness has continued for a long time without abating. He has lost his wits and he has become demented. He cannot continue the imperial line or perform the sacrifices in ancestral temples, nor can he be entrusted with the care of the empire. May [you courtiers] discuss [how to] replace him.

This edict in *History of the Han* contrasts the ideal relationship between the subject and the ruler with Liu Gong's supposed inability to fulfill the responsibilities of a ruler. From a certain historiographic perspective, the author(s)' use of official documents in this chapter increases the credibility of *History of the Han*. The work also serves as an archive for important documents (on the assumption that they are presented accurately).[56] However, as the public and official means by which information was transmitted, these documents were carefully polished and refined, not only for aesthetic purposes but also with an eye toward hiding the real purpose of a certain policy or an action. *History of the Han* quickly introduces Liu Gong's discovery before quoting the edict, but by quoting the edict at length, *History of the Han* establishes its documentary reliability at the expense of the logical chain.[57]

It is impossible to know why Ban Gu or any other author of *History of the Han* made the changes from *Records of the Historian* to form the "Gaohou ji" chapter in *History of the Han*. Hans van Ess holds that the purpose of depersonalization, through cutting episodes concerning the Liu princes and inserting edicts, was to depict the empress dowager as a usurper.[58] However, the practice of limiting details and quoting edicts is also found in other "Basic Annals" chapters in *History of the Han*, such as those devoted to rulers after Emperor Wu. How do we account for these chapters? According to Tang historian Liu Zhiji's 劉知幾 (661–721 CE) explanation of the *ji-zhuan* 紀傳 (annal) form, the *zhuan* (tradition) chapters use related events to explain the "Basic Annals" chapters just as exegeses such as *Zuo Commentary* use related events to explain *Annals of the Spring and Autumn*.[59] Although this opinion partially accords with *History of the Han*, the analogy is not entirely convincing because it contradicts the case of *Records of the Historian*. As the first book to employ the *ji-zhuan* form, *Records of the Historian* has a section of "Basic Annals" chapters more than half of which consist of highly detailed narrations of related events. These chapters are not fundamentally different from those in the division of "Arrayed Traditions." Although the compiling principles of *History of the Han* are agnostic, its current form, as manipulated by the historian(s), emphasizes isolated historical facts rather than the interconnection of events as a coherent chain.

Conclusion

Examining the different versions of the usurpation of the Tian lineage and the rise of Empress Lü to power reveals not merely the various ways in which *Zuo Commentary*, *Records of the Historian*, and *History of the Han* employ their narrative speed but also the importance of structure in shifting the emphases of histories. In the case of the Tian lineage, these details actually weaken the protagonists' morality to some degree; in the case of Empress Lü, her stratagems presented in the text draw more notice to her extraordinary political competence than to the legitimacy of her rule. In both case studies examined in this chapter, *Records of the Historian*'s detailed narration of protagonists' step-by-step operations over a long period directs the readers to pay more attention to the protagonists' actions in a chain rather than judging the morality of their individual actions at face value. In a sense, all of these protagonists were successful schemers who at least fulfilled their ambitions and reached the highest political positions.

Records of the Historian places the stairs ascending to power instead of the moral standing of characters at the center, exhibiting a recurring pattern of recounting important historical processes in detail. This feature of *Records of the Historian* becomes visible only when its narrative speed is compared with that of *Zuo Commentary* and *History of the Han*. *Zuo Commentary* is less concerned with historical process than with moral judgment based on individual episodes; *History of the Han* asserts its own factuality by prioritizing single facts and quoting edicts at length. The narrative speed of these two works emphasizes *what* is done, whereas *Records of the Historian* is interested in teaching *how* the past proceeds in a given direction. For any premodern readers in the political realm, this was no less important than learning from moral models, because all readers needed to deeply understand how power actually rises little by little and what tactics may be employed in state affairs. This is exactly where the value of the stories of *Records of the Historian* lies. By laying out the historical processes, *Records of the Historian* provokes the reader to extract their own lessons freely; the narrator does not intrude heavily to promote any particular takeaways.

Chapter 4

Multiple Points of View

Illuminating Desires and Dynamics

In the preceding chapters, I have analyzed the manipulation of temporal sequence of events and the speed of narration in *Records of the Historian* by comparing it with other early Chinese histories. Like these narrative devices, point of view is a device that regulates a narrative's information and the reader's reception, referring to the perceptual or conceptual position in terms of which the narrated situations and events are presented. As Gérard Genette pointed out, to narrate from a point of view means to narrate with a restrictive mode.[1] This chapter examines the substantial use of multiple, correspondive points of view in *Records of the Historian* to showcase the triggering and intensification of conflicts aroused within political relationships. This remarkable feature, which is rarely seen in *Records of the Historian*'s predecessors and even later histories, enables *Records of the Historian* to trace the development of characters' desires and their effects upon dynamics within political relationships.

A storyteller and every character in a story can have their individual points of view regarding the same moments and events along the storyline. Their divergent or even completely opposite perceptions regarding the same facts mean that a narrator must choose one or multiple perspectives to recount a story. Historians cannot fictionalize events like fiction writers, but they also must adopt one or multiple points of view to recount the past. When a history reports an event from one point of view, readers have access only to information seen from that single perspective, and their understanding of that event is constrained by that limited access; in contrast, if a text provides multiple points of view, readers will be able to view the same facts from different perspectives.[2] Since a character's desires, thoughts, speeches, and sometimes actions, too, can all indicate one's point of view, multiple points of view seen through these portrayals effectively advance a text's presentation of interpersonal relationships. For historical works, although the majority of nonaction descriptions are speculations or even completely invented, the historians' way of tackling the issue of point of view casts light on the historical knowledge available to readers, which determines the text's rhetorical function as a history.[3]

Records of the Historian demonstrates a pattern of employing a variety of characters' points of view to report the same events, shedding light on desires and emotions as root factors impacting the interactions and critical twists among characters. Through the developing portrayals of these psychological aspects, the text does not simply report what conflicts, competition, distrust, and disasters occurred, but how they evolved to become issues within typical political relationships in early China, such as those between rivals, fathers and sons, patrons and retainers, and so on. Two of the most significant are those between a ruler and his wives and between a ruler and his ministers, which together form the core of early Chinese politics. *Records of the Historian* represents both in great detail, shedding light on what the text teaches us.

Tracing the transformation of the same character's point of view and the interactions between multiple figures' perceptions, I investigate how *Records of the Historian* takes advantage of point of view as a narrative device to showcase how historical changes spark, develop, and come to an end framed within political relationships. I shall first introduce the concept of point of view, its various categories, and the advantages of applying this concept in Chinese historical writings. I then move on to the ruler-consort relationship within the harems and the ruler-minister relationship in public administration to illustrate *Records of the Historian*'s use of points of view. Comparing the different ways in which *Zuo Commentary* and *Records of the Historian* narrate the same stories from the Spring and Autumn period shows two patterns: first, characters' perceptions develop and interact over time, articulating the direction and outcome of events; second, *Records of the Historian* consistently features the ruler's perception as an active, sometimes even decisive factor in shaping the aforementioned two relationships. My exploration of accounts devoted to the Warring States period and the Qin-Han dynasties finds that these patterns also extend to the rest of the book, forming a consistent characteristic.

Point of View

Different types of point of view provide readers with various amounts of information. In a text, an author can use a single point of view throughout a narrative or switch to a variety of points of view in different sections of the story. To adopt a consistent point of view, the narrator can be a character in the story or an analytic or omniscient viewer outside the story.

The former situation is known as an internal perspective. Since readers understand the story only through a particular character's point of view, what information a reader gets access to strictly depends upon that character's knowledge and perception. In the latter case, the narrator is an outside observer who knows all of the events and characters, meaning that the narrator knows everything when they narrate. Space and time do not prevent them from knowing events that happen at the same time or in different locations; they also know what will happen next when readers are still engaged with the current passage.

Yet the degree to which an omniscient narrator elaborates a story varies from text to text. Two typical subtypes of the omniscient viewer are author observer and omniscient author. Author observers narrate from an external perspective, having no access to the characters' intentions, feelings, thought process, and so on, whereas omniscient authors are able to penetrate characters and thereby depict their internal world. Omniscient authors also have the freedom to move from one point of view to another, reporting the same story from multiple perspectives.

When an omniscient author narrates from a character's point of view, we know more about the character's perception of an event; on the other hand, when an author ignores a character's point of view, we lose the character's perceptions of the same facts. In both cases, the author reveals the characters' points of view primarily through reporting psychological descriptions and verbal exchanges. The use of an internal perspective means that psychological descriptions are of particular importance, because the authors do not fake them; no character would be able (or need) to forge their thoughts in front of the reader, as everyone thinks honestly to themselves and the internal world is safely exclusive from other characters; conversational quotations, by contrast, are not always believable, because villains often need to hide their true destructive intentions in seemingly proper speeches. The reliability of the characters' thoughts allows an omniscient author to establish coherent relations between visible conduct and intangible motivations.

Chinese historians tend to be omniscient narrators recounting historical events retrospectively, but the historians' degree of omniscience is forceful enough to shift textual emphases. *Zuo Commentary* and *Records of the Historian* represent the author observer and omniscient author respectively, despite fluctuation of the degrees of omniscience from one account to another, or even within the same account. One feature of employing an author observer's perspective is that *Zuo Commentary* appears to contain a great number of conversations, but they do not often reflect the characters' real feelings and thoughts in scenarios.[4] Often, without streamlining the logic between a character's speeches and behavior, an insignificant or even negligible action at the beginning of an entry leads to a weighty outcome at the end.[5] The exchanges are mostly filled with the author's elaboration of moral principles and evaluative analyses according to contemporary rituals and customs. Many of these artificial speeches do not even explain the characters' subsequent behavior later in the plot.[6]

Another feature of *Zuo Commentary*'s external point of view is that the text's narrative frame relies heavily on the characters' actions to drive the entries forward. The frame either centers on ritual propriety, which decides the outcome of many events, or divinations and dreams, which are likely to be fulfilled.[7] Sometimes, a narrative has a mixed framework of the two. This feature is convenient for highlighting ritual propriety and moral codes: the conduct of characters elicits good or bad outcomes. Ending with a formulaic structure—wrapping with one or more quotation(s) from either Confucius, a nobleman, or the *Book of Odes*[8] to reiterate a moral principle or ritual propriety—entries in *Zuo Commentary* only reveal the author's own perception, primarily fulfilling a didactic purpose, rather than directly or logically exposing the characters' internal world. The results are that the true, subterranean causes of political affairs, such as unsatisfied desire, dangerous calculation, or improper pursuits are not presented as the root cause of many conflicts, and that the real daily interactions, which take time to crack interpersonal relationships and gradually snowball into severe consequences, are not integrated to account for the outcomes.

By contrast, *Records of the Historian*'s accounts primarily adopt the view of an omniscient author, narrating from multiple characters' points of view to minimize the author's intrusion within the plot. Three forms of portrayals present the diverse invented perceptions. The first is mental processes, which distinguish *Records of the Historian* among the received texts and excavated manuscripts in terms of the amount and quality of psychological descriptions. For instance, "The Arrayed Traditions of Bi, the King of Wu" (ch. 106) relies on a series of penetrating descriptions of the protagonist Liu Bi's 劉濞 (216–154 BCE) thoughts before he initiates the rebellion against the central court, known as the "Chaos of the Seven Kingdoms"; in "The Hereditary Houses of the Imperial Family's Maternal Relatives" (ch. 49) all of the Han empresses' life experiences are filled with expansive depictions of feelings and intentions that vividly illustrate their demands, desires, and decisions. From the first one, Empress Lü, to the last in this chapter, Empress Chen, their internal thoughts are accessible to readers, explaining their conduct in various events.

The second form is direct speech within conversations. The characters in *Records of the Historian*'s narratives appear to say what they *would naturally* say, instead of what the author has *forced* them to say. In other words, the direct and indirect speeches of characters match well with their identities, even at different stages of their life. Modern scholar Qian Zhongshu 錢鐘書 (1910–1998) once compared the speeches in *Zuo Commentary* and *Records of the Historian* and expressed his appreciation of the latter's skills.[9] Unlike the characters in *Zuo Commentary*, who speak for the authors behind the text as the authors try to convey moral lessons, *Records of the Historian* gives more freedom to its characters, including both protagonists and those supporting characters. Indeed, comparisons of parallel stories in *Zuo Commentary* and *Records of the Historian* show that the latter regularly cuts down principle-illustrating parts in a conversation and preserves exchanges contributing to driving the plot.[10] Thus, readers of *Records of the Historian* have the feeling that many chapters—the "Arrayed Traditions" section in particular—read like a novel or short story.

In addition to the internal thoughts and conversational speeches, *Records of the Historian* contains the third form of point of view, monologues of protagonists. In the text, it is common to find characters speaking or even shouting out their thoughts without any audience. This kind of situation usually appears at the most important or dramatic moment of their life, such as a foreshadowing episode at the beginning of their career, a turning point of their life, or right before the end of their life. On these occasions, there is no need to set a clear border between the thoughts and speeches of a character because their difference is very vague. Xiang Yu's blaming of Heaven before committing suicide, Qu Yuan's poem expressing resentment before he sinks in the river, and Li Si's sigh of the rats' different living environments at the courtyard (discussed in the first chapter)—only readers know what the characters have said.[11]

Whether public speeches, internal thoughts, or expressive monologues, the three aforementioned forms of invented perceptions demonstrate the actors' different understandings of the same events from their individual perspectives. The concept of point of view has three advantages in the current study. First, point of view allows us to treat the same character as a whole to trace his or her developing perception over time. As I pointed out in the first chapter, due to *Records of the Historian*'s outstandingly vivid characters, previous scholarship has tended to focus on the separate categories of descriptions such as appearance, action, speech, thoughts, feelings, and so on.[12] By focusing on these aspects of character, this method does, to some degree, explain particular aspects of *Records of the Historian*'s lifelike characterization, but it does not contribute to understanding correlations between the same character's mind and conduct.

Second, point of view redirects our attention from skillful descriptions of one character to the interactive perceptions between multiple characters. In particular, psychological descriptions and conversational speeches demonstrate how one character's mind, feelings, and conduct directly or indirectly stimulate other characters' reactions within a relationship, alerting readers to the diverse factors of the dynamics. The reactions from all actors, back and forth, together accumulate to result in the outcomes.

Third, point of view is a device that assists us in understanding the function of histories. *Records of the Historian* has numerous psychological portrayals that do not contribute to teaching morality or ritual propriety. As we have seen in *Zuo Commentary*, without these descriptions, readers can judge the characters and the outcomes of events clearly; in contrast, *Records of the Historian* does not inherit this feature but rather strives to include these seemingly unnecessary and even redundant descriptions, many of which prevent an easy moral judgment of the characters.[13] Previously, scholars have treated the text either as a masterpiece of literature or a collection of historical records; it seems that the rich descriptions of characters' perceptions only have one function—to portray vivid characters. However, we cannot assume that Sima Qian's choice of including descriptive details was to build characters or simply to highlight the decisive role of humans in shaping history.[14] The vivid characters are compositional or editorial results of tracing the main logical chain that drives the history forward. Indeed, without denying scholars' consensus concerning the text's extraordinary characterization skills, we can still affirm that events are the center of narration. The multiple points of view of *Records of the Historian* greatly contribute to presenting the story's logic embedded into the characters' perceptions.

Comparing the different narrations of the same accounts in *Zuo Commentary* and *Records of the Historian* shows that the latter has a consistent pattern of employing blended, developing, and interactive points of view. This pattern recurs in a wide range of narratives devoted to various historical periods and illustrates the dynamics of two of the most important but hard-to-tackle relationships: those between rulers and their consorts and between rulers and their ministers, as analyzed in detail in this chapter.

Rulers and Their Consorts

During the late Western Zhou and Chunqiu period, a primary wife enjoyed the apex title of *di* 嫡. In theory, only her (eldest) son could succeed to the throne, a privilege that is referred to as the inheritance policy of *dizhangzi*.[15] However, in practice, the ruler's favor toward a concubine could easily make him transgress the hierarchy between primary and secondary wives, directly impacting the line of succession, sometimes even leading to a political disaster. During the later eras, from the Warring States period to the Qin and Han dynasties, rulers also frequently challenged this inheritance policy in their implementation. For these reasons, the authors of early Chinese historical writings showed great concern about the relationship between the two genders in their writings.

In *Zuo Commentary* and *Records of the Historian*, numerous political crises, such as dynastic downfalls, succession struggles, and usurpations, start within the royal family and are closely related to women; but the two histories' representations of the same political affairs differ significantly, particularly in terms of the role of male rulers. The historians, without altering the basic facts of historical events, manipulate the points of view to which readers gain access.

The story of the most notorious woman of the Spring and Autumn period (770–481 BCE), Lady Li 驪姬, appears in both *Zuo Commentary* and *Records of the Historian*. She was the favorite concubine of Lord Xian of Jin 晉獻公 (r. 676–651 BCE), who defeated her tribe and took her and her sister back to Jin. The basic storyline is that, after the lord establishes Shensheng as his heir, Lady Li bears the lord a son called Xiqi 奚齊; in order to install Xiqi as the crown prince, the woman calculates a way to generate conflict within the royal family, eventually leading to the suicide of the legitimate crown prince and the expulsion of Xiqi's other brothers outside of Jin. This severe succession struggle among the lord's sons lasts for decades, eventually developing into a long-term turmoil known as the five-generation chaos 五世之亂. Although both texts depict Lady Li as a destructive woman who took advantage of her husband's favor to achieve her illegitimate goal, *Records of the Historian*'s rewriting of the story does not inherit *Zuo Commentary*'s wide use of external point of view but adopts an internal perspective to bring in the lord's developing perception over time. This transformation enables *Records of the Historian* to incorporate the impacts of multiple characters, particularly the couple's interactions, into its narration, to shed light on inappropriate desires and conduct between the genders.

Zuo Commentary presents Lady Li as an evil woman in two entries. One entry (Lord Zhuang 28.2) recounts that after she gives birth to Xiqi, she schemes to estrange the lord with his other sons (except for her sister's), eventually ascending her own son to the throne. Mostly posited from an outside focal point, the entry includes little information on feelings and thoughts, mainly focusing on the participants' public speeches and actions: in order to achieve her goal, she bribes two male favorites of Lord Xian to persuade the lord to send her son's rivals (i.e., the crown prince and other sons) outside of the capital. The entry primarily narrates from an external point of view to report her allies' implementation of the scheme—deceitful speeches.

> 驪姬嬖，欲立其子，賂外嬖梁五，與東關嬖五，使言於公曰：「曲沃，君之宗也；蒲與二屈，君之疆也；不可以無主。宗邑無主，則民不威；疆場無主，則啟戎心。戎之生心，民慢其政，國之患也。若使大子主曲沃，而重耳夷吾主蒲與屈，則可以威民而懼戎，且旌君伐。」使俱曰：「狄之廣莫，於晉為都，晉之啟土，

不亦宜乎！」晉侯說之。夏，使大子居曲沃，重耳居蒲城，夷吾居屈。群公子皆鄙，唯二姬之子在絳。二五卒與驪姬譖群公子，而立奚齊。晉人謂之二耦。[16]

Lady Li enjoyed great favor of the lord and wanted to have her son Xiqi established [as the crown prince]. She [accordingly] bribed Liang Wu and Wu from Dongguan, the lord's two [male] favorites living outside of the harem. [She] had them speak to the lord: "Quwo is the site of our lord's ancestral temple. Pu and the two Qus are the lord's frontier. [They] must not be left without overseers. Lacking an overseer in the city of the ancestral temple will cause people to lack awe; lacking an overseer on the frontier will provoke the harboring of ambition of the Rong tribes. [If] their harbored ambition is provoked, people will despise our government. This is the concern of our state. If you let the crown prince oversee Quwo and [let] Chong'er and Yiwu oversee Pu and Qu respectively, then it will awe the people, frighten the Rong, and at the same time make a display of the ruler's merit." [Lady Li] had them both say [to the lord]: "Since the lands of the barbarians are so broad and vast, Jin should make Pu and Qu into cities of importance. Jin will thus open new territory. Would that not be great?" The lord was pleased at their suggestions. In the summer, he ordered the crown prince to reside in Quwo, Chong'er to reside in the city of Pu, and Yiwu to reside in Qu. Various sons were sent to outlying areas. Only the two sons of two concubines, [Lady Li and her younger sister], stayed in Jiang. The two Wus eventually joined Lady Li in slandering various sons of the lord and established Xiqi as the crown prince. People of Jin referred to it as "the teamwork of the two Wus."

This passage reveals little about the characters' perceptions except for Lady Li's intention at the beginning and the lord's pleasure toward the end. Despite his power, the lord is depicted as a passive receiver of the scheme who, accordingly, dispatches the crown prince and the other sons outside the capital while keeping Xiqi in the capital. The passage does not concern itself with the source of Lady Li's treacherous intention. The woman's wicked conduct is apparent, making it easy for readers to judge her morality. But due to the lack of descriptions of the couple's interactions, how the relationship between the ruler and the woman impacts succession issues is overshadowed by the scheme.

The other *Zuo Commentary* account about Lady Li, the later entry Lord Xi 4.6 (568 BCE), highlights her inborn power of destruction through a flashback. The narration of Lady Li's other scheme again takes an external point of view. Limited to registering the characters' public words and actions, the entry begins with two divinations that predict whether it is auspicious to install her as a concubine. Although one result appears to be inauspicious, Lord Xian follows the other, the auspicious one, taking her as a concubine. Unfortunately, as the inauspicious divination foretells, disaster happens. Lady Li incriminates the innocent legitimate crown prince, Shensheng, and directly causes his suicide: the woman fabricates a story that Lord Xian has dreamed of Shensheng's deceased mother and urges Shensheng to make a sacrifice for his mother's ghost by going to the ancestral temple in Quwo. Shensheng does so, and upon his return he brings blessed meat for his father. However, before she presents the meat to the lord, Lady Li secretly poisons it and attributes the misdeed to Shensheng. Facing the accusation of attempting to murder his father, Shensheng hangs himself without revealing Lady Li's crime.[17]

Like the first entry, this episode mostly uses an author observer's point of view and presents little perception of the characters, except for Shensheng's speech at the end. As a filial son, before committing suicide, the crown prince declines to flee to other states in his conversation with someone. He expresses his concerns about whether his father could live well without Lady Li, and he laments that no state will receive him, after hearing of his damaged reputation. But overall, the text's incarnation of the woman does not reveal the woman's own feelings despite her immoral conduct. In addition, again, the ruler is like a puppet who simply believes in the woman and behaves rather passively. His perception of the crisis is not available, as the author does not report the story from his perspective. Instead, the text focuses on Lady Li and Shensheng, placing the conflict between them. They respectively display predetermined evil and unconditional filial piety, which together explain the result, not the development of the narrative.

In contrast to *Zuo Commentary*, *Records of the Historian* narrates this fierce succession dispute from both the ruler's and Lady Li's points of view. Without changing the basic facts, the *Records of the Historian* account in

"The Hereditary House of Jin" (ch. 39) places the dispute within the couple's relationship. By disclosing their interactions, the text presents the crisis as a consequence of inappropriate conduct and provoked desires of the two genders. Unlike *Zuo Commentary*, with its lack of characters' points of view, *Records of the Historian* presents the ruler's and the woman's authentic perceptions, in the sense that these understandings change and match the characters' relationship at three stages over fifteen years in the story. As shown in the following *Records of the Historian* version, the ruler not only transfers his favor from the concubine to her son but also completely neglects the potential consequence of his dangerous feelings and thoughts, which I have underlined. The excerpts read:

(1) 五年，伐驪戎，得驪姬、驪姬弟，俱<u>愛幸之</u>。...

In the fifth year (672 BCE), [Lord Xian] led an expedition against the Lirong and obtained Lady Li and her younger sister. He <u>loved and favored both of them</u>.

(2) 十二年，驪姬生奚齊。<u>獻公有意廢太子</u>，乃曰：「曲沃吾先祖宗廟所在，而蒲邊秦，屈邊翟，不使諸子居之，我懼焉。」於是使太子申生居曲沃，公子重耳居蒲，公子夷吾居屈。獻公與驪姬子奚齊居絳。晉國以此知太子不立也。...

In the twelfth year (665 BCE), Lady Li gave birth to Xiqi. Lord Xian, <u>intending to depose the crown prince</u>, said, "Quwo is the place where my ancestral temple is located, Pu is along the border of Qin; Qu is along the border of Di. If I do not charge my sons to reside at these [places], I would fear [Qin and Di]." He then sent Crown Prince Shensheng to oversee Quwo, the noble scion Chong'er to oversee Pu, and the noble scion Yiwu to oversee Qu. Lord Xian and Lady Li's son Xiqi [still] resided in Jiang. The people of Jin, because of this, knew that the crown prince would not be invested.

(3) [十九年]<u>獻公私謂驪姬</u>曰：「<u>吾欲廢太子，以奚齊代之。</u>」驪姬泣曰：「太子之立，諸侯皆已知之，而數將兵，百姓附之，奈何以賤妾之故廢適立庶？君必行之，妾自殺也。」驪姬詳譽太子，而陰令人譖惡太子，而欲立其子。[18]

[In the nineteenth year (658 BCE)], <u>Lord Xian said to Lady Li in private,</u> "<u>I intend to depose the crown prince</u> and replace him with Xiqi." Lady Li wept and said, "All territorial lords have known of the crown prince's establishment. And he has commanded troops several times. The families of the hundred cognomens follow him. How can you remove the oldest son borne by the principal wife just because of me, a humble concubine? If my lord is bound to do that, I will kill myself." Lady Li falsely praised the crown prince, but secretly ordered people to slander and denounce him, intending to establish her son [in his place].[19]

In comparison to *Zuo Commentary*, *Records of the Historian* adds the ruler's developing point of view in the succession struggle and thus pinpoints the gradual changes within the ruler-consort interactions, from the triggering to the climax. The rewritten narrative traces Lord Xian's own increasingly strong motive to replace the legitimate crown prince over the years: he extends his favor for Lady Li to her son; he at first keeps his intention to depose Shensheng to himself, then implements the thought that estranges Shensheng and creates the problematic administrative arrangement; finally, he frankly shares his idea in a spoken announcement to Lady Li, which eventually stimulates her improper desire to install her own son as the successor. The lord's transformation in emotion, attitude, and conduct within the ruler-consort relationship illuminates how succession crisis forms, deteriorates, and breaks out.

Although Lady Li is still cunning in *Records of the Historian*, just like her representation in *Zuo Commentary*, *Records of the Historian* moves her depraved speeches and attaches them to the ruler as his own internal thoughts and administrative deployment. These editorial changes have two specific effects. First, the *Records of the Historian* account increases the importance of the ruler's role in the long-term development of the disaster. In contrast to the passive puppet in *Zuo Commentary*, Lord Xian in *Records of the Historian* not only initiates the struggle but also actively articulates the direction of the matter most of the time. The formation of the catastrophe is directly related to his failure in restraining his desires and to his inappropriate interactions with his concubine. Second, the *Records of the Historian* account humanizes and rationalizes Lady Li's image, which is much less mechanically and instrumentally evil than in *Zuo Commentary*. In *Records of the Historian*, her dangerous desire and later incrimination of the crown prince are not the only cause of the disaster, but a mixed result provoked by the lord's repeated misconduct. Although the *Records of the Historian* account does introduce the inauspicious divination showing that attacking the Li tribe would bring disaster at the end of the account, the sin of Lady Li is less mortal because the lord's point of view, evolving over the decade, greatly blurs the divination's importance in explaining the crisis.

In *Records of the Historian*, the pattern of presenting the rulers' points of view as a dominant and sometimes even the decisive factor in succession crises is consistent. It appears not only in the narration of Jin but also in accounts devoted to other states, demonstrating that, in the composition of the text, similar narratives compiled from the *Zuo Commentary* accounts probably went through a systematic editing process. For example, Lord Xuan of Wei's killing of his legitimate heir in *Records of the Historian* shows an application of the same editing principle.[20] In addition, in "The Hereditary House of Lu" (ch. 33), Lord Zhuang (r. 693–662 BCE) and Lord Wen (r. 627–609 BCE) both unwisely insist on installing their respective younger sons to be the crown princes, causing two disasters of power transition.[21] In *Records of the Historian*'s consistent records of succession issues dated to the Spring and Autumn period, the rulers' proper governance of their sexual desire and domestic conduct are critical for a regime's stability.

Emphasizing the rulers' role among multiple factors upon succession issues continues into the narrations of the Han dynasty. The dynasty's founder, Liu Bang 劉邦 (r. 202–195 BC) had to face the same problem, but unlike the aforementioned rulers, he saved the Han Empire from suffering a severe shock to its power by gradually giving up the idea of replacing his legitimate crown prince over a period of six years (201–195 BCE). As a counterexample, it suggests that if a ruler can correct himself, succession struggles are avoidable. As introduced in chapter 3, Liu Bang had appointed his oldest son Liu Ying 劉盈 born to Empress Lü 呂后 (241–180 BCE) to be the crown prince; later, the emperor wanted to replace Liu Ying with one of the younger sons, Liu Ruyi 劉如意, born to the concubine Lady Qi. The primary reason was that the crown prince was "humane and weak" (*renruo* 仁弱), not resembling him, whereas Liu Ruyi resembled him,[22] as the emperor expresses in "The Hereditary House of the Marquis of Liu" (ch. 55).[23]

This account is devoted to Zhang Liang, an adviser who played a critical role in assisting Liu Bang in seizing the throne and was deeply involved in the succession crisis. This chapter narrates from multiple points of view, with an emphasis on the emperor's desires and emotions, to report from the beginning to the end of the crisis. Note, in this case, the emperor and the empress were not only a couple who strove together to found the Han Empire but also political rivals representing their respective families. In terms of the succession issue, their conflict is even more dramatic. The chapter recounts that, although the emperor installs Liu Ying as the crown prince in 205 BCE,[24] he regrets this decision and takes actions to correct it in the next few years. In this process, and in response to the emperor's change in attitude, Empress Lü immediately reacts with various approaches to secure her son's position.

"The Hereditary House of the Marquis of Liu" reveals the emperor's perception as the beginning of the crisis when the emperor was still the king of Han. When he comes up with the idea of replacing Liu Ying with Liu Ruyi, Empress Lü panics and seeks help from Zhang Liang, the marquis of Liu. Following the marquis's advice, she finds the four reclusive elders whom the emperor has not been able to recruit to his court. These scholars, regarding the emperor as haughty and rude, have hidden themselves away in the mountains and refused on principle to pledge any allegiance to the house of Han; however, from this time onward, the four elders serve the crown prince as his advisers because of his humanity.

Next, we read, in 196 BCE, the emperor wants to send the crown prince to lead forces to fight against a rebellion. This is the second time that the emperor's perception is revealed in the account. The text then brings in the four elders' understanding that the emperor's desire to send Liu Ying into battle is a clear signal that the emperor intends to replace him, because a crown prince's regular duty is to stay at the capital and take care of the administration. Following the four advisers' suggestion, the empress weeps in front of the emperor and begs him to go and pacify the rebellion himself. The emperor, considering that the crown prince lacks military competence, accepts the empress's proposal, temporarily relieving the conflict.

Later, the text for the third time traces the driving factor of the crisis to the emperor's motive: in 195 BCE, the emperor shows an even stronger desire to remove the legitimate crown prince (愈欲易太子), since the emperor becomes seriously ill after returning from the battlefield. He insists on this idea even after the crown prince's grand tutor remonstrates with the emperor by threatening to commit suicide. In the face of such dire circumstances, the crown prince brings his four advisers before the emperor at a banquet. The emperor is astonished, asking why they have deigned to come and wait upon the crown prince. The four men fearlessly contrast the emperor and the crown prince to emphasize the latter's benevolence, filial piety, kindness, and reverence toward scholars.²⁵ This is very likely an arrangement by the empress, as the text narrates that, realizing Empress Lü's strong influence in the court, Liu Bang gives up his dream for Liu Ruyi. The emperor leaves the banquet and sadly calls Lady Qi to his side, explaining to her:

「我欲易之，彼四人輔之，羽翼已成，難動矣。呂后真而主矣。」戚夫人泣，上曰：「為我楚舞，吾為若楚歌。」歌曰：「鴻鵠高飛，一舉千里。羽翮已就，橫絕四海。橫絕四海，當可奈何！雖有矰繳，尚安所施！」歌數闋，戚夫人噓唏流涕，上起去，罷酒。竟不易太子者，留侯本招此四人之力也。²⁶

"I had hoped to change the crown prince, but these four men have come to his aid. Like a pair of great wings, they have borne him aloft where it is hard to remove [him]. Empress Lü is the real master now." Lady Qi wept. The emperor said, "If you will do a dance of Chu for me, I will make you a song of Chu," and he sang:

> The great swan soars aloft,
> In one swoop a thousand miles.
> He has spread his giant wings
> And spans the four seas.
> He who spans the four seas—
> Ah, what can we do?
> Though we bear stringed arrows to down him,
> Where can we aim them?

As Lady Qi sobbed and wept, the emperor sang the song through several times; then he rose and stopped drinking. The fact that in the end the emperor did not change the crown prince was due to the powerful influence of these four men whom Zhang Liang had originally [suggested the empress] summon.²⁷

This excerpt describes the emperor's shifting attitudes in great detail. The crown prince and Liu Ruyi are contrasted: the former is backed by Empress Lü, the Han officials, and the scholars, represented by the four men, whereas the latter only has the emperor's personal favor. The display of the four men wakes up the emperor and causes his compromise, which allows the enthronement of Liu Ying as Emperor Hui to be a peaceful transition. The details of dance, singing, and sad speeches in the preceding excerpt seem unnecessary for reporting the outcome, but they clearly explain how a ruler's mind articulates succession issues. From the original idea of replacing the crown prince to the helpless abandonment of the idea, the emperor's perception develops over time, stimulating the other figures' reactions. This counterexample shows that if a ruler is levelheaded, many of the chaotic situations that are caused by other rulers are avoidable.

When Sima Qian recounts later eras that are closer to his own time, *Records of the Historian*'s narration follows the same pattern of emphasizing the ruler's feelings in the succession issues, only in a more complicated fashion. Although the emperors are still at the center of the story, the text incorporates perceptions from a wider range of members of the imperial harem to demonstrate their impacts upon the emperor's feelings and how the emperor's emotions lead him to make a decision. "The Hereditary Houses of the Families Related to the Emperors by Marriage" (Waiqi Shijia 外戚世家; ch. 49) carefully documents the interactions of the characters' perceptions as the causes of their subsequent actions.

Emperor Jing's (r. 157–141 BCE) deposition of his original crown prince, Liu Rong, results from his increasing dislike of the crown prince's mother, Concubine Li 栗姬, through three stages. The narrative traces the disfavor first to the negative attitude that the emperor's elder sister, the grand princess, has toward Concubine Li. Originally, in order to secure her wealth and status, the princess wants to marry her daughter to the crown prince; but Concubine Li declines out of envy—the princess has introduced several ladies to fill the emperor's palace. The grand princess becomes furious and switches to another concubine of the emperor, Lady Wang, who happily accepts the marriage proposal between her son and the princess's daughter. The princess thus speaks ill of Concubine Li every day, weakening the relationship between Concubine Li and the emperor. Next, the narrative represents the couple's interactions, which lead to further cracks between them. When the emperor feels unease due to a health issue and thinks he might die soon, he tries to entrust all of his sons to the woman who will become the empress dowager and be in charge of the imperial household thereafter. Concubine Li refuses to accept this trust, and the emperor hates her in his heart but does not vent his hate (心嗛之而未發).[28] Finally, the account reports how Lady Wang fuels the emperor's anger, indirectly pushing the emperor to confirm his intention to depose Concubine Li and the crown prince. Reading the emperor's mind, Lady Wang secretly arranges a minister to suggest the emperor make Concubine Li empress. The emperor is enraged and immediately deposes the crown prince, vacating the position for Lady Wang's son, who later ascended the throne as Emperor Wu.

The narrative tells the historical fact that Emperor Jing removed his original crown prince. The court's archives or rumors may contain the basic elements of the story such as characters' actions and the outcome of events; but the author has edited or even invented some figures' conversations and emotions such as envy, hidden fury, and external temper, which are highly interactive and cohesive, each matching well with the role of the figure to whom it is attributed. Concubine Li's envy causes her to reject the grand princess's marriage proposal; the grand princess's anger with Concubine Li leads to Emperor Jing's discontent with Concubine Li; Concubine Li's envy further destroy the emperor's remaining favor toward her; as Concubine Li's rival, Lady Wang takes advantage of the emperor's silent resentment, eventually destroying the emperor's favor toward Concubine Li. The text relies on these reconstructed perceptions to rationalize the core actions of the character with a focus on the ruler-consort relationship. The crown prince's deposition is thus determined by the emperor but impacted by Concubine Li, the grand princess, and Lady Wang, throughout the aforementioned three stages. Reporting the story from all the participants' perceptions builds the logic of the story, and thus the text demonstrates that the emperor's deposition of the crown prince was the culmination of an interactive and developing series of actions taking place within the ruler's harem.

In the preface of "The Hereditary Houses of the Families Related to the Emperors by Marriage," *Records of the Historian* theoretically alerts readers to the difficulty of achieving harmonious interactions between the *yin* and *yang* forces (male and female) and calls upon the rulers' discretion to maintain the domestic relationship.[29] Unlike the earlier histories, which primarily focus on the characters' morality and ritual propriety, *Records of the Historian* repeatedly highlights the characters' concrete desires and stimulating interactions to show the boundary in practical relations. From the dissipated king to the mature emperor to the emotional emperor, the text pays particular attention to the rulers' perceptions and traces the development of their emotions, depicting how their changing mind stimulates the consorts' different responses and vice versa.

Rulers and Ministers

The relationship between a ruler and his minister is another important theme of early Chinese texts. *Zuo Commentary* and *Records of the Historian* portray a great number of rulers, but their ways of representing the rulers are remarkably different.[30] Because of the use of external point of view, *Zuo Commentary* pays substantial attention to the rulers' public actions, such as their travels, court meetings, reception of visitors, consultation with advisers, and so on. In these scenarios, the rulers often speak little; most of the time, they either heed an official's advice or refuse his remonstrances. The result is that many entries inform readers of what a ruler does at the superficial level but do not reveal much of his motivation and emotion behind the actions. Many of the rulers are like puppets without feelings. Only readers who are familiar with the entire text and have trained eyes can infer a ruler's internal thoughts from his actions or from a supporting character's comments on the ruler's actions.

Records of the Historian seems to be unsatisfied with this feature of *Zuo Commentary*, attempting to illuminate rulers' emotions and motivations in events, which truly impact their relationship with the ministers. In order to emphasize rulers' influence upon their ministers' careers, *Records of the Historian* abandons the external point of view of *Zuo Commentary*. It often narrates from the characters' perspectives and pays particular attention to setting up a link between rulers' psychological feelings and their public decisions. *Records of the Historian*'s rewriting of the recruitment of Guan Zhong by Lord Huan of Qi (r. 685–643 BCE), who was known as Gongzi Xiaobai before his seizure of the throne, is a typical example. Gongzi Xiaobai and his brother Gongzi Jiu, two princes of Qi, fled to other states to avoid the chaos in the court of their older brother, Lord Xiang of Qi (r. 698–686 BCE). Gongzi Xiaobai escaped to Ju with his tutor Bao Shu, also known as Bao Shuya; Gongzi Jiu went into exile to Lu with two advisers, Guan Zhong (i.e., Guan Yiwu) and Shao Hu. Later, Lord Xiang was assassinated during the chaos and he had not clearly appointed or indicated his heir. Thus, each prince tried to enter Qi before the other in order to seize the throne. In an effort to help Gongzi Jiu, Guan Zhong even attempted to assassinate Gongzi Xiaobai. Pretending to be shot and dead, Gongzi Xiaobai actually arrived first in Qi and ascended the throne as Lord Huan of Qi.

The following entry in *Zuo Commentary* recounts that Bao Shu has the state of Lu kill Gongzi Jiu but takes his adviser Guan Zhong from Lu back to Qi, although Guan Zhong has sided with Lord Huan's rival. Thereafter, Bao Shu immediately recommends that Lord Huan appoint this former enemy to be a high official. This worthy advice was verified by history, as Guan Zhong did help Lord Huan become the first hegemon (*ba* 霸) in the Spring and Autumn period. Reporting from an external point of view, the text does not reveal any perception on the part of the ruler. The text portrays him as a passive character who follows Bao Shu's suggestion. Heeding right suggestions is not an easy task for a ruler, but *Zuo Commentary* emphasizes Guan Zhong's selflessness and worthiness more than the ruler's feelings and thoughts.[31]

> 鮑叔帥師來言曰：「子糾，親也，請君討之，管召，讎也，請受而甘心焉。」乃殺子糾于生竇，召忽死之。管仲請囚，鮑叔受之，及堂阜而稅之。歸而以告曰，管夷吾治於高傒，使相可也，公從之。[32]

Bao Shu led troops here [i.e., Lu] and explained, "Gongzi Jiu is our kinsman. We ask you to chastise him. Guan Zhong and Shao Hu are our enemies. We ask you to hand them over, and we will be satisfied." So Gongzi Jiu was put to death at Shengdou, and Shao Hu chose to die with him. Guan Zhong asked to become a prisoner, and Bao Shu accepted this, but when they reached Tangfu, Bao Shu released him. Bao Shu returned to the capital and reported, "Guan Zhong's talent for governing surpasses that of Gao Xi.[33] It would be appropriate to make him a minister." The Lord of Qi heeded this advice.[34]

The entry in *Zuo Commentary* represents the text's two narrative features. One is that the passage contains many action words. Almost all of the characters appearing in this story act, but we know nothing about their internal thoughts, such as their feelings, purpose, and intentions, that drove their actions. The meaning of Bao Shu's speech is clear, but its impact upon the plot is vague because it's not immediately understandable whether the speech is a scheme. Even experienced readers might not be able to understand why Bao Shu releases Guan Zhong until they reach Guan Zhong's advice to Lord Huan toward the end of the passage. In contrast, the *Records of the Historian* version is very clear in this regard. In addition, Guan Zhong's request to be imprisoned also seems ambiguous in the passage. Does he take Bao Shu's summons as a rescue? Is he grateful for the help, or regretful of his previous support to Gongzi Jiu? Without descriptions of their perceptions, the reasons why the characters take certain actions are not apparent.

The other narrative feature of *Zuo Commentary* is that the text does not concern itself much with the influence of characters' desires and thoughts upon the development of events. As a didactic text, *Zuo Commentary* always judges characters on the basis of their external speeches or conduct. In the case of the aforementioned passage, an experienced reader may grasp that Guan Zhong's request to be a prisoner indirectly suggests his appreciation; Bao Shu's recommendation of a capable man surpassing himself is worthy; heeding advice is a good quality of a ruler. But the motivations behind these actions seem to be of little importance. For the authors of the text, the striking change in the relationship between Guan Zhong and Lord Huan, from enemies to teammates, does not need much explanation. The core is that every character's conduct is aligned with their individual duties: as a righteous minister, Bao Shu recommends a talented figure; as a ruler, the lord accepts the right advice. Readers can only speculate about the characters' mind from the text's description of words and speeches or appeal to other, related entries to build a logical chain by themselves.

In "The Hereditary House of the Grand Lord of Qi" (ch. 32), *Records of the Historian* recounts the same story without changing the basic facts. The major edits are the embellishments on the characters' points of view, such as the fear of the Lu people, Bao Shu's objective comment on Guan Zhong, and the gratitude of Guan Zhong. In particular, the passage illustrates Lord Huan's change in attitude toward Guan Zhong.

> 齊遺魯書曰：「子糾兄弟，弗忍誅，請魯自殺之。召忽、管仲讎也，請得而甘心醢之。不然，將圍魯。」魯人患之，遂殺子糾于笙瀆。召忽自殺，管仲請囚。桓公之立，發兵攻魯，心欲殺管仲。鮑叔牙曰：「臣幸得從君，君竟以立。君之尊，臣無以增君。君將治齊，即高傒與叔牙足也。君且欲霸王，非管夷吾不

可。夷吾所居國國重，不可失也。」於是桓公從之。乃詳為召管仲欲甘心，實欲用之。管仲知之，故請往。鮑叔牙迎受管仲，及堂阜而脫桎梏，齋祓而見桓公。桓公厚禮以為大夫，任政。³⁵

Qi sent the state of Lu a letter, saying, "Gongzi Jiu is my brother. I cannot bear to kill him. I beseech Lu to kill him. Shao Hu and Guan Zhong are our enemies. I ask permission to take them back and mince them up with satisfaction; otherwise, I will surround Lu." The Lu people were worried about this issue and then killed Gongzi Jiu at Shengdou. Zhao Hu committed suicide. Guan Zhong asked to be imprisoned. Upon his installment, Lord Huan sent troops to attack Lu, wanting to kill Guan Zhong. Bao Shuya said, "I fortunately followed your majesty. You eventually were able to ascend [the throne]. Regarding your reverence, I have nothing to add to you. If you are administrating Qi in order, then only Gao Xi and Shuya would be adequate; if you want to claim [the title of] hegemon in the future, no one except for Guan Yiwu [i.e., Guan Zhong] is able [to help you]. The state where Yiwu lives is always weighty. You cannot lose him." Thus, Lord Huan followed this suggestion. He <u>then</u> pretended to summon Guan Zhong, wanting to satisfy his will [of killing him], but actually wanting to use him. Guan Zhong was aware of this. He thus asked to go to [Lord Huan]. Bao Shuya greeted and received Guan Zhong. When [they] arrived in Tangfu, Guan Zhong was allowed to take his shackles off. He fasted and bathed to meet Lord Huan. Lord Huan treated him with great respect and appointed him minister, letting him be in charge of government.

In the *Records of the Historian* version, Lord Huan is active throughout the story. Although the subjects of the sentences in the letter are omitted, my translation inserts "I," referring to Lord Huan, for two reasons: first, the beginning of the letter refers to Gongzi Jiu as a brother; and second, Bao Shu's recommendation of Guan Zhong is part of the flashback initiated with the phrase "Upon the installment of Lord Huan," which indicates the rollback of time. The word *nai* 乃 (then; thereupon), underlined in the excerpt, signals the resumption of the chronology, connecting with the letter at the beginning, which indicates that the lord at least participates in implementing the letter scheme. Thus, when reading this account, readers have the feeling that the lord has deeply joined the planning and implementation involved in getting Guan Zhong back to Qi. Although Bao Shu's analysis prompts the lord to change his mind, Lord Huan plays a determinative role in the arrangement and implementation of the tactic.

This passage in *Records of the Historian* has two features. The incorporation of Lord Huan's internal thought illuminates the purpose of all the actions, making the whole storyline more comprehensible. The text not only informs readers that the letter sent to Lu was a tactic to take Guan Zhong back to Qi, a necessary step before employing him, but also highlights that the minister's career path heavily depends on the ruler's mind. Moreover, a character's thought is closely linked with his subsequent actions, which greatly strengthens the significance of the figures' desire and motivations, rather than their conduct at the superficial level, in shaping the direction of history.

Records of the Historian's emphases upon the interactive perceptions between rulers and ministers continues into its narration of the Qin and Han periods. As I mentioned in chapter 3, Sima Qian once lamented his lack of sources for the Qin dynasty; not coincidentally, the chapters devoted to the Qin ministers and generals tend to use more psychological descriptions to build the narrative framework, which account for the subtle relationships between the emperors and their ministers. Through these descriptions, the text is able to recount how shifts and turns take place within a ruler-minister relationship.

Lü Buwei 呂不韋 (d. 205 BCE) was an influential prime minister of Qin. Starting as a merchant, he served two generations of the Qin kings: first, he helped King Zhuangxiang of Qin (also known as Zichu in *Records of the Historian*; r. 250–247 BCE) to inherit the throne; then, he paved the way for King Zhuangxiang's son, Ying Zheng, to unify China and become the First Emperor. In "The Arrayed Traditions of Lü Buwei" (ch. 85) in *Records of the Historian*, Lü's psychological portrayals form a thread that logically links his plans, actions, and speeches. Two episodes are filled with extremely detailed descriptions of how Lü perceives himself and his contemporary ruler.

The first episode appears at the beginning of the chapter when the protagonist first meets Zichu 子楚 in Handan, the capital of Zhao. Lü Buwei, who has acquired wisdom through his business experiences, applies this wisdom to political subjects and immediately realizes the value of investing in Zichu, a miserable Qin prince who seems to have no chance at all to inherit the throne. As one of the middle sons, he has rarely received any attention from the old king and was sent to Handan as a hostage several years earlier. The text narrates this meeting between Lü Buwei and the prince in a mixed description of internal thoughts and secret speeches of both sides, illustrating the importance of shared ambition between ministers and rulers. As the two characters have sensed, this meeting turns out to be so crucial that both of their futures change dramatically.

> 子楚，秦諸庶孽孫，質於諸侯，車乘進用不饒，居處困，不得意。呂不韋賈邯鄲，見而憐之，曰「此奇貨可居」。乃往見子楚，說曰：「吾能大子之門。」子楚笑曰：「且自大君之門，而乃大吾門！」呂不韋曰：「子不知也，吾門待子門而大。」子楚心知所謂，乃引與坐，深語。³⁶

Zichu was one of the grandsons of [the king of Qin] from the lineage of a concubine. He was sent as a hostage to one of the other states. His carriages and other equipment were poorly provisioned. He had to live in straitened circumstances and was not able to do as he pleased. Lü Buwei was doing business in Handan.

He saw Zichu, sympathized with him, and said, "This is a rare piece of merchandise to put in storage." He then went to meet Zichu, trying to persuade him, saying, "I know how to enlarge your gate for you!"

Zichu laughed and said, "You'd better enlarge your own gate before you enlarge mine."

Lü Buwei said, "You do not understand. The enlarging of my gate depends on the enlargement of yours!" Zichu, heartily understanding what [he] referred to, therefore guided and seated him and started a deep conversation.

In this episode, Lü Buwei successfully attracts Zichu's attention by proposing a mutually beneficial plan. From the beginning to the end, a series of psychological words and covert exchanges illustrate the duo's cooperation. While Lü *lian* 憐 (pities) Zichu after learning his situation, Lü's keen eyes immediately recognize Zichu as a *qihuo* 奇貨 (rare piece of merchandise) that deserves to be stored because this hopeless prince will bring Lü fortune and power. This comment by Lü is not part of a conversation, nor said to any audience in the text; rather, it targets readers, revealing Lü's thought that triggers the entire plan of helping Zichu become the inheritor of his father and thus getting enormous benefits for Lü.

Next, the word, *nai* 乃 (then; therefore) highlights the logical connection between Lü's thought and his subsequent action. At their first meeting, Zichu's sneer apparently shows that he initially does not believe in Lü Buwei's proposal; only when Lü smartly intertwines Zichu's aspiration to improve his current situation with Lü's own ambition of investment does Zichu realize the sincerity of Lü's proposal and become willing to discuss the matter in depth. Thereafter, Lü Buwei's tissue of schemes significantly increases Zichu's importance within Qin's royal family. The prince becomes much more visible and eventually succeeds his father. After he ascends the throne as King Zhuangxiang, he appoints Lü as the chancellor of Qin and enfeoffs him as the Marquis of Wenxin with the revenue from a hundred thousand households in Henan and Luoyang.

Lü Buwei reaches the prime of his life in the next decade, when King Zhuangxiang passes away and his son, Ying Zheng, ascends the throne. Since the new king is too young, Lü Buwei serves as the regent and the new king addresses him as the "second father." But Lü's two chief actions during this period cause Ying Zheng concern. One is that Lü Buwei sponsors thousands of *ke* 客 (retainers). As seen in the example of noble scion of Wei in chapter 1 of the current study, during the Warring States period, it was popular for various aristocrats with high social status and political positions to humble themselves and sponsor talented retainers. The patron's ability to attract retainers depended on their power, wealth, proximity to the court, and other factors. Qin's competitors, such as Qi, Chu, and other states in the east, all had influential patrons. Again, through psychological portrayal, we learn that Lü *feels* disgraced by the failure of the powerful Qin to obtain influential patrons. Therefore, after he becomes the chancellor of Qin, he obtains thousands of followers. Nonetheless, as we will see, Lü Buwei's sponsorship of retainers is a sensitive matter in the young king's mind. The other action raising Ying Zheng's anxiety is that Lü is involved in the rebellion initiated by Lao Ai (?–238 BCE), a male servant whom Lü disguises as a eunuch and sends to the queen dowager, that is, Ying Zheng's mother. Lao Ai has two sons with the queen dowager and schemes to install one of his sons as the king's successor.[37]

The aforementioned two matters alarm the king. The account records the changes in the king's mind in detail: although Lao Ai's threatened rebellion prompts the king to kill Lü Buwei, in light of Lü's enormous contribution in enthroning the previous king and the continuing attempts of retainers to persuade the king to pardon Lü Buwei, the king doesn't punish him immediately.[38] But one year later, the king dismisses him from the post of prime minister and sends him back to his own fief, while allowing Lü to retain his title as marquis of Wenxin.[39] Unfortunately, in another year or so, the king sends Lü a letter to exile him. The following excerpt, through their respective points of view, presents the king's concern and Lü's regret, which jointly cause the previous chancellor's final collapse.

歲餘，諸侯賓客使者相望於道，請文信侯。秦王恐其為變，乃賜文信侯書曰：「君何功於秦？秦封君河南，食十萬戶。君何親於秦？號稱仲父。其與家屬徙處蜀！」呂不韋自度稍侵，恐誅，乃飲酖而死。[40]

Over a year, emissaries from the various regional rulers and retainers would gaze at each other on the way to invite the marquis of Wenxin [to join them]. The king of Qin was afraid that the marquis would make a coup and thus gave him a letter, saying, "What merits have you contributed to Qin? Qin enfeoffed you with the region of Henan and nourishments of households of one hundred thousand. What kinship do you have with Qin? You are addressed as the second father. You and your family are exiled to the Shu region!" Lü Buwei pondered [these matters] himself and sensed that he had been excessive. He was afraid of being executed,[41] thus drank poison, and died.

This excerpt shows Ying Zheng's anxiety and suspicion about a potential rebellion that the king deems to be started by Lü's guests; meanwhile, the passage reveals Lü's self-reflection that leads him to commit suicide, presenting the protagonist's final self-awareness of his deeds. The rise and decline of Lü Buwei both contain detailed perceptions of Lü and the two kings. The contrast between these perceptions in the opposite contexts shows the importance of shared ambition between a ruler and his minister: when Lü and Zichu have the common goal of enthroning

Zichu, they quickly unite to cooperate; when Lü serves Ying Zheng, due to his extreme high position in the court, he is not aware that he has little in common with the young king, at least nothing presented in the account. On the contrary, they contest in many aspects in the king's eyes. Lü's interference within the harem and intense interactions with non-Qin rulers and retainers cross the line and directly lead to his suicide. From his attracting Zichu's attention to losing Ying Zheng's trust, the protagonist experiences prosperity and tragedy. Although the ups and the downs seem contrasting, they are both subject to the two rulers' perceptions, as seen in the textual representation here.

When *Records of the Historian* depicts the historical figures of the Han dynasty, the same pattern of emphasizing the points of view within the ruler-minister relationship reappears. As seen in the pre-Han examples, again, the emperors' feelings and concerns develop across different phases, driving changes in the political dynamics between the rulers and their ministers from time to time. One typical example is "The Hereditary House of the Prime Minister Xiao" (ch. 53) devoted to Xiao He 蕭何 (d. 193 BCE), an honest, upright adviser who assisted Liu Bang from his humble beginning as a commoner to his promotion to the king of Han, and further to his becoming the founding emperor of the Han dynasty. As each is elevated to a higher position, the relationship between Xiao He and Liu Bang changes throughout the chapter. Their dynamics are driven by psychological descriptions of Liu Bang, which are directly and indirectly introduced in the narrative.

According to the chapter, the king places his full trust in Xiao He when the king first establishes his base in the Shu region and explores the Sanqin area between 206 and 205 BCE. Whereas the king leads his army to fight in the battlefield, Xiao He stays in Shu and ensures supplies to the front line, serves the crown prince, and handles administrative affairs. The king relies on Xiao He to make numerous decisions: when Xiao He asks for his approval, he gives it; when it is hard to send letters, the king allows the adviser to flexibly exercise power, even including deployment of soldiers.

Two years later, when the king confronts Xiang Yu near Xingyang, the relationship between the king and Xiao He cracks. The king's point of view is not directly revealed through his own thoughts or actions, but indirectly provided through Xiao He's subordinate, whose surname is Bao. According to Bao, the king is fighting miserably on the front line but has several times contacted Xiao He at this sensitive moment of the battle, which means that the king doubts Xiao He's loyalty. Xiao

He heeds Bao's suggestion of sending sons from the Xiao family to the front line in order to relieve the king's unease. At the end of this episode, we read that the king is very happy, which verifies Bao's analysis. The king's temporary ease leads him to rank Xiao He as top among the ministers who have contributed to his possession of the empire. At a court meeting, the king declares Xiao He's merits incomparable. This announcement shows that, despite some suspicion, the king still remembers the minister's help during his difficult years at this time.

After the founding of the Han, Liu Bang enfeoffed his early followers with lands and the title of kings as he promised; nonetheless, soon the emperor felt the threats brought by their growing power and distinguished capabilities. Xiao He's account reports that by 196 BCE the emperor and his empress had put down Chen Xi and Han Xin's rebellion and killed the two generals. In this context, the emperor appointed Xiao He as the prime minister, further increased his revenue, and sent five guards to protect him. When all Xiao He's colleagues come to congratulate him, a person named Zhao Ping alerts him to the hidden danger behind the promotion. Zhao analyzes the emperor's discomfort within the ruler-minister interaction. The excerpt reads:

「禍自此始矣。上暴露於外而君守於中，非被矢石之事而益君封置衛者，以今者淮陰侯新反於中，疑君心矣。夫置衛衛君，非以寵君也。願君讓封勿受，悉以家私財佐軍，則上心說。」相國從其計，高帝乃大喜。⁴²

"The disaster will begin with this. While the emperor has been exposed to the outside, you stand within the city walls. Your business has nothing to do with immersing oneself in arrows and rocks, but [the emperor] further increased your fief and set up guards. This is because now the marquis of Huaiyin [i.e., Han Xin] has just rebelled within the court and the [emperor] doubts your heart. The setting of guards to protect you is not because he favors you. I hope you yield the fief and do not accept anything; if you use all of the private wealth of your house to aid the troops, then the emperor will be happy at heart." The prime minister followed Zhao Ping's plan. Emperor Gaozu was thus very delighted.

One year later, another general, Qing Bu, rebelled. While the emperor went to put down the rebel armies in person, he sent emissaries to Xiao

He, asking what he was doing in the Han capital. The prime minister, considering that the emperor was out in the army, had been placating the people and had exhausted his personal belongings to help with the army. However, the emperor had less and less trust with his early followers who were powerful and influential in the court. One of Xiao He's guests suggested that he defame himself to retrieve the king's trust, as seen in the following passage.

> 客有說相國曰：「君滅族不久矣。夫君位為相國，功第一，可復加哉？然君初入關中，得百姓心，十餘年矣，皆附君，常復孳孳得民和。上所為數問君者，畏君傾動關中。今君胡不多買田地，賤貰貸以自汙？上心乃安。」於是相國從其計，上乃大說。⁴³

A guest came to the prime minister and said, "It won't be long before your clan is eradicated. Your position is that of prime minister, and your merit ranks first. Can anything be added? But since you moved to the region within the Guanzhong area [i.e., the capital region], you have won the people's heart for over ten years. [The people] all submit to you, and you are often diligent to achieve harmony with the people. The reason why the emperor asked for you several times is that he is afraid you may make moves in the Guanzhong area. Now why don't you buy many parcels of land and then lend them at a low price to deprive yourself? The emperor's heart would then be at rest." Thereafter, the prime minister followed the guest's plan; the emperor was thus very delighted.

In these two episodes, the emperor's point of view is indirectly presented through the mouths of Zhao Ping and the nameless guest. At the end of both episodes, we read that the emperor is very happy after Xiao He accepts the suggestions, which indicates that Zhao Ping's and the guest's analyses reflect the emperor's feelings precisely. The linear sequence of this account outlines a change in the relationship between Liu Bang and Xiao He—Liu Bang's ascendence to the throne and Xiao He's elevation to prime minister provoke a constant development of the emperor's point of view. Liu Bang's greater and greater suspicion of Xiao He forces the hero to take action and resolve the issue. The hero's chapter represents the relationship between a ruler and his merited ministers, most of whom end up being suspected.

The three previous examples of ruler-minister relationship occur across various eras, from the Spring and Autumn period to the early Han era. All of these accounts are devoted to the ministers, describing the protagonists' entire career trajectories, but the development and outcome of events are presented in the interactions between the rulers and their ministers. Although the descriptions of rulers are not necessarily elaborated, *Records of the Historian* regularly adds the rulers' points of view as a dominant factor to account for the ministers' decisions and reactions and how their lives ended. In addition to these examples, we see the same pattern in a wide arrange of other accounts: in Wu Zixu's account (ch. 66), the protagonist's successful revenge for his father and his failure to protect Wu from collapse are associated with the two generations of Wu kings respectively; in Jia Yi's chapter (ch. 84), his promotion and deposition heavily depend on Emperor Wen's changing attitude toward him; in General Li Guang's account (ch.109), his failure to achieve recognition is primarily due to his relationship with Emperor Wen and Emperor Wu. This model is seen in accounts devoted to various historical periods recounted by *Records of the Historian*.

Broadly speaking, the ruler-minister dynamics are not limited to the interactions between rulers and their officials but extend to the relationships between patrons and retainers, between rulers and entertainers, between emperors and regional kings, and between central government and local powers. In this sense, *Records of the Historian*'s "Arrayed Traditions" chapters, which are devoted to lives of promising or influential individuals, provide concrete examples to manifest changes in and boundaries of interactions within the ruler-minister model.

Conclusion

In the postface of *Records of the Historian* (ch. 130), *Annals of the Spring and Autumn* is described as *kongwen* 空文 (empty words);[44] *Zuo Commentary* embellishes the *Annals* with more details, explicating the significance of individual events and moral stance of isolated actions. In this regard, *Records of the Historian* distances itself from its predecessors.

The ruler-consort and ruler-minister relationships examined in this chapter demonstrate that *Records of the Historian* shows a consistent pattern of narrating from multiple characters' points of view. In comparison to *Zuo Commentary* and other early Chinese histories, the text increases the variety of perspectives of historical narratives to an unprecedented level. *Records of the Historian* represents ever-changing relationships: a small idea in a ruler's mind can grow into a succession disaster; a former deadly enemy can turn into the best adviser; a previously appreciated capability of a follower may be considered a threat later by a ruler; a fully trusted minister may suffer suspicion that leads to death. Characters change over time, grow close or estranged within the harem, and rise and fall at court. Emphasizing present factors in long-term relationships, *Records of the Historian* does not rigidly apply moral codes and ritual rules to characters' individual actions. Rather than narrating what is right and what is wrong at face value, the text penetrates into characters' desires, motives, and emotions, which alert readers to boundaries of political relationships. In particular, the text concerns rulers' visible and invisible perceptions of the world. With this added lens, they are no longer puppets, but active figures who decide the direction of their relationships with the surrounding characters.

By correlating all the participants' perceptions with their own behavior and mutual interactions, *Records of the Historian* presents violations of morality, of political hierarchy, and of ritual propriety as results of mutual reactions emerging from submerged moves and constant dynamics within political relationships. The text does not represent the past in *kongwen* but in concrete, tangible turns, retelling *how* changes start, develop, and come to an end. Instead of offering absolute and abstract lessons, it unfolds the past in incessant processes and multiple perspectives, promoting multifarious historical understandings. This is wherein the power of Sima Qian's retelling lies.

Conclusion

I opened the introduction to this book by quoting a statement by General Wang Feng in which he expressed concern about giving a copy of *Records of the Historian* to a prince. The general's concern had nothing to do with Sima Qian's authorial intentions but was instead directed toward the wily schemes and unusual measures documented in the text. This is how *Records of the Historian* was read before the lens of biographical reading was applied from early in the Six Dynasties (220–589). Thereafter, the center of attention shifted to Sima Qian's misfortune throughout most of the history of *Records of the Historian*'s reception. Based on the traditional Chinese author-reader model, the biographical approach advocates an ideal communicative situation in which readers can grasp an author's hidden intentions from his writing; but in practice, readers following this approach have overemphasized Sima's persona (inevitably reconstructing it in their minds) and have thus overlooked the text itself, the only medium that they are truly interacting with. In this book, I have suggested reading *Records of the Historian* from a narratological perspective. Bringing the text's narrative form to light, I believe that the goal of analysis should be to reveal the text's retelling pattern and interpretive openness in the context of early Chinese historiography.

To this end, I have located *Records of the Historian* in the history of the evolution of texts from preimperial China to the early Han. As a text that has survived the tides over millennia and gained classical status since the Tang dynasty (618–907), *Records of the Historian* has been widely miscast as a seamless and integral composition by Sima Qian, just like many later works of prose and poetry produced in the post-Han era. Tracing the textual composition and transmission of the manuscripts that preceded it, I have redefined the text's place in Chinese textual history. The text was born at a turning point, when short, open, and fragmentary passages began to be assembled into long, closed, and coherent accounts. On the one hand, Sima strove to streamline multiple preexisting accounts regarding the same personage or theme into coherent narratives; on the other hand, he wrote original chapters on the basis of raw materials to build character consistency and development. Rather than a single-authored work, *Records of the Historian* is actually a combination of rewritings (with various degrees of editing) and original composition. In both types of accounts, by locking the reading sequence, Sima Qian greatly reduced textual fluidity and improved textual unity.

The methodological limitations and textual complexity sketched in this book prompt the need for an alternative approach. Believing that the same story can be told in different ways to produce distinctive effects, Genette treats narratives as the sculpted outcomes of narrative devices. Since histories represent the past through narration, it is rational that Chinese historiographical works would acquire a narrative nature, which adds another dimension to studying the text. The primary advantage of this method is that it brackets off Sima's life experiences and examines how *Records of the Historian*'s narrative structure affects its conveyance of messages. Moreover, with this framework, puzzles that have lingered around the *Records of the Historian* studies, such as whether Sima Qian or his father composed certain accounts and whether a passage is an interpolation by later writers, do not impinge on the overall narrative patterns of the text. The third advantage is that the narratological method can deal with accounts with various levels of literary quality and degrees of integration. I have studied the use of three narrative devices—temporal order, narrative speed, and point of view—in *Records of the Historian*, *Zuo Commentary*, and *History of the Han*. These devices collaboratively play a significant role in the rhetorical function of these histories.

More specifically, *Records of the Historian*'s mix of four temporal orders helps it represent a more interwoven network of causality than earlier histories. Entries in *Zuo Commentary* tend to constrain their logical chain to one primary connection between the "beginning" (cause) and "end" (outcome) of a story defined by the author; but *Records of the Historian* is interested not only in the connection between the two time points but also in the various factors that play a role through a subject's "entire life track." With its revolutionary linear structure, *Records of the Historian* knits the overall chronological order together with simultaneous

Conclusion | 143

events, prolepses, and analepses to bring in manifold factors over the historical course of a subject's progression from the rise to fall, regardless of a dynasty, a state, a family, or a historical figure. On the one hand, therefore, the earlier texts relate the beginning and end of an account to reinforce codes of righteousness and morality; in *Records of the Historian*'s chapters, on the other hand, each episode is merely one of many factors that build up the entire hybrid network, which prevents a neat and simple explanation of a subject's prosperity and failure.

Moreover, the varied uses of narrative speed in early histories lead to their diverse priorities. The distribution of uneven narrative speed in historical writings help identify where the historian's efforts are concentrated, as they slow down to detail certain events while speeding up to summarize others. By examining this device across *Zuo Commentary*, *Records of the Historian*, and *History of the Han*, I find that *Records of the Historian* takes pains to account for how a big change takes place through a series of small, interrelated moves. For *Records of the Historian*, it is more vital to explain *how* a subject ascends to power in a continuous and cumulative process over long periods, whether the subject is morally exemplary or not. Placing the fluctuation of power at the center, the text prevents neat moral messages. In contrast, many entries in *Zuo Commentary* and accounts in *History of the Han* break up the continuity of the historical course to recount multiple individual shots of the past, which instrumentally serve both didactic teaching and moral judgment.

Finally, *Records of the Historian*'s use of multiple points of view is unprecedented. As another instrument to regulate readers' reception, point of view informs readers' access to one or multiple characters' perceptual or conceptual position. Since *Zuo Commentary* mostly reports from an omniscient *viewer*'s perspective, the text narrates from an external angle, which tremendously reduces readers' access to characters' intentions, feelings, and thought processes. In contrast, *Records of the Historian* has an omniscient *author*, attentively developing blended, evolving, and interactive points of view to increase readers' consciousness of ruler-consort and ruler-minister relationships in early China. In *Records of the Historian*'s accounts, rulers are often placed in the central position in these relationships. Unlike silent puppets who passively accept or reject suggestions, as in other earlier texts, they are proactive participants, often driving the direction of the narratives. Overall, the text endeavors to match the major characters' internal world with their external deeds. In this highly concrete manner, *Records of the Historian* defines the boundary of interactions between the two relationships rather than simply denouncing violations of ritual propriety and political hierarchy.

My analyses of the three narrative devices in *Records of the Historian* bring me to my major conclusion: separating Sima Qian's biographical experiences from interpreting *Records of the Historian* enables the discovery of repeated narrative patterns in the text. My comparison between *Records of the Historian* and other early Chinese historical writings distinguishes *Records of the Historian* as an outlier, one that prioritizes continuous historical processes rather than single events or isolated facts. The text's unparalleled emphasis upon *how* historical events occurred, from small beginnings to momentous consequences, invites readers to extract a great variety of lessons, impeding a simple and didactic understanding of the past. In this sense, *Records of the Historian* challenges the cliché of Chinese historiography that the function of history is to *cheng'e quan shan* 懲惡勸善 (condemn the wicked and commend the good).

Meanwhile, the continuity of historical processes that Sima Qian endeavors to shape in *Records of the Historian* is the true and endless source that keeps the text fresh and intriguing generation after generation, appealing to readers premodern and modern, from both the east and the west. The text easily engages readers like many fascinating movies that we can watch repeatedly. Even though the ending is already known to us, we still want to delve into the narrative from beginning to end yet again. As viewers, we may even obtain different perceptions every time we experience the whole process. In the same principle, readers are enchanted by *Records of the Historian* not because they are curious about the facts, but because the historical processes recounted in the text are appealing. Historical processes are always open for interpretation. The strong correspondence between causes and outcomes in *Zuo Commentary* and the highlight of isolated facts in *History of the Han* constrain the readers' interpretation to some degree.

This discrepancy between *Records of the Historian* and *History of the Han* also sheds light on the development of Chinese narrative works in two tracks. *Records of the Historian*'s unbroken progression (in not all but many chapters) provides a prototype for later narrative literature, such as short stories and tales in the medieval era and novels and fiction in the later imperial period. *History of the Han* serves as an admirable model for historians compiling dynastic histories, which often collect the historical figures' deeds and judge them on the basis of moral codes.

Many subsequent dynastic histories are thus modeled after *History of the Han* rather than *Records of the Historian*.

Where do we go from here, then, as regards the future of *Records of the Historian* studies and our understanding of Chinese historiography? In light of the retellings that have been examined in this book, perhaps it is wise to recognize that, although there is only one past, historians have many techniques to shape their peculiar version of it. Their job is demanding in that they must be loyal and creative at the same time: on the one hand, they have to care about historical accuracy; on the other hand, they create new ways to learn from old events. Even when the basic facts are the same, different historians can still retell them in profoundly different ways. The value of the histories lies not only in their preservation of facts but also in the manner in which the facts are explained.

These concepts shed light on future studies. Several other interesting issues that remain unresolved include how the biographical tradition arose, why readers in the medieval and late imperial periods created, accepted, and even reconfirmed Sima Qian's persona as a frustrated scholar, and what the benefits of this hermeneutic strategy are. Answers to these questions will advance our understanding of the Chinese author-reader model. Furthermore, *Records of the Historian* represents a vast treasury from which we can continually discover new insights. It is also rewarding to investigate in what respect narratological theories based on a structural approach can be valuable for studying other early historical texts.

Finally, we can examine numerous large-scale works from later periods of Chinese history that take the form of narrative. Works such as the *Shuihu zhuan* (Water Margin) and *Sanguo yanyi* (Romance of the Three Kingdoms) were produced by multiple hands over a long time. As with *Records of the Historian*, we know little about the authors; with collective and repeated revisions, these works evolved from oral and open accounts into written and closed texts. Looking for repeated narrative patterns within these texts may provide new directions for study. The interdisciplinary dialogue between Chinese texts and Western theories is worth continuing.

Notes

Introduction

1. The title *Shiji* is an abbreviation of *Taishigong shu* and "Taishi" refers to the office of historian in the Han court; I thus translate the title *Shiji* as *Records of the Historian*. See Zhu Ziqing (1893–1948), *Jingdian changtan* 經典常談 (1946; rpt., Hong Kong: Sanlian, 2001), 54; and Zhu Dongrun 朱東潤 (1896–1988), *Shiji kaosuo* 史記考索 (1940; rpt., Hong Kong: Taiping, 1962), 242–43.

2. *Shiji* 80.3324–25. Unless otherwise noted, all translations of Chinese texts are mine.

3. As discussed later in this introduction, Sima Qian's father also contributed to *Records of the Historian*, but it is very difficult and sometimes impossible to identify the authorship of individual chapters. Since the son was responsible for finalizing the text, for the most part, I refer to its author as Sima Qian.

4. Gerald Prince, *Narratology: The Form and Functioning of Narrative*, Janua Linguarum: Series Maior 108 (Berlin: Mouton, 1982), 1.

5. This is not to say that all narratives are equally believable. See Paul van Els and Sarah A. Queen, "Anecdotes in Early China," in *Between History and Philosophy: Anecdotes in Early China*, ed. Paul van Els and Sarah A. Queen (Albany: State University of New York Press, 2017), 5–7, 10; Lü Zongli, *Handai de yaoyan* 漢代的謠言 (Hangzhou: Zhejiang daxue chubanshe, 2011).

6. Examples are Dirk Meyer, *Documentation and Argument in Early China: The "Shàngshū" (Venerated Documents) and the Shū Traditions* (Berlin/Boston: De Gruyter Mouton, 2021); Yuri Pines, *Zhou History Unearthed: The Bamboo Manuscript "Xinian" and Early Chinese Historiography* (New York: Columbia University Press, 2020); and Rens Krijgsman, "Cultural Memory and Excavated Anecdotes in 'Documentary' Narrative—Mediating Generic Tensions in the Baoxun Manuscript," in *Between History and Philosophy: Anecdotes in Early China*, ed. Paul van Els and Sarah A. Queen (Albany: State University of New York Press, 2017), 301–29.

7. The Han dynasty consisted of two periods: the Western Han (202–8 CE) and Eastern Han (25–220 CE), also known as the Former Han and the Later Han, respectively.

8. William G. Boltz, "The Composite Nature of Early Chinese Texts," in *Text and Ritual in Early China*, ed. Martin Kern (Seattle: University of Washington Press, 2007), 50–78; Li Ling, *Jianbo gushu yu xueshu yuanliu* 簡帛古書與學術源流 (Beijing: Sanlian, 2008), 209–14; Sun Shaohua and Xu Jianwei, *Cong wenxian dao wenben: Xian Tang jingdian wenben de chaozhuan yu liubian* 從文獻到文本：先唐經典文本的抄撰與流變 (Shanghai: Shanghai guji chubanshe, 2016), 10–16.

9. *Shiji* 130.3319.

10. Griet Vankeerberghen, "Texts and Authors in the *Shiji*," in *China's Early Empires: A Re-appraisal*, ed. Michael Nylan and Michael Loewe, University of Cambridge Oriental Publications 67 (Cambridge: Cambridge University Press, 2010), 461–79; Martin Kern, "Kongzi as a Han author," in *Confucius and Analects Revisited: New Perspectives on Composition, Dating, and Authorship*, ed. Martin Kern and Michael Hunter (Leiden: Brill, 2018), 268–307; Kern, "The 'Masters' in the *Shiji*," *T'oung Pao* 101, no. 4–5 (2015): 335–62; Wai-yee Li, "The Letter to Ren An and Authorship in the Chinese Tradition," in *The Letter to Ren An and Sima Qian's Legacy*, ed. Stephen W. Durrant, Wai-yee Li, Michael Nylan, and Hans van Ess (Seattle: University of Washington Press, 2016), 96–124.

11. As introduced later, *Zuozhuan* has been transmitted as a commentary to the Confucian classic *Chunqiu* (Annals of Spring and Autumn). Therefore, I translate the former title as *Zuo Commentary*.

12. Starting with the dawn of the Western Han and ending with the year 23 CE, *Hanshu* does not recount the entire Han dynasty; nonetheless, the meaning of its title is the history of the Han dynasty. I thus translate *Hanshu* as *History of the Han*.

13. Considering the long history of *Shiji* studies and the broad attention that scholars have devoted to the text, scholarly attention to its narratives is unreasonably brief. Joseph R. Allen is the pioneer of the study of the narratives as such and also the only scholar who has shown interest in such studies; yet he constrained his scope of research merely within chapter 109. See "An Introductory Study of Narrative Structure in the *Shi ji*," *Chinese Literature: Essays, Articles, Reviews* (CLEAR) 3, no. 1 (1981): 31–66. *Zuo Commentary*'s narratives have caught the eye of more scholars than *Records of the Historian*. John C. Y. Wang examined how the plot, character, point of view, and meaning are mingled together to reinforce each other in the text. See "Early Chinese Narrative: The *Tso-chuan* as Example," in *Chinese Narrative: Critical and Theoretical Essays*, ed. Andrew H. Plaks (Princeton: Princeton University Press, 1977), 3–20. Ronald C. Egan was primarily concerned with whether *Zuo Commentary* is a history or fiction. He analyzed the text's style to explain its didactic purpose. See "Narratives in *Tso chuan*," *Harvard Journal of Asiatic Studies* 37, no. 2 (1977): 323–52.

14. It is not realistic to divide the labor of the two historians. Over a long time, according to the postface of *Records of the Historian*, scholars have reached the consensus that the son did most of the work.

15. The letter is collected in two later works, *History of the Han* and *Wenxuan* (文選; *Literary Selections*). See "Sima Qian zhuan" 司馬遷傳 (The Arrayed Traditions of Sima Qian), in *Hanshu* 62.2725–36; Xiao Tong, comp., *Wenxuan*, with commentary by Li Shan (Beijing: Zhonghua, 1977), 41.1854–66. In addition, Xun Yue 荀悅 (148–209) also cites a long portion of this letter in *Hanji* 漢紀 (Annals of the Han).

16. Zhang Hanmo, in his *Authorship and Text-Making in Early China* (Boston: De Gruyter Mouton, 2018), 241–305, suspects that the letter was composed by Sima Qian's grandson Yang Yun; similarly, Esther Sunkyung Klein, *Reading Sima Qian from Han to Song: The Father of History in Pre-modern China*, Studies in the History of Chinese Texts 10 (Leiden: Brill, 2018), 47–54, contends that we do not have enough evidence to be assured of the letter's authenticity. Stephen Durrant disagrees, believing in the letter's authenticity. See "Seeking Answers, Finding More Questions," in Durrant, Li, Nylan, and van Ess, *The Letter to Ren An and Sima Qian's Legacy*, 39–50.

17. David Knechtges, "'Key Words,' Authorial Intent, and Interpretation: Sima Qian's Letter to Ren An," *Chinese Literature: Essays, Articles, Reviews (CLEAR)* 30 (2008): 75–84.

18. Mark Edward Lewis, *Honor and Shame in Early China* (Cambridge: Cambridge University Press, 2020), 186–218. For a year-by-year reconstruction of Sima Qian's entire life, see Wang Guowei, "Taishigong xingnian kao" 太史公行年考, in *Guantang jilin* 觀堂集林 (Taipei: Yiwen yinshu guan, 1956).

19. The locus classicus for *liyan* is in *Zuo Commentary*, Duke Xiang 24. See Yang Bojun 楊伯峻, *Chunqiu "Zuozhuan" zhu* 春秋左傳註 (Beijing: Zhonghua, 1981), 1088.

20. Li Shaoyong contends that Sima Qian, like Confucius, intended to stimulate and satire (*ciji* 刺譏). See *Sima Qian zhuanji wenxue lungao* (Chongqing: Chongqing xinhua, 1987), 21. On the basis of the conversation between Sima Qian and Hu Sui in *Records of the Historian*, Durrant argues that Sima Qian intended to be a second Confucius. See *The Cloudy Mirror: Tension and Conflict in the Writings of Sima Qian*, SUNY Series in Chinese Philosophy and Culture (Albany: State University of New York Press, 1995), 62–65. Burton Watson's position stands somewhere between Li's and Durrant's: he believes that Sima Qian intended to show that his *Records of the Historian* was both similar to and different from Confucius's *Annals of the Spring and Autumn*. See *Ssu-ma Ch'ien: Grand Historian of China* (New York: Columbia University Press, 1958), 90. In *The Ambivalence of Creation: Debates concerning Innovation and Artifice in Early China* (Stanford, CA: Stanford University Press, 2001), 177–81, Michael Puett argues that *Records of the Historian* is not a work that models on *Annals of the*

Spring and Autumn and promotes moral patterns, as its presentation of the rise of empire is much more complicated.

21. For example, Burton Watson, like many other scholars, accepts the view that many of Sima Qian's writings are hidden critiques of Emperor Wu. See *Ssu-ma Ch'ien: Grand Historian of China*, 33–36. Grant Hardy contends that Sima Qian builds a world that relies on Confucian morality and that his target was the First Emperor of Qin. See Hardy's *Worlds of Bronze and Bamboo: Sima Qian's Conquest of History* (New York: Columbia University Press, 1999). Other examples are Itō Tokuo, *"Shiki" to Shiba Sen* (Tokyo: Yamakawa Shuppansha, 1996); Takeda Taijun cho, *Shiba Sen* (Tokyo: Nihon Hyoronsha, 1943); Ruan Zhisheng, "Sima Qian zhi xin—Bao Ren Shaoqing shu xilun" 司馬遷之心《報任少卿書》析論, *Taida lishi xuebao* 臺大歷史學報 26 (2000): 151–205.

22. These scholars' comments are preserved respectively in *Hanshu* 87B.3580; *Hou Hanshu* 40.1325; *Hanshu* 62.2737–38.

23. Klein, *Reading Sima Qian from Han to Song*.

24. Jin Dejian identified at least eighty philosophical and historical texts as sources of *Shiji*. See his *Sima Qian suojian shu kao* (Shanghai: Shanghai renmin chubanshe, 1963).

25. Martin Kern, "'The Biography of Sima Xiangru' and the Question of the *Fu* in Sima Qian's *Shiji*," *Journal of the American Oriental Society* 123, no. 2 (2003): 303–16; Cheng Sudong, "Shikong de wenben yu shiyu de wenxue piping—yi *Shiji* ji qi yanjiushi weili" 失控的文本與失語的文學批評—以《史記》及其研究史為例, *Zhongguo shehui kexue* 中國社會科學1 (2017): 164–208.

26. Paul R. Goldin, "Appeals to History in Early Chinese Philosophy and Rhetoric," *Journal of Chinese Philosophy* 35, no. 1 (2008): 81–91.

27. W. K. Wimsatt Jr. and Monroe C. Beardsley, *The Verbal Icon: Studies in the Meaning of Poetry* (Lexington: University Press of Kentucky, 1954), 1–2. Also see Seán Burke, *The Death and Return of the Author: Criticism and Subjectivity in Barthes, Foucault, and Derrida*, 3rd ed. (Edinburgh: Edinburgh University Press, 2010).

28. Hans-Georg Gadamer, *Wahrheit und Methode*, 4th ed. (Tübingen: J. C. B. Mohr, 1975); David Weberman, "Gadamer's Hermeneutics and the Question of Authorial Intention," in *The Death and Resurrection of the Author?*, ed. William Irwin (Westport, CT: Greenwood, 2002), 55–58, 45. For specific discussions on how narratives produce meanings, see Gerald Prince, "Narrative Pragmatics, Message, and Point." *Poetics* 12, no. 6 (1983): 527–36; as to readers' role in interpreting texts, see Dan Sperber and Deirdre Wilson, *Relevance: Communication and Cognition* (Cambridge, MA: Harvard University Press, 1986).

29. In the "Basic Annals" section, both "Basic Annals of Qin" (*Shiji* 5) and "Basic Annals of the First Emperor" (*Shiji* 6) describe rulers of Qin from the time it was established as a state until it became an empire unified by the First Emperor (259–210 BCE).

30. There is no general consensus on how to translate the two characters. Stephen Durrant proposes to translate *zhuan* as "biography" instead of "tradition." See *Cloudy Mirror*, 212–17. William H. Nienhauser does not agree with the point that *lie* means "arrayed"; he believes that *lie* is a plural marker. See William H. Nienhauser, ed., *The Grand Scribe's Records: The Memoirs of Pre-Han China* (Bloomington: Indiana University Press, 1994), 7: vii. Chapter 1 of the present book discusses these issues in detail.

31. Genette's systematic theory of narrative builds upon an analysis of the writings of Marcel Proust, particularly *Remembrance of Things Past*. Gérard Genette, *Narrative Discourse: An Essay in Method* (Ithaca, NY: Cornell University Press, 1983), 121.

32. Genette, *Narrative Discourse*, 29.

33. Hayden White, *Metahistory: The Historical Imagination in Nineteenth-Century Europe* (Baltimore: Johns Hopkins University Press, 2014), ix.

34. The famous poet Qu Yuan is an example. See Ke Mading, "*Shiji* li de 'zuozhe' gainian" 史記裡的作者概念, in "*Shiji*" *xue yu shijie Hanxue lunji xubian* 史記學與世界漢學論集續編, ed. Ke Mading [Martin Kern] and Li Jixiang (Taipei: Tangshan chubanshe, 2016), 51–57.

35. Zhang Gaoping, "Shufa, shixue, xushi, guwen yu bishi zhuci: Zhongguo chuantong xushixue zhi lilun jichu" 書法, 史學, 敘事, 古文與比事屬辭: 中國傳統敘事學之理論基礎, *Journal of Chinese Studies* 64 (2017): 1–33; Pan Mingji, "Hanshu" *ji qi "Chunqiu" bifa* 漢書及其春秋筆法 (Beijing: Zhonghua, 2019).

36. Paul R. Goldin, "The Hermeneutics of Emmentaler," *Warring States Papers* 1 (2010): 75–78.

37. Because of the complicated textual history of *History of the Han*, the authorship of each chapter is difficult to determine. Several compilers took on the labor over a century after the ambitious father, Ban Biao 班彪 (3–54 CE), initiated it. His son Ban Gu continued and probably wrote the "Basic Annals" and "Arrayed Traditions" chapters but left the rest of the book unfinished when he died. Thereafter, Ban Gu's sister Ban Zhao 班昭 (b. ca. 48 CE) and two other scholars, Ma Rong 馬融 (79–166 CE) and Ma Xu 馬續 (d. ca. 141 CE), took up the project and likely finalized it.

Chapter 1. The Turn to Textual Unity

1. A systematic survey of inconsistences in *Records of the Historian* is Takigawa Kametarō, *Shiki kaichū kōshō* 史記會注考證 (1934; rpt., Taipei: Hongshi, 1986). For the most recent studies, see Cheng, "Shikong de wenben yu shiyu de wenxue piping," 164–84; Xu Jianwei, *Wenxian kaogu: guanyu "Zuo Commentary" "Shiji" guanxi de yanjiu* 文獻考古：關於左傳史記關係的研究 (Beijing: Commercial Press, 2021), 50–56.

2. For the public character of early texts, see Li Ling, *Jianbo gushu yu xueshu yuanliu*, 209–14; Sun and Xu, *Cong wenxian dao wenben*, 116–20; Matthias L. Richter, "Manuscript Formats and Textual Structure in Early China," in *Confucius and "Analects" Revisited: New Perspectives on Composition, Dating, and Authorship*, ed. Michael Hunter and Martin Kern (Leiden: Brill, 2018), 198.

3. Yu Jiaxi 餘嘉錫 makes this observation in his book *Gushu tongli* 古書通例 (Shanghai: Shanghai guji chubanshe, 1985), 30. Li Ling adds that, unlike private collections, which rarely had book titles, official collections owned by the imperial library did have titles. See *Jianbo gushu yu xueshu yuanliu*, 214–15; Paul Fischer, "Authentication Studies (辨偽學) Methodology and the Polymorphous Text Paradigm," *Early China* 32 (2008–2009): 1–43.

4. Lai Guolong emphasizes the fluidity of texts caused by ancient scribes' reading habits in the process of oral transmission, copying, and collation. See "Textual Fluidity and Fixity in Early Chinese Manuscript Culture," *Chinese Studies in History* 50, no. 3 (2017): 172–84.

5. Boltz, "Composite Nature of Early Chinese Texts," 70.

6. For example, among the excavated manuscripts, all those that predate the great scale of collation by Liu Xiang 劉向 (79–8 BCE) have an internal arrangement that differs from their received counterparts. See Martin Kern, "Early Chinese Literature: Beginnings through Western Han," in *The Cambridge History of Chinese Literature*, vol. 1, *To 1375*, ed. Kang-i Sun Chang and Stephen Owen (Cambridge: Cambridge University Press, 2010), 62.

7. Li Ling, *Jianbo gushu yu xueshu yuanliu*, 294, 297.

8. Sun and Xu, *Cong wenxian dao wenben*, 218.

9. The historicity of anecdotes is not a primary concern for these texts, as their value lies in instruction, persuasion, and entertainment. Els and Queen, "Anecdotes in Early China," 10.

10. See Wai-yee Li, *The Readability of the Past in Early Chinese Historiography* (Cambridge, MA: Harvard University Press, 2007), 37; Stephen W. Durrant, "Ssu-ma Ch'ien's Conception of *Tso-chuan*," *Journal of the American Oriental Society* 112, no. 2 (1992): 295–301; Xu Jianwei, *Wenxian Kaogu*, 111–47.

11. The relationship between *Zuo Commentary* and *Discourses of the States* remains unclear. Zhang Yiren 張以仁 argues that the two books are not a result of division of the same book. See his "Lun *Guoyu* yu *Zuozhuan* de guanxi" 論國語與左傳的關係, *Lishi yuyan yanjiu suo jikan* 歷史語言研究所輯刊 33 (1962): 233–86. Li Ling, in *Jianbo gushu yu xueshu yuanliu*, 298–99, holds that the compiler of *Zuo Commentary* could also have put *Discourses of the States* together, simply by using different materials.

12. See Tsuen-hsuin Tsien, "Chan Kuo Ts'e 戰國策," in *Early Chinese Texts: A Bibliographical Guide*, ed. Michael Loewe (Berkeley: University of California Press, 1993), 2, 4–5; Fan Xiangyong, annotation, *Zhanguoce jianzheng* 戰國策箋證 (Shanghai: Shanghai guji chubanshe, 2006), 1–6.

13. According to *Hanshu* 30.1714, *Shiben* originally had fifteen chapters, but now only some of its fragments are extant. The extant passages are collected in Chen Qirong's *Shiben*, in *Shiben bazhong* 世本八種, ed. Qin Jiamo 秦嘉謨 and annotated by Song Zhong 宋衷 (Beijing: Zhonghua, 2008).

14. Zhou Jingjing, "Shiben yanjiu" 《世本》研究, PhD diss., Zhejiang University, 2011, 22–26.

15. Xiao Yunxiao, "Restoring Bamboo Scrolls: Observations on the Materiality of Warring States Bamboo Manuscripts," *Chinese Studies in History* 50, no. 3 (2017): 235–54; David J. Lebovitz, "Molecular Incoherence, Continuity, and the Perfection of the *Laozi*," *Early China* 44 (2021): 1–83.

16. The manuscript was copied over a period between 195 and 188 BCE from at least three sources. See Yomiko Fukushima Blanford, "Studies of the 'Zhanguo Zonghengjia shu' Silk Manuscript," PhD diss., University of Washington, 1989, 1–3. Eleven of the twenty-seven passages from the silk scroll also appear in the aforenoted received text *Stratagems of the Warring States* and *Records of the Historian*. See *Changsha Mawangdui Hanmu jianbo jicheng* 長沙馬王堆漢墓簡帛集成, ed. Qiu Xigui 裘錫圭 (Beijing: Zhonghua shuju, 2014), 2: 201.

17. Jin, *Sima Qian suo jian shu kao*, 323–24.

18. Hayden White, "The Value of Narrativity," in *On Narrative*, ed. W. J. T. Mitchell (Chicago: University of Chicago Press, 1980), 8.

19. Gao Shiqi, *"Zuozhuan" jishi benmo* 左傳紀事本末 (Beijing: Zhonghua shuju, 1959).

20. Prince, *Narratology*, 71.

21. Wai-yee Li, *Readability of the Past*, 29–58.

22. Paul R. Goldin, *The Art of Chinese Philosophy: Eight Classical Texts and How to Read Them* (Princeton: Princeton University Press, 2020), 7.

23. Yang Bojun, *Chunqiu "Zuozhuan" zhu*, Xuan 3.3, 2: 669–72, which describes the king's arrogance, and Xuan 12.1, 2: 719–20, which praises the king for his humane treatment of his enemy.

24. See *Hanshu* 30.1701 (in "Yi wen zhi" 藝文志; "Monograph on Arts and Letters").

25. *Hanshu* 30.1701. Christopher Connery argues that this Han official effort was a continuation of Qin's bibliographic control. See his *The Empire of the Text: Writing and Authority in Early Imperial China* (Lanham, MD: Rowman & Littlefield, 1998), 54. For the influence of Liu Xiang and Liu Xin's catalog, see Wang Chongmin, "Lun 'Qilue' zai woguo muluxue shi shang de chengjiu he yingxiang" 論《七略》在我國目錄學史上的成就和影響, *Lishi yanjiu* 歷史研究 4 (1963): 177–90.

26. *Shiji* 130.3319. Here *gushi* (historical events) probably refers to a wide body of accounts including oral transmissions from various regions, as we learn from the authorial voice interspersed throughout *Records of the Historian* from time to time.

27. See *Hanshu* 30.1701. Lu Yaodong 逯耀東 argues that the scale of the two Simas' collection and collation of previous texts might be even larger than Liu Xiang and Liu Xin's work. See his *Yiyu yu chaoyue: Sima Qian yu Hanwudi shidai* 抑鬱與超越：司馬遷與漢武帝時代 (Beijing: Sanlian, 2008), 36–44, 239–40.

28. With the establishment of a strict correspondence between a text and a name, texts were closed and their fluidity was lost. Sima actively participated in shaping this transformation by compiling the monumental *Records of the Historian*. In his accounts devoted to masters such as Confucius, Mencius, and Han Feizi, he strengthened the strict relationship between a text and an author by explicitly linking these names to the composition of some texts. As Martin Kern argues, Sima coined the image of Confucius not only as a sage but also as an author of the classic *Annals of the Spring and Autumn*. Vankeerberghen, "Texts and Authors in the *Shiji*," 461–79; Kern, "Kongzi as a Han Author"; Kern, "'Masters' in the *Shiji*." *Records of the Historian* developed models of authorship by connecting writers' personal experiences with specific texts.

29. Sun Zuoyun, "Du *Shiji* 'Qu Yuan liezhuan'" 讀史記屈原列傳, *Shixue yuekan* 9 (1959): 25–29; Martin Kern points out the patchy narratives depicting Confucius and Qu Yuan in "*Shiji* li de 'zuozhe' gainian," 49–52; for a detailed analysis of Qu Yuan's biography in *Records of the Historian*, see Kern's "Cultural Memory and the Epic in Early Chinese Literature: The Case of Qu Yuan 屈原 and the *Lisao* 離騷," *Journal of Chinese Literature and Culture* 9, no. 1 (2022): 131–69.

30. *Shiji* 130.3299.

31. On the one hand, Liu Xie 劉勰 (ca. 465–522), in his *Wenxin diaolong* 文心雕龍 (The Literary Mind and the Carving of Dragons, Annotated), ed. Fan Wenlan 范文瀾 (Beijing: Renmin wenxue, 1958), elevates *Records of the Historian* as the beginning of historical narration because Sima Qian took the initiative to elaborate historical figures rather than events, which makes the text easy to read; on the other hand, the famous Tang historiographical critic Liu Zhiji 劉知幾 (661–721), condemned the *ji-zhuan ti*, as the same events have to be narrated in multiple participants' accounts, which caused the split of events and redundant narration in several chapters. Discussions by later critics and scholars favoring either *biannian* or *ji-zhuan ti* did not go beyond the comparison of the two representative critics.

32. Modern scholar Grant Hardy briefly discusses the readability of *Records of the Historian* and points out that the text's form is complicated. Since the same event may be narrated in several accounts, readers need to read across chapters to gain a complete picture of particular events and characters. See Hardy, "Form and Narrative in Ssu-ma Ch'ien's *Shih chi*," *Chinese Literature: Essays, Articles, Reviews* (CLEAR) 14 (1992): 1–23. Yet the focus of the current study is on the individual accounts rather than the relationship across chapters.

33. I have chosen to translate *liezhuan* as "Arrayed Traditions" rather than "Biography." First, *zhuan* is the nominal form of *chuan* (the same Chinese char-

acter as is used for *zhuan*), which means to transmit. Then, the literal meaning of *liezhuan* is the transmitted stories laid out in order. The translation "Arrayed Traditions" helps to convey the sense of transmission and arrangement. Second, "traditions" is probably a better translation than "biography" (a practical translation of *zhuan*) because the latter only represents a partial connotation of *zhuan* in *Records of the Historian*. In addition to accounts depicting historical figures, six chapters in the *liezhuan* section revolve around the history of people and foreign lands. The titles of these chapters—such as "Traditions of Xiongnu" and "Traditions of Southern Yue"—show that a chapter reporting the rise and fall of a regional power could also be called *zhuan*. In order to universally translate *liezhuan*, I would use "traditions" in the titles of chapters in this division.

34. Li Shaoyong, *Sima Qian zhuanji wenxue lungao*, 57–59.

35. Name, age, kinship, and ancestral temples are tools for positioning a person in early China. An individual was considered dispersed from a network. See K. E. Brashier, *Public Memory in Early China* (Cambridge, MA: Harvard University Asia Center, 2014).

36. *Shiji* 77.2377.

37. *Shiji* 107.2839–56.

38. Including the "Basic Annals" chapters devoted to the Five Emperors (ch. 1), the First Emperor of Qin (ch. 6), Xiang Yu (ch. 7), Emperor Gaozu (ch. 8), Empress Dowager Lü (ch. 9), Emperor Wen (ch. 10), Emperor Jing (ch. 11), and Emperor Wu (ch. 12). Note that Emperor Wu's chapter has been lost and the current one is a copy of "The Treatise on the Feng and Shan Sacrifices" (ch. 28), from the "Treatises" division of *Records of the Historian*.

39. Lu Yaodong, *Yiyu yu chaoyue*, 261–63.

40. They are Xiongnu (ch. 110), Nanyue (ch. 113), Dongyue (ch. 114), Chaoxian (ch. 115), Xi'nanyi (ch. 116), and Dayuan (ch. 123).

41. Lei Yang, "From Evil Women to Dissolute Rulers: Changes in Gender Representation across *Zuozhuan*, *Guoyu*, and *Shiji*," *Journal of the Royal Asiatic Society* 3 (2020): 727–30.

42. *Shiji* 77.2380.

43. *Shiji* 48.1949.

44. Similarly, Fotis Jannidis emphasizes that the virtual nature of characters, arguing that they are figures based on texts and media. See Jannidis, "Character," in *The Living Handbook of Narratology*, ed. Peter Hühn, Jan Christoph Meister, John Pier, and Wolf Schmid (Hamburg: Hamburg University Press, 2009).

45. As Liang Qichao 梁啟超 (1873–1929) pointed out at the turn of the twentieth century, *Records of the Historian* is the earliest history that revolves around humans rather than events. Liang Qichao, *Zhongguo lishi yanjiu fa* 中國歷史研究法 (Shijiazhuang: Hebei jiaoyu, 2000), 19. Li Shaoyong 李少雍 believes that early Chinese histories show a tendency to emphasize the power of gods as superior to that of man and that *Historian of the Records* makes great progress in

freeing historiography from this emphasis. See *Sima Qian zhuanji wenxue lungao*, 16–19. Burton Watson also contends that Sima Qian fully recognizes the effects of individuals upon shaping history in his *Ssu-ma Ch'ien: Grand Historian*, 126–27.

46. Some examples include the chapters focusing on Xiang Yu, Liu Bang, and Chen She. For a study of the relationship between coherence and meaning in the *Zuo Commentary*, see Egan, "Narratives in *Tso Chuan*."

47. Durrant, *Cloudy Mirror*, 129–43.

48. *Shiji* 7.296. According to "The Basic Annals of the First Emperor of Qin" (ch. 6), the emperor went to Kuaiji—that is, the Wu area where Xiang Yu grew up—in 210 BCE. Using the rule of age calculation in the Qin-Han period, we can conclude that Xiang Yu was twenty-three at that time.

49. *Shiji* 7.34.

50. *Shiji* 87.2539.

51. *Shiji* 87.2540.

52. *Shiji* 87.2539–40.

53. *Shiji* 87.2547.

54. Paul R. Goldin, *After Confucius: Studies in Early Chinese Philosophy* (Honolulu: University of Hawai'i Press, 2005), 72.

55. Huhai later succeeded the First Emperor and was known as the Second Emperor (r. 210–207 BCE).

56. Zhao Gao had served and taught Huhai secretly. Therefore, he must have known that "Huhai was a foolish and malleable lording. He encouraged the young prince to seize the throne for himself, hinting darkly that the empire would not rebel if Fusu were to be assassinated." See Goldin, *After Confucius*, 73.

57. *Shiji* 81.2562.

58. Li Si's hope of returning to his hometown as a commoner is an example of "the disnarrated," which refers to hypothetical events that only appear in characters' imagination, hopes, desires, ponderings, and so on. Although the disnarrated did not happen, it functions as a characterization device. See Gerald Prince, "The Disnarrated," *Style* 22, no. 1 (Spring 1988): 1–8.

Chapter 2. Temporal Order: Weaving a Synthesized Causality

1. Edward Hallett Carr, *What Is History?* (New York: Knopf, 1962); W. H. Walsh, *An Introduction to Philosophy of History* (1961; rpt., London: Thoemmes Press, 1992). Louis O. Mink argues that historians, at least partially, depend on sequential explanation to account for historical events. Locating an event in a narrative sequence allows the historians to provide the event's antecedents and consequences, which fosters the reader's understanding. See his "The Autonomy of Historical Understanding," *History and Theory* 5, no. 1 (1966): 33.

2. Paul Veyne, *Writing History: Essay on Epistemology*, trans. Mina Moore-Rinvolucri (Middletown, CT: Wesleyan University Press, 1984), 31–36; Ted Honderich, *The Oxford Companion to Philosophy* (Oxford: Oxford University Press, 1995), 366.

3. Genette, *Narrative Discourse*, 34.

4. Christian Metz, *Film Language: A Semiotics of the Cinema*, trans. Michael Taylor (New York: Oxford University Press, 1974), 18, cited in Genette, *Narrative Discourse*, 33. I have altered Taylor's translation slightly so as to align its terms with the terms used throughout this book.

5. Genette, *Narrative Discourse*, 35.

6. Genette, *Narrative Discourse*, 35.

7. Modern scholar Li Jixiang 李紀祥 also points out the impossibility of recounting two events simultaneously in a text. When narrating a complicated event with at least two linear orders (two characters), the narrator (the historian in most historical writings) has to go back and forth among various orders. Li defines this solution as *zhuanshu* 轉述, "U-turn narration." To him, *zhuanshu* is possible in historical narratives because history is capable of being edited. A counter example could be found in film. Normally, a movie cannot tell two episodes at the same time: it is possible only if the editor mutes the two episodes and includes them in one shot. Sacrificing the voice makes this narration possible. Li Jixiang, *Shijian, lishi, xushi: shixue chuantong yu lishi lilun zaisi* 時間·歷史 敘事：史學傳統與歷史理論再思 (Taipei: Maitian, 2001), 82–86.

8. William Labov, *The Language of Life and Death: The Transformation of Experience in Oral Narrative* (Cambridge: Cambridge University Press, 2013), 14–20.

9. Jin Dejian, *Sima Qian suojian shukao*, 105–11. For specific principles of how Sima Qian used *Zuo Commentary* as a source, see Gu Lisan, *Sima Qian zhuanxie "Shiji" caiyong "Zuo Commentary" de yanjiu* 司馬遷撰寫史記採用左傳的研究 (Taipei: Zhongzheng shuju, 1980); Xu Jianwei, "*Shiji* Chunqiu lishi de xiezuo shijian yu wenben jiegou" 史記春秋歷史的寫作實踐與文本結構, *Wenxue yichan* 文學遺產 1 (2020): 29.

10. *Zuozhuan* Huan 2.5 in Yang Bojun, *Chunqiu Zuozhuan zhu*, 1: 91–95; *Shiji* 39.1637.

11. For a full discussion of naming in the context of Chinese political thought, see Cao Feng, *Zhongguo gudai "ming" de zhengzhi sixiang yanjiu* 中國古代名的政治思想研究 (Shanghai: Shanghai guji chubanshe, 2017).

12. Wai-yee Li, *Readability of the Past*, 90–91.

13. Li Feng, *Landscape and Power in Early China: The Crisis and Fall of the Western Zhou, 1045–771 BC* (Cambridge: Cambridge University Press), 2006.

14. In "The Table by Year of the Twelve Regional Lords," *Records of the Historian* records that it is King Huan of Zhou, rather than King Ping of Zhou, that sends troops to save Jin. See *Shiji* 14.551. The commentators of *Zuo Com-*

mentary suggest not following "Hereditary Houses" but the "Tables," which is in line with *Zuo Commentary*. See *Zuozhuan*, Yin 5.3, in Yang Bojun, *Chunqiu Zuozhuan zhu*, 1: 45.

15. A full description of the event is recorded in "The Hereditary House of Zheng." See *Shiji* 42.1762.

16. *Records of the Historian* calculates sixty-seven years, starting with 745 BCE when Chengshi was enfeoffed in Quwo.

17. *Shiji* 39.1637–40; Liu Caonan, *"Shiji" Chunqiu shi'er zhuhou shishi jizheng* 史記春秋十二諸侯史事輯證 (Tianjin: Tianjin guji chubanshe, 1992), 93–97.

18. *Shiji* 39.1638.

19. Yuri Pines examines the collapse of the interstate order that depended on ritual during the Spring and Autumn period. See his *Foundations of Confucian Thought: Intellectual Life in the Chunqiu Period, 722–453 B.C.E.* (Honolulu: University of Hawai'i Press, 2002), 105–35.

20. Tong Shuye 童書業 uses entries in *Zuo Commentary* to analyze the historical situation of the Chunqiu period. He holds that Zhou's influence had declined; however, as the central court, Zhou was still able to intervene in interstate order at the beginning of the Spring and Autumn period. See Tong Shuye, *"Chunqiu" "Zuozhuan" yanjiu* 春秋左傳研究 (Shanghai: Shanghai renmin chubanshe, 1980), 358.

21. The excavated manuscript from a looted tomb, *Zhushu jinian* 竹書紀年 (The Bamboo Annals), also has records related to the Jin-Quwo struggle, and some are very similar to the entries in *Zuo Commentary*. But the reliability of the annals is questionable; thus, its availability to Sima Qian is not discussed here.

22. For example, *Records of the Historian* does not include a statement that the Zhou once helped Quwo to attack Jin but later switched to help Jin because Quwo rebelled against the Zhou. The *Zuo Commentary* entries Yin 5.2 and 5.5 recount this change without explaining what caused Zhou's change of position. See *Zuozhuan* Yin 5.2 and 5.5, in Yang Bojun, *Chunqiu Zuozhuan zhu*, 1: 44–45.

23. Lu is not considered one of the twelve regional states, which are Qi, Jin, Qin, Chu, Song, Wei, Chen, Cai, Cao, Zheng, Yan, and Wu. See Xu Jianwei, "*Shiji* Chunqiu lishi de xiezuo shijian yu wenben jiegou," 29. Grant Hardy believes that Sima Qian drew upon *Zuo Commentary* to embed specific meanings to his table that provides a synopsis of the Spring and Autumn era, which is somewhat independent of the rest of the *Records of the Historian*. See Hardy, "The Interpretive Function of *Shih Chi* 14, 'The Table by Years of the Twelve Feudal Lords,'" *Journal of the American Oriental Society* 113, no. 1 (1993): 14–24.

24. See *Shiji* 17.795 (in "The Table by Months of the Times of Qin and Chu").

25. The name Henei refers to the county of Henei, located in modern Henan Province.

26. *Shiji* 7.327–28.

27. For Jin Ke's commemoration in the imperial period and modern China, see Yuri Pines's "A Hero Terrorist: Adoration of Jing Ke Revisited," *Asia Major* 21, no. 2 (2008): 1–34.

28. *Shiji* 86.2534–35.

29. *Shiji* 86.2535.

30. Wai-yee Li, *Readability of the Past*, 86.

31. Burton Watson, *Early Chinese Literature* (New York: Columbia University Press, 1962), 75; Jean-Paul Reding, *Les fondements philosophiques de la rhétorique chez les sophists grecs et chez les sophists chinois* (Bern: Peter Lang, 1985), 341.

32. Fan Xiangyong, *Zhanguoce jianzheng*, 1260–62.

33. See *Lüshi Chunqiu*, "Chang jian" 長見 in the "Zhongdong ji" section in Wang Liqi, ed., *Lüshi Chunqiu zhushu* 呂氏春秋註疏 (Chengdu: Bashu shushe, 2002), 1130–34.

34. *Shiji* 68.2227–28.

35. The most revealing passage concerning *xingming* (here translated as "performance and title") is attributed to Master Shen—that is, Shen Buhai (d. 337 BCE). Extant quotations of his lost doctrine articulate that rulers should demand reality (實 *shi*, which refers to the performance of ministers), according to the name (名 *ming*, which refers to the ministers' titles). This method allows a ruler to test the abilities of the ministers, thus keeping the power in his own hand. See Herrlee G. Creel, *What Is Taoism? and Other Studies in Chinese Cultural History* (Chicago: University of Chicago Press, 1982), 81–82.

36. During the Battle of Chenggao, Liu Bang had already considered Han Xin a rising power. Near the end of the battle, Liu Bang seizes Han Xin's troops by force and leads them to fight against Xiang Yu's troops. See *Shiji* 92.2619.

37. *Shiji* 92.2625.

38. *Shiji* 89, "The Arrayed Traditions of Zhang Er and Cheng Yu." Zhang Er wins, and Chen Yu is defeated, at the cost of his own life.

39. *Shiji* 41, "The Hereditary House of King of Yue." According to this chapter, page 1746, Fan fled to Qi and earned substantial wealth by running a business. He once sent a letter from Qi to Wen Zhong, suggesting that the latter should flee. The letter reads, "When the flying birds are all [caught], the good bow is hidden; when the wily hares are dead, the hunting dog will be boiled . . ." (蜚鳥盡，良弓藏；狡兔死，走狗烹).

40. *Shiji* 92.2627.

41. *Shiji* 92.2629. The word "lackey" refers to the fact that Empress Lü tricked Han Xin into coming to the palace.

42. Han Xin's account is in *Hanshu* 34, "Han, Peng, Ying, Lu, Wu zhuan" 韓彭英盧吳傳 (The Arrayed Traditions of Han, Peng, Ying, Lu, and Wu); Kuai Tong's account is in *Hanshu* 45, "Kuai, Wu, Jiang, Xifu zhuan" 蒯伍江息夫 (The Arrayed Traditions of Kuai, Wu, Jiang, and Xifu).

43. *Hanshu* 45.1874–78.

160 | Notes to Chapter 3

44. Pak Chae-u, *"Shiji" "Hanshu" bijiao yanjiu* 史記漢書比較研究 (Beijing: Zhongguo wenxue, 1994), 61–62. In Pak's discussion, he concludes that Sima Qian integrated his own emotions into his writing, whereas Ban Gu's *History of the Han* is less emotional and therefore more objective. He argues that Sima Qian was more emotional because of the experiences he underwent through his disastrous involvement in the Li Ling affair.

45. *Shiji* 42.1763. The same event appears in *Zuo Commentary*, but the entry only has one narrative level. The entry only uses one logical conjunction, *gu* (therefore), to explain Zhai Zhong's refusal to join the trip. See *Zuozhuan*, Huan 18.2, in Yang Bojun, *Chunqiu Zuozhuan zhu*, 1: 153.

46. *Shiji* 49.1978–79.

Chapter 3. Narrative Speed: Elaborating Stairs Ascending to Power

1. For the definition of narrative speed, see Genette, *Narrative Discourse*, 87–88. Genette first discussed narrative speed with the category of verbal narratives in 1972. Seymour Chatman later expanded this definition to nonverbal forms, such as film. See his *Story and Discourse: Narrative Structure in Fiction and Film* (Ithaca, NY: Cornell University Press, 1980).

2. For example, the part pertaining to the Han history occupies two-thirds of *Records of the Historian*. In the section "Basic Annals," six among twelve chapters are about the Han rulers; among the ten tables, seven are devoted to the history after Han was established in 206 BCE; twelve out of thirty chapters in the section "Hereditary Houses" are occupied by Han families; in the "Arrayed Traditions" section, which has seventy chapters, forty-two describe figures of the Han.

3. *Shiji* 15.684.

4. *Zuozhuan*, Yin 1.3 and 1.4, in Yang Bojun, *Chunqiu Zuozhuan zhu*, 1: 7 and 10–16; *Shiji* 42.1759.

5. The calculation of numbers of characters in *Zuo Commentary* and *Records of the Historian* does not include punctuation, which would not have been present in most premodern editions.

6. Alun Munslow, *Narrative and History* (London: Red Globe Press, 2019), 53–54, discusses a slightly different spectrum of narrative speed under the category of duration. His analysis is based on Genette's categories, but within the context of historiography.

7. Genette considers direct quotation of a character's speech as more imitative than indirect summary, because direct speech most resembles the words spoken during an event. See Genette, *Narrative Discourse*, 163–72. In a Chinese historical work, however, a character's speech may be dry and tortuous, offering merely stereotypical platitudes that bear little resemblance to what was probably

said. We can observe this in the case of *Zuo Commentary*'s account of the Tian lineage, which I discuss later.

8. *Shiji* 109.2870–71.

9. *Hanshu* 54.2443.

10. This is probably one reason why Édouard Chavannes considered Sima Qian no more than a cut-and-paste compiler of earlier documents. This opinion, however, is hard to reconcile with my evidence in this chapter. See his *Les mémoires historiques de Se-ma Ts'ien*, 5 vols. (Paris: Ernest Leroux, 1895–1905; rpt., with 6th vol., Paris: Adrien Maisonneuve, 1967–1969), 1: ccxxv. Page references are to the Maisonneuve edition.

11. *Records of the Historian* refers to all the members of this lineage by the family name of Tian, whereas *Zuo Commentary* mostly uses the original family name of Chen. To avoid confusion, I follow the naming conventions used in *Records of the Historian*. Several episodes concerning the Tian lineage also appear in the chapter "The Hereditary House of the Grand Lord of Qi" (ch. 32) because the rise of the Tian lineage was closely involved in the decline of Qi (the Jiang family)—for instance, through the Tian lineage's establishing and then murdering of Lord Jian of Qi and its competing with other powerful families in Qi's court.

12. At times in *Zuo Commentary*, an entry may include another, earlier event. These analepses are indicated by the character *chu* 初 (at an earlier time). As Wai-yee Li points out, *Zuo Commentary* uses this approach to offer more information, mostly such as omens and prophecy about the main event related by the narrative. See her *Readability of the Past*, 86–87.

13. David Schaberg notes that the majority of the anecdotes in *Zuo Commentary* emphasize reported speech or, in Genette's words, direct speech. But to tell a story, one need not use these quoted exchanges naturally. In contrast, Schaberg points out that *Records of the Historian* tells more of its tales without quoted speech. Earlier, he argued that speeches and anecdotes in *Zuo Commentary* are carefully presented with patterns to make moral sense of the past. See Schaberg, *A Patterned Past: Form and Thought in Early Chinese Historiography* (Cambridge, MA: Harvard University Asia Center, 2001), 19.

14. *Zuozhuan*, Zhuang 22.1, in Yang Bojun, *Chunqiu Zuozhuan zhu*, 1: 220–24. The use of divination is a major narrative device in *Zuo Commentary*. For the function of divination in *Zuo Commentary* and the relation between *Zuo Commentary* and the *Book of Changes*, see Wai-yee Li, *Readability of the Past*, 209–11.

15. *Zuozhuan*, Zhao 3.3, in Yang Bojun, *Chunqiu Zuozhuan zhu*, 4: 1234–36.

16. Many people lost their legs to penal amputation, indicating the lord's overuse of punishment as an incentive for obeying the law.

17. Before Tian Qi installed Yangsheng, he first incited a court feud so serious that Tu and his followers' troops fought a battle and were defeated. Tu therefore fled to Lu. Once Yangsheng was successfully enthroned, Tu was assas-

sinated on the orders of Tian Qi. See *Zuozhuan*, Ai 6.3, in Yang Bojun, *Chunqiu Zuozhuan zhu*, 4: 1633–34. This story is also described in *Shiji* 46.1881–82.

18. *Zuozhuan*, Ai 6.6, in Yang Bojun, *Chunqiu Zuozhuan zhu*, 4: 1637–39.

19. *Shiji* 46.1879–1904. Several important episodes involving this power struggle are narrated in chapter 32 of *Records of the Historian*, "Qi Taigong Shijia" 齊太公世家 (The Hereditary House of the Grand Lord of Qi). Nonetheless, due to its focus on the lineage of Qi's ruling house, only part of this chapter is concerned with the Tian lineage.

20. *Shiji* 46.1881. Emphasis here and in the following translation is mine.

21. *Shiji* 46.1882.

22. *Shiji* 46.1883. Liu Zhiji doubted that such a song existed. He argued that it was impossible that people were using the posthumous name of Tian Chang—namely, Chengzi—to refer to him while he was alive. See *Shitong xin jiaozhu* 史通新校註 (Chongqing: Chongqing chubanshe, 1990), 1070–71 (ch. 12, in "Outer Chapters"). Although *Zuo Commentary* does not include this song, a similar version of the song appears in *Hanfeizi*; see Wang Xianshen, ed. and comm., *Han Feizi jijie* 韓非子集解, Xinbian zhuzi jiecheng 新編諸子集成 edition (Beijing: Zhonghua shuju, 2003), 312.

23. According to *Zuo Commentary*, Lord Jian escaped to a different place, Shuzhou. See *Zuozhuan*, Ai 14.3, in Yang Bojun, *Chunqiu Zuozhuan zhu*, 4: 1680–81.

24. *Shiji* 46.1884.

25. *Shiji* 46.1884.

26. *Shiji* 46.1884.

27. Some scholars argue precisely the reverse: some chapters in the extant *Records of the Historian* were actually copied from *History of the Han*. For a full discussion of overlapping chapters between these two works, see Pak Chae-u, "*Shiji*" "*Hanshu*" *bijiao yanjiu*, 67–75. As noted in the introduction, the textual history of *History of the Han* is complicated. Ban Biao, Ban Gu, Ban Zhao, Ma Rong, and Ma Xu all contributed to it. For the role of each participant, particularly Ban Zhao and the Ma brothers, see Homer H. Dubs, "The Reliability of Chinese Histories," *Far Eastern Quarterly* 6 (1946): 25–27.

28. See *Shiji* 9.395–412. Other passages in *History of the Han* that record events related to Empress Dowager Lü are found in "Gaozu wu wang zhuan" 高五王傳 (The Arrayed Traditions of Five Princes of Emperor Gaozu, *Hanshu* 38.1987–2002) and "Waiqi zhuan" 外戚傳 (The Arrayed Traditions of the Families Related to the Emperors by Marriage, *Hanshu* 97.3933–72). Hans van Ess, in his "Praise and Slander: The Evocation of Empress Lü in the *Shiji* and the *Hanshu*," *Nan nü* 8, no. 2 (2006): 221–54, analyzes the different representations of Empress Lü found in *Records of the Historian* and *History of the Han*. Van Ess's study focuses on *Shiji* 49 and the contention for the throne between Liu Ying

and Liu Ruyi, whereas the present study has a wider scope, analyzing Lü's life in both harem and court.

29. For a discussion of the full chapter devoted to Empress Lü in *Records of the Historian* and the issue of a female ruler as regent, see Lisa Ann Raphals, *Sharing the Light: Representations of Women and Virtue in Early China* (Albany: State University of New York Press, 1998), 70–78.

30. Although *History of the Han* relates her claim to be able to issue imperial decrees (*zhi* 制), a privilege reserved only for the emperor himself, it refers to these decrees as *zhao* 詔, which could be issued on behalf of the emperor. Raphals, *Sharing the Light*, 70.

31. Liu Hong's original name was Liu Yi 劉義. When he ascended the throne, his name was changed to Liu Hong. Normally, when a new emperor succeeded to the throne, the calendar would restart to Year One (of the new reign). This practice is known as *gaiyuan* 改元, but it was not followed in the case of Liu Hong. So, officially, the first year of Liu Hong's reign was the fifth year. See *Shiji* 9.403.

32. *Shiji* 9.395.

33. The successful appointment of Liu Ying as the crown prince was an important contribution to the many efforts of Empress Dowager Lü, who used her connections with ministers to influence Liu Bang's decision.

34. *Shiji* 9.396.

35. Although Han Xin and Peng Yue helped to shift the balance of power in Liu's favor during the fierce contention between Liu Bang and Xiang Yu 項羽 (232–202 BCE), both of them were charged with revolting. For how Empress Lü eliminates Han Xin, see details in chapter 2. As for Peng Yue, *Shiji* 90.2594 records that Liu Bang does not kill him; but Empress Lü shows great concern. She lies to Peng Yue, claiming to save him from exile but actually persuading her husband to kill him.

36. *Hanshu* 3.95.

37. *Shiji* 3.397. Whether the maltreatment really happened is at issue; undoubtedly, the Han historians had access to rumors and gossip transmitted in the palace. See David Schaberg's "Word of Mouth and the Sources of Western Han History," in *Idle Talk: Gossip and Anecdote in Traditional China*, ed. Jack W. Chen and David Schaberg (Berkeley: University of California Press, 2014), 17–37.

Scholarly debate continues over the question of these detailed descriptions. Were they intended to condemn Empress Lü, or merely to demonstrate her robust sense of resolution? Nienhauser contends that Sima Qian used this recording of history to condemn Empress Lü. Van Ess, on the other hand, holds that Sima Qian neither criticizes Empress Lü for promoting her relatives to ensure power nor considers her a usurper. He contends that she did what she did merely for the sake of survival and that Sima presents her as a good mother, ruler, and wife.

See the translator's note in Nienhauser, *The Grand Scribe's Records*, 2: 139–41; van Ess, "Praise and Slander," 251.

38. The romanization of 張辟彊 follows the entry for him in Michael Loewe's *Biographical Dictionary of the Qin, Former Han, and Xin Periods (221 BC–AD 24)* (Leiden: Brill, 2000). See 674.

39. *Shiji* 9.399. This episode is narrated identically in *Hanshu* 97.3938–39.

40. This contrasts with her mournful weeping later in this episode, when her relatives' positions were secured. It is probably thinly veiled criticism.

41. *Shiji* 9.400. The oath is referred to as the "Oath of the White Horse" because Liu Bang sealed it by sacrificing a white horse.

42. *Shiji* 9.400.

43. *Shiji* 9.401. For example, in the fourth year of her reign, the empress dowager enfeoffed Lü Xu 呂嬃 (her sister) as marchioness of Linguang, Lü Ta 呂他 as marquis of Yu, Lü Gengshi 呂更始 as marquis of Zhuiji, and Lü Fen 呂忿 as marquis of Lücheng. She also appointed five other members of the family as chancellors of feudal states. *Shiji* 9.402.

44. Liu Ruyi was the first king of Zhao. Liu You was the second and was slandered by his queen, a Lü daughter. Liu Hui, formerly king of Liang, became the third. His queen, also a Lü daughter, murdered the concubine he favored, and because he was under constant surveillance from the queen and her followers, he felt hopeless and decided to end his life. *Shiji* 9.404.

45. *Shiji* 9.404–05.

46. *Hanshu* 3.95.

47. *Hanshu* 97.

48. *Hanshu* 97.3939: This account is so abbreviated that perhaps the authors of *History of the Han* expected the readers to have known the underlying details. Van Ess also notes the removal of details, particularly those indicating the sequence of promotion—that is, Empress Dowager Lü always ennobled others before her relatives. He argues that Ban Gu deleted these details to prove her wickedness. See van Ess, "Praise and Slander," 244.

49. Of the eleven titles of marquis that Empress Dowager Lü granted in that year, only four were granted to the sons of Emperor Hui; and the remaining seven were granted to members of the Lü family. In the same year, the empress dowager bestowed the title of king on four individuals: two were Emperor Hui's sons, and two were her nephews. She installed Liu Qiang as the king of Huiyang, Liu Buyi as the king of Hengshan, Liu Shan as marquis of Xiangcheng, Liu Chao as marquis of Zhi, and Liu Wu as marquis of Huguan, and Liu Da as marquis of Changping. *Records of the Historian* and *History of the Han* agree on who were promoted and when they were promoted. See *Shiji* 17 and 19; *Hanshu* 3 and 6.

50. *Hanshu* 97.

51. *Hanshu* 38 and 35.

52. The empress dowager's resolve in eliminating powerful ministers is also briefly mentioned in *Hanshu* 34, "Han, Peng, Ying, Lu, Wu zhuan" 韓彭

英盧吳傳 (The Arrayed Traditions of Han, Peng, Ying, Lu, and Wu), and 41, "Zhang, Chen, Wang, Zhou zhuan" 張陳王周傳 (The Arrayed Traditions of Zhang, Chen, Wang, and Zhou). Shi Ding also discusses the redistribution of materials concerning Empress Lü. See his "Ma–Ban yitong sanlun" 班馬異同三論, in *Sima Qian yanjiu xinlun* 司馬遷研究新論, ed. Shi Ding施丁 and Chen Keqing 陳可青 (Zhengzhou: Henan renmin chubanshe, 1982), 214.

53. In *Records of the Historian*, the "Basic Annals" devoted to Empress Dowager Lü cites edicts twice. The first citation is in *Shiji* 9.397: "That summer, [Empress Lü] issued an edict bestowing the posthumous title Marquis of Lingwu on the father of the marquis of Li" (夏, 詔賜酈侯父追諡為令武侯). The second appears in *Shiji* 9.406: "The empress of Gaozu passed away. In her testamentary edict, she bestowed thousands of catties of gold to each of the kings, gave gifts of gold appropriate to their ranks to the generals, ministers, marquises, and lower palace officials, and proclaimed a general amnesty to the empire. She appointed Lü Chan, the king of Lü, as prime minister, and the daughter of Lü Lu as empress of the [child] emperor" (高后崩, 遺詔賜諸侯王各千金, 將相列侯郎吏皆以秩賜金。大赦天下。以呂王產為相國, 以呂祿女為帝后).

54. *Hanshu* 3.96. "The third degree" refers to executing the entire lineage of the father, the mother, and the wife of an offender. Lü Zongli defines "monstrous words" as heretical speeches and writings, which confuse the common people and cause chaos. See Lü, *Handai de yaoyan*, 36. In the same book, he also introduces laws related to *yaoyan*. See 64–67.

55. *Hanshu* 3.98. A slightly different version of the edict appears in the "Basic Annals" chapter in *Records of the Historian*, which has *qi dai zhi* 其代之 (May he be replaced), but *Records of the Historian* puts it in the mouth of the empress dowager, rather than beginning the quote with *zhaoyue* 詔曰 (The edict says . . .). The text introduces the background information of this event immediately before the conversation, explaining why the emperor was not a biological son of the widowed empress but the murdered concubine. See *Shiji* 9.403. In contrast, the "Basic Annals" account in *History of the Han* skips the reason and simply informs us that the emperor found out the truth. See *Hanshu* 3.98. My translation of this passage is a slight adaptation of that found in Watson, *Ssu-ma Chi'en*, 273.

56. For doubts regarding Ban Gu's use of documents, see Gary Arbuckle, "Restoring Dong Zhongshu (BCE 195–115): An Experiment in Historical and Philosophical Reconstruction," PhD diss., University of British Columbia; Michael Loewe, *Dong Zhongshu, a "Confucian" Heritage and the "Chunqiu Fanlu"* (Leiden: Brill, 2011), 118–20; Sun Jingtan, "Dong Zhongshu de *Tianren sance* shi Ban Gu de weizuo" 董仲舒的《天人三策》是班固的偽作, *Nanjing shehui kexue*, no. 10 (2000): 29–35.

57. *History of the Han* provides detailed public policies that are useful for modern scholars, but the authenticity of the edicts is sometimes doubtful. See Shi, "Ma–Ban yitong sanlun," 211–13.

58. Van Ess, "Praise and Slander," 244.

59. By the end of late Zhou times, *zhuan* had become the name of a genre of commentaries that explicated classics and transmitted their great principles. For a translation of Liu Zhiji's assertion and a discussion of the relationship between the "Basic Annals" and "Arrayed Traditions" sections in standard dynastic histories, see D. C. Twitchett, "Chinese Biographical Writing," in *Historians of China and Japan*, vol. 3, ed. William G. Beasley and Edwin George Pulleyblank (London: Oxford University Press, 1961), 97–98; Chen Shih-hsiang, "An Innovation in Chinese Biographical Writing," *Far Eastern Quarterly* 13 (November 1953): 49–62; Watson, *Ssu-ma Ch'ien: Grand Historian*, 121.

Chapter 4. Multiple Points of View: Illuminating Desires and Dynamics

1. Genette prefers another term, "focalization," to refer to the same concept; but since there is little fundamental difference between "point of view" and "focalization," particularly for Chinese historical writings, in the current study, I follow the majority of narratological theorists in using the former for its "wide usage in narratological analysis." Genette, *Narrative Discourse*, 189.

2. Tamara T. Chin analyzes the contradictory perspectives presented in the "Arrayed Traditions of the Xiongnu" in "Defamiliarizing the Foreigner: Sima Qian's Ethnography and Han-Xiong Marriage Diplomacy," *Harvard Journal of Asiatic Studies* 70, no. 2 (2010): 311–37.

3. Anthony C. Yu, also known by Yu Guofan, scrutinizes the imagination in historical narratives by comparing historical writings, which are considered serious knowledge by historians, and historical novels, which have more freedom to embed imaginative material. Yu uses the word "verisimilitude" (*sizhengan* 似真感) to refer to the efforts of the historian, that is, to let the heroes act and speak naturally. See Yu Guofan, "Lishi, xugou, yu Zhongguo xushi wenxue zhi yuedu," in *Yu Guofan Xiyouji lun ji* 余國藩西遊記論集 (Taipei: Liaojing, 1989), 221–25.

4. Egan, "Narratives in *Tso chuan*," 323–26.

5. Wai-yee Li, *Readability of the Past*, 92–105.

6. For the authenticity and sources of the speeches in *Zuo Commentary* see Yuri Pines, "Speeches and the Question of Authenticity in Ancient Chinese Historical Records," in *Historical Truth, Historical Criticism and Ideology: Chinese Historiography and Historical Culture from a New Comparative Perspective*, ed. Helwig Schmidt-Glintzer, Achim Mittag, and Jörn Rüsen (Leiden: Brill, 2005), 207–13, in which the author argues that the speeches come from *Zuo Commentary*'s sources—the written records of several states; for an opposite opinion that connects the speeches to oral traditions, see David Schaberg, "Remonstrance in Eastern Zhou Historiography," *Early China* 22 (1997): 133–79.

7. Mori Hideki, "Saden no yogen kiji ni mieru shisô no jôkyô" 左傳の預言記事にみえる思想の狀況, *Chûtetsubun gakkaihô* 中哲文學會報 2 (1976): 35–55. The role of predictions in *Zuo Commentary*'s narratives can be found in Schaberg, *Patterned Past*, 182–83, 192–95.

8. Eric Henry, "'Junzi Yue' versus 'Zhongni Yue' in *Zuozhuan*," *Harvard Journal of Asiatic Studies* 59, no. 1 (1999): 125–61; Mao Zhenhua, "Zuo zhuan fu shi yanjiu bainian shu ping" 《左傳》賦詩研究百年述評, *Hunan daxue xuebao* (Shehui kexue) 湖南大學學報（社會科學）21, no. 4 (2007): 87–92; David Schaberg, "Platitude and Persona: Junzi Comments in *Zuozhuan* and Beyond," in Schmidt-Glintzer, Mittag, and Rüsen, *Historical Truth, Historical Criticism and Ideology*, 177–96.

9. Qian Zhongshu, *Guan Zhui pian* (Beijing: Sanlian, 2001), 1: 166.

10. Gu Lisan, *Sima Qian zhuanxie "Shiji" caiyong "Zuo Commentary" de yanjiu*.

11. For how the Han authors give songs individual narrative frames, see David Schaberg, "Song and the Historical Imagination in Early China," *Harvard Journal of Asiatic Studies* 59, no. 2 (1999): 305–61.

12. See Han Zhaoqi, *"Shiji" yu zhuanji wenxue ershi jiang* 史記與傳記文學二十講 (Beijing: Shangwu chubanshe, 2016), 23; Ke Yongxue 可永雪 collects and summarizes *Shiji*'s techniques of building characters in her *"Shiji" wenxue yanjiu jicheng* 史記文學研究集成 (Beijing: Huawen chubanshe, 2005), 9: 118–21.

13. Many scholars, although acknowledging the complexity of the accounts in *Records of the Historian*, believe that Sima Qian's composition of the text is an emulation of Confucius's compilation of *Annals of the Spring and Autumn*. With a Confucian lens, they extract moral lessons and clear judgments from Sima's writing. See Hardy, *Worlds of Bronze and Bamboo*; Wai-yee Li, "The Idea of Authority in the *Shih chi* (*Records of the Historian*)," *Harvard Journal of Asiatic Studies* 54, no. 2 (1994): 352–61.

14. Qian Mu 錢穆 contends that the emphasis upon humans in *Records of the Historian* is a continued practice from the Warring States period. See his *Zhongguo shixue mingzhu* 中國史學名著 (Beijing: Sanlian, 2000), 70. Li Shaoyong 李少雍 holds a similar opinion that Sima Qian's history is a turning point in history making in early China, and Li underscores that *Records of the Historian* marks the change from histories of gods to the beginning of histories of humans. See his *Sima Qian zhuanji wenxue lungao*. For a contrary opinion, see Liu Xianxin, *Liu Xianxin xueshu lunwen ji* 劉咸炘學術論文集, ed. Huang Shuhui (Guilin: Guangxi shifan daxue chubanshe, 2018), 18.

15. For the system of inheritance and government establishment, see Xu Fuguan, *Liang Han sixiangshi* 兩漢思想史 (Shanghai: Huadong shifa daxue chubanshe, 2001), 1: 8–12.

16. *Zuozhuan*, Lord Zhuang 28.2, in Yang Bojun, *Chunqiu Zuozhuan zhu*, 1: 239–40.

17. *Zuozhuan*, Lord Xi 4.6, in Yang Bojun, *Chunqiu Zuozhuan zhu*, 1: 299.

18. *Shiji* 39.1640.

19. The translation is based on Zhao Hua and William H. Nienhauser Jr.'s translation with minor modifications. See Nienhauser, *Grand Scribe's Records*, 1: 305–09.

20. Yang, "From Evil Women to Dissolute Rulers," 721–36.

21. *Shiji* 33.1531.

22. *Shiji* 9.395. The resemblance between a father and a son is probably a trope confirming Ruyi's legitimacy, since a son who does not "resemble" the father might be a bastard.

23. The same reason is also mentioned in "The Basic Annals of Empress Dowager Lü" (ch. 9). See *Shiji* 9.395.

24. *Shiji* 22.1119.

25. *Shiji* 55.2047.

26. *Shiji* 55.2047.

27. Burton Watson's translation with minor changes. See his *Records of the Grand Historian: Han Dynasty*, 1: 112.

28. *Shiji* 49.1976.

29. Yang, "From Evil Women to Dissolute Rulers," 726.

30. Yuri Pines discusses the widening gap between the ruler and minister, illustrating the changing relationship between the rulers and the educated elite from the late Spring and Autumn period to the early imperial era. See Pines, "From Teachers to Subjects: Ministers Speaking to the Rulers from Yan Ying 晏嬰 to Li Si 李斯," in *Facing the Monarch: Modes of Advice in the Early Chinese Court*, ed. Garret P. S. Olberding (Cambridge, MA: Harvard University Press, 2009), 87–118.

31. Eric Henry, "The Motif of Recognition in Early China," *Harvard Journal of Asiatic Studies* 47, no. 1 (1987): 5–30.

32. *Zuozhuan*, Lord Zhuang 9.5, in Yang Bojun, *Chunqiu Zuozhuan zhu*, 1: 180.

33. Gao Xi was a capable high official at the court of Lord Xiang of Qi. According to "The Hereditary House of the Grand Lord of Qi" (ch. 32) in *Records of the Historian*, he was close to Gongzi Xiaobai and aided the latter to seize the throne.

34. The translation is from Stephen W. Durrant, Wai-yee Li, and David Schaberg, trans., *Zuo Tradition / Zuo Commentary: Commentary on the "Spring and Autumn Annals*," 3 vols. (Seattle: University of Washington Press, 2016), 1: 158.

35. *Shiji* 32.1486.

36. *Shiji* 85.2507.

37. The tension between the king and his mother is elaborated in "The Annals of the First Emperor of Qin" (ch. 6) but only alluded to in Lü Buwei's account. The queen dowager's support enables Lao Ai to come to power. Modern scholar Yang Kuan 楊寬 believes that the Lao Ai rebellion was the result of an

intensive rivalry between Lao Ai and Lü Buwei for political influence, although they were once allied. See Yang Kuan, *Zhanguo shi* 戰國史, revised version (rpt. Zonghe: Gufeng, 1986), 474–75. For a detailed analysis of the relationship between the king and queen dowager, see Durrant, "Ssu-ma Ch'ien's Portrayal of the First Ch'in Emperor," 44–45.

38. See *Shiji* 85.2512.

39. For further discussion, see Paul R. Goldin, *The Culture of Sex in Ancient China* (Honolulu: University of Hawai'i Press, 2002), 75–85.

40. *Shiji* 85.2513.

41. If Lü Buwei had been *executed*, his family and property would all have been seized. To commit suicide would save both.

42. *Shiji* 53.2017.

43. *Shiji* 53.2017.

44. *Shiji* 130.3299.

Bibliography

Allen, Joseph Roe, III. "An Introductory Study of Narrative Structure in the *Shi ji*." *Chinese Literature: Essays, Articles, Reviews* (CLEAR) 3, no. 1 (1981): 31–66.

Arbuckle, Gary. "Restoring Zhongshu (BCE 195–115): An Experiment in Historical and Philosophical Reconstruction." PhD diss., University of British Columbia, 1983.

Ban Gu 班固. *Hanshu* 漢書 [History of the Han]. Beijing: Zhonghua, 1962.

Blanford, Yomiko Fukushima. "Studies of the 'Zhanguo Zonghengjia shu' Silk Manuscript." PhD diss., University of Washington, 1989.

Boltz, William G. "The Composite Nature of Early Chinese Texts." In *Text and Ritual in Early China*, edited by Martin Kern, 50–78. Seattle: University of Washington Press, 2005.

Brashier, K. E. *Public Memory in Early China*. Cambridge, MA: Harvard University Asia Center, 2014.

Burke, Seán. *The Death and Return of the Author: Criticism and Subjectivity in Barthes, Foucault, and Derrida*. 3rd ed. Edinburgh: Edinburgh University Press, 2010.

Cao Feng 曹峰. *Zhongguo gudai "ming" de zhengzhi sixiang yanjiu* 中國古代名的政治思想研究 [A Study of Names in Political Thought in Premodern China]. Shanghai: Shanghai guji chubanshe, 2017.

Carr, Edward Hallett. *What Is History?* New York: Knopf, 1962.

Changsha Mawangdui Hanmu jianbo jicheng 長沙馬王堆漢墓簡帛集成 [Collection of Manuscripts on Bamboo and Silk from Han Tombs at Mawangdui, Changsha]. Edited by Qiu Xigui 裘錫圭. Beijing: Zhonghua shuju, 2014.

Chatman, Seymour. *Story and Discourse: Narrative Structure in Fiction and Film*. Ithaca, NY: Cornell University Press, 1980.

Chavannes, Édouard, trans. *Les mémoires historiques de Se-ma Ts'ien*. 5 vols. Paris: Ernest Leroux, 1895–1905. Reprint, with 6th vol., Paris: Adrien Maisonneuve, 1967–1969. Page references are to the Maisonneuve edition.

Chen Qirong 陳其榮. *Shiben*. In *Shiben bazhong* 世本八種 [The Eight Categories of *Shiben* Texts], edited by Qin Jiamo 秦嘉謨, Wang Mo 王謨, Sun Fengyi 孫馮翼, Chen Qirong 陳其榮, Zhang Shu 張澍, Lei Xueqi 雷學淇, Mao Panlin 茆泮林, Wang Zicai 王梓材 and annotated by Song Zhong 宋衷, fl. 192. Beijing: Zhonghua, 2008.

Chen Shih-hsiang. "An Innovation in Chinese Biographical Writing." *Far Eastern Quarterly* 13 (November 1953): 49–62.

Cheng Sudong 程蘇東. "Shikong de wenben yu shiyu de wenxue piping—yi *Shiji* ji qi yanjiushi weili" 失控的文本與失語的文學批評—以史記及其研究史為例 [The Unruled Texts and Silent Literary Criticism—*Records of the Historian* and Its Research History as an Example]. *Zhongguo shehui kexue* 中國社會科學 [Social Science in China] 1 (2017): 164–208.

Chin, Tamara T. "Defamiliarizing the Foreigner: Sima Qian's Ethnography and Han-Xiong Marriage Diplomacy." *Harvard Journal of Asiatic Studies* 70, no. 2 (2010): 311–37.

Connery, Christopher. *The Empire of the Text: Writing and Authority in Early Imperial China*. Lanham, MD: Rowman & Littlefield, 1998.

Creel, Herrlee G. *What Is Taoism? and Other Studies in Chinese Cultural History*. Chicago: University of Chicago Press, 1982.

Dubs, Homer H. "The Reliability of Chinese Histories." *Far Eastern Quarterly* 6 (1946): 23–43.

Durrant, Stephen W. *The Cloudy Mirror: Tension and Conflict in the Writings of Sima Qian*. SUNY Series in Chinese Philosophy and Culture. Albany: State University of New York Press, 1995.

———. "Seeking Answers, Finding More Questions." In *The Letter to Ren An and Sima Qian's Legacy*, edited by Stephen Durrant, Wai-yee Li, Michael Nylan, and Hans van Ess, 39–50. Seattle: University of Washington Press, 2016.

———. "Ssu-ma Ch'ien's Conception of *Tso-chuan*." *Journal of the American Oriental Society* 112, no. 2 (1992): 295–301.

———. "Ssu-ma Ch'ien's Portrayal of the First Ch'in Emperor." In *Imperial Rulership and Cultural Change in Traditional China*, edited by Frederick P. Brandauer and Chun-chieh Huang, 28–50. Seattle: University of Washington Press, 2015.

Durrant, Stephen W., Wai-yee Li, and David Schaberg, trans. *Zuo Tradition / Zuo Commentary: Commentary on the "Spring and Autumn Annals."* 3 vols. Seattle: University of Washington Press, 2016.

Egan, Ronald C. "Narratives in *Tso chuan*." *Harvard Journal of Asiatic Studies* 37, no. 2 (1977): 323–52.

Eno, Robert. *The Confucian Creation of Heaven: Philosophy and the Defense of Ritual Mastery*. Albany: State University of New York Press, 1990.

Fan Xiangyong 范祥雍, annotation. *Zhanguoce jianzheng* 戰國策箋證 [Annotated Stratagems of the Warring States]. Shanghai: Shanghai guji chubanshe, 2006.

Fischer, Paul. "Authentication Studies (辨偽學) Methodology and the Polymorphous Text Paradigm." *Early China* 32 (2008–2009): 1–43.

Gadamer, Hans-Georg. *Wahrheit und Methode*. 4th ed. Tübingen: J. C. B. Mohr, 1975.

Gao Shiqi 高士奇. *"Zuozhuan" jishi benmo* 左傳紀事本末 [Zuo Commentary Accounts of Events Arranged from Roots to Branches]. Beijing: Zhonghua, 1979.

Genette, Gérard. *Narrative Discourse: An Essay in Method*. Ithaca, NY: Cornell University Press, 1983.

Goldin, Paul R. *After Confucius: Studies in Early Chinese Philosophy*. Honolulu: University of Hawai'i Press, 2005.

———. "Appeals to History in Early Chinese Philosophy and Rhetoric." *Journal of Chinese Philosophy* 35, no. 1 (2008): 79–96.

———. *The Art of Chinese Philosophy: Eight Classical Texts and How to Read Them*. Princeton: Princeton University Press, 2020.

———. *The Culture of Sex in Ancient China*. Honolulu: University of Hawai'i Press, 2002.

———. "The Hermeneutics of Emmentaler." *Warring States Papers* 1 (2010): 75–78.

Gu Lisan 顧立三. *Sima Qian zhuanxie "Shiji" caiyong "Zuozhuan" de yanjiu* 司馬遷撰寫史記採用左傳的研究 [A Research of Sima Qian's Use of Zuo Commentary in the Composition of Records of the Historian]. Taipei: Zhongzheng shuju, 1980.

Guoyu 國語 [Discourses of the States]. Sibu beiyao series.

Han Zhaoqi 韓兆琦. *Shiji jianzheng* 史記箋證. Jiangxi: Xinhua shudian jingxiao, 2005.

———. *Shiji yu zhuanji wenxue ershi jiang* 史記與傳記文學二十講 [Twenty Sessions on Records of the Historian and Biographical Literature]. Beijing: Shangwu chubanshe, 2016.

Hardy, Grant. "Form and Narrative in Ssu-ma Ch'ien's *Shih chi*." *Chinese Literature: Essays, Articles, Reviews (CLEAR)* 14 (1992): 1–23.

———. "The Interpretive Function of *Shih Chi* 14, 'The Table by Years of the Twelve Feudal Lords.'" *Journal of the American Oriental Society* 113, no. 1 (1993): 14–24.

———. *Worlds of Bronze and Bamboo: Sima Qian's Conquest of History*. New York: Columbia University Press, 1999.

Henry, Eric. "'Junzi Yue' versus 'Zhongni Yue' in *Zuozhuan*." *Harvard Journal of Asiatic Studies* 59, no. 1 (1999): 125–61.

———. "The Motif of Recognition in Early China." *Harvard Journal of Asiatic Studies* 47, no. 1 (1987): 5–30.

Hideki, Mori 森秀樹. "Saden no yogen kiji ni mieru shisô no jôkyô" 左傳の預言記事にみえる思想の狀況 [The Zuo Commentary Mindset as Observed from Its Usage of Predictions to Depict Events]. *Chûtetsubun gakkaihô* 中哲文學會報 2 (1976): 35–55.

Hightower, James Robert, trans. "Letter to Jen An (Shao-ch'ing)." In *Anthology of Chinese Literature: From Early Times to the Fourteenth Century*, edited by Cyril Birch, 95–102. New York: Grove Press, 1995.

Honderich, Ted. *The Oxford Companion to Philosophy*. Oxford: Oxford University Press, 1995.

Hou Hanshu 後漢書 [History of the Later Han]. Beijing: Zhonghua, 1965.

Huainanzi jishi 淮南子集釋 [Collected Commentaries on *Huainanzi*]. Beijing: Zhonghua, 1998.

Hucker, Charles O. *A Dictionary of Official Titles in Imperial China*. Stanford, CA: Stanford University Press, 1985.

Hühn, Peter, Jan Christoph Meister, John Pier, and Wolf Schmid, eds. *Handbook of Narratology*. Berlin: De Gruyter, 2014.

Itō Tokuo 伊藤德男. *"Shiki" to Shiba Sen* 「史記」と司馬遷 [*Records of the Historian* and Sima Qian]. Tokyo: Yamakawa Shuppansha, 1996.

Jannidis, Fotis. "Character." In *The Living Handbook of Narratology*, edited by Peter Hühn, Jan Christoph Meister, John Pier, and Wolf Schmid, 1–45. Hamburg: Hamburg University Press, 2009.

Jin Dejian 金德建. *Sima Qian suojian shu kao* 司馬遷所見書考 [An Examination of Books Seen by Sima Qian]. Shanghai: Shanghai renmin chubanshe, 1963.

Ke Mading. *See* Kern, Martin.

Ke Yongxue 可永雪. *"Shiji" wenxue yanjiu jicheng* 史記文學研究集成 [A Collection of the Literary Studies of *Records of the Historian*]. Vol. 9. Beijing: Huawen chubanshe, 2005.

Kern, Martin. "'The Biography of Sima Xiangru' and the Question of the *Fu* in Sima Qian's *Shiji*." *Journal of the American Oriental Society* 123, no. 2 (2003): 303–16.

———. "Cultural Memory and the Epic in Early Chinese Literature: The Case of Qu Yuan 屈原 and the *Lisao* 離騷." *Journal of Chinese Literature and Culture* 9, no. 1 (2022): 131–69.

———. "Early Chinese Literature: Beginnings through Western Han." In *The Cambridge History of Chinese Literature*, vol. 1, *To 1375*, edited by Kang-i Sun Chang and Stephen Owen, 1–115. Cambridge: Cambridge University Press, 2010.

———. "Kongzi as a Han Author." In *Confucius and Analects Revisited: New Perspectives on Composition, Dating, and Authorship*, edited by Martin Kern and Michael Hunter, 268–307. Leiden: Brill, 2018.

———. "The 'Masters' in *Shiji*." *T'oung Pao* 101, no. 4–5 (2015): 335–62.

———. "The Poetry of Han Historiography." *Early Medieval China*, no. 1 (2004): 23–65.

———. "*Shiji* li de 'zuozhe' gainian" 史記裡的作者概念 [The Concept of Author in *Records of the Historian*]. In *Shiji xue yu Records of the Historiane Hanxue lunji xubian* 史記學與世界漢學論集選編 [Collection of Papers on *Shiji* Studies and Global Sinology], edited by Ke Mading 柯馬丁 [Martin Kern] and Li Jixiang 李紀祥, 23–61. Taipei: Tangshan chubanshe, 2016.

Klein, Esther Sunkyung. *Reading Sima Qian from Han to Song: The Father of History in Pre-modern China*. Studies in the History of Chinese Texts 10. Leiden: Brill, 2018.

Knechtges, David. "'Key Words,' Authorial Intent, and Interpretation: Sima Qian's Letter to Ren An." *Chinese Literature: Essays, Articles, Reviews (CLEAR)* 30 (2008): 75–84.

Krijgsman, Rens. "Cultural Memory and Excavated Anecdotes in 'Documentary' Narrative—Mediating Generic Tensions in the Baoxun Manuscript." In *Between History and Philosophy: Anecdotes in Early China*, edited by Paul van Els and Sarah A. Queen, 301–29. Albany: State University of New York Press, 2017.

Labov, William. *The Language of Life and Death: The Transformation of Experience in Oral Narrative*. Cambridge: Cambridge University Press, 2013.

Lai Guolong. "Textual Fluidity and Fixity in Early Chinese Manuscript Culture." *Chinese Studies in History* 50, no. 3 (2017): 172–84.

Lebovitz, David J. "Molecular Incoherence, Continuity, and the Perfection of the *Laozi*." *Early China* 44 (2021): 1–83.

Lewis, Mark Edward. *Honor and Shame in Early China*. Cambridge: Cambridge University Press, 2020.

——. *Writing and Authority in Early China*. Albany: State University of New York Press, 1999.

Li Changzhi 李長之. *Sima Qian zhi renge yu fengge* 司馬遷之人格與風格 [The Character and Style of Sima Qian]. Reprint, Taipei: Kaiming shudian, 1976.

Li Feng. *Landscape and Power in Early China: The Crisis and Fall of the Western Zhou, 1045–771 BC*. Cambridge: Cambridge University Press, 2006.

Li Jixiang 李紀祥. *Shijian, lishi, xushi: shixue chuantong yu lishi lilun zaisi* 時間 歷史・敘事: 史學傳統與歷史理論再思 [Time, History, Narrative: Reconsidering the Tradition and Theory of Chinese History]. Taipei: Maitian, 2001.

Li Ling 李零. *Jianbo gushu yu xueshu yuanliu* 簡帛古書與學術源流 [Ancient Books Written on Bamboo and Silk and the Origins of Scholarship]. Beijing: Sanlian, 2008.

Li Shaoyong 李少雍. *Sima Qian zhuanji wenxue lungao* 司馬遷傳記文學論稿 [Draft Essays on the Biographical Literature of Sima Qian]. Chongqing: Chongqing xinhua, 1987.

Li, Wai-yee. "The Idea of Authority in the *Shih chi* (Records of the Historian)." *Harvard Journal of Asiatic Studies* 54, no. 2 (1994): 345–405.

——. "The Letter to Ren An and Authorship in the Chinese Tradition." In *The Letter to Ren An and Sima Qian's Legacy*, edited by Stephen W. Durrant, Wai-yee Li, Michael Nylan, and Hans van Ess, 96–124. Seattle: University of Washington Press, 2016.

———. *The Readability of the Past in Early Chinese Historiography*. Cambridge, MA: Harvard University Asia Center, 2007.
Liang Qichao 梁啟超. *Zhongguo lishi yanjiu fa* 中國歷史研究法 [Research Methods for Chinese History]. Shijiazhuang: Hebei jiaoyu, 2000.
Liang Yusheng 梁玉繩. "*Shiji*" *zhiyi* 史記志疑 [A Record of Doubts about *Records of the Historian*]. Beijing: Zhonghua, 1981.
Liu Caonan 劉操南. "*Shiji*" *Chunqiu shi'er zhuhou shishi jizheng* 史記春秋十二諸侯史事輯證 [Collected Evidence of Historical Events in *Records of the Historian* Regarding the Twelve Regional Lords during the Spring and Autumn Period]. Tianjin: Tianjin guji chubanshe, 1992.
Liu Xianxin 劉咸炘. *Liu Xianxin xueshu lunwen ji* 劉咸炘學術論文集 [Collected Essays by Liu Xianxin], edited by Huang Shuhui. Guilin: Guangxi shifan daxue chubanshe, 2018.
Liu Xie 劉勰. *Wenxin diaolong zhu* 文心雕龍注 [Literary Mind and the Carving of Dragons, Annotated]. Edited by Fan Wenlan 范文瀾. Beijing: Renmin wenxue, 1958.
Liu Zhiji 劉知幾, comp. *Shitong xin jiaozhu* 史通新校注 [A New Annotated Comprehensive Understanding of Historiography]. Annotated by Zhao Lüfu 趙呂甫. Chongqing: Chongqing chubanshe, 1990.
Loewe, Michael. *A Biographical Dictionary of the Qin, Former Han, and Xin Periods (221 BC–AD 24)*. Leiden: Brill, 2000.
———. *Dong Zhongshu, a "Confucian" Heritage and the "Chunqiu Fanlu."* Leiden: Brill, 2011.
———, ed. *Early Chinese Texts: A Bibliographical Guide*. Berkeley: University of California Press, 1993.
Lu Yaodong 逯耀東. *Yiyu yu chaoyue: Sima Qian yu Hanwudi shidai* 抑鬱與超越：司馬遷與漢武帝時代 [Melancholy and Transcendence: The Era of Sima Qian and Emperor Wu of the Han]. Beijing: Sanlian, 2008.
Lü Zongli 呂宗力. *Handai de yaoyan* 漢代的謠言 [Rumors in the Han Dynasty]. Hangzhou: Zhejiang daxue chubanshe, 2011.
Mao Zhenhua 毛振華. "Zuo zhuan fu shi yanjiu bainian shu ping" 《左傳》賦詩研究百年述評 [A Review of Research on *Zuo Commentary*'s Citation of the "Book of Odes" over the Last One Hundred Years]. *Hunan daxue xuebao* (Shehui kexue) [Journal of Hunan University (Social Sciences)] 21, no. 4 (2007): 87–92.
Mengzi zhu shu 孟子注疏 [A Commentary of Mencius]. Beijing: Beijing daxue, 1999.
Metz, Christian. *Film Language: A Semiotics of the Cinema*. Translated by Michael Taylor. New York: Oxford University Press, 1974.
Meyer, Dirk. *Documentation and Argument in Early China: The "Shàngshū" (Venerated Documents) and the Shū Traditions*. Berlin/Boston: De Gruyter Mouton, 2021.

Mink, Louis O. "The Autonomy of Historical Understanding." *History and Theory* 5, no. 1 (1966): 24–47.
Munslow, Alun. *Narrative and History*. London: Red Globe Press, 2019.
Nienhauser, William H. "A Century (1895–1995) of *Shih chi* Studies in the West." *Asian Culture Quarterly* 24, no. 1 (1996): 1–51.
Nienhauser, William H., ed. *The Grand Scribe's Records*. Vols. 1–2; and 7. Bloomington: Indiana University Press, 1994–.
Nivison, David S., and Bryan William Van Norden. *The Ways of Confucianism: Investigations in Chinese Philosophy*. Chicago and La Salle: Open Court, 1996.
Pak Chae-u 朴宰雨. "*Shiji*" "*Hanshu*" *bijiao yanjiu* 史記漢書比較研究 [A Comparative Study of *Records of the Historian* and *History of the Han*]. Beijing: Zhongguo wenxue, 1994.
Pan Mingji 潘銘基. "*Hanshu*" *ji qi* "*Chunqiu*" *bifa* 漢書及其春秋筆法 [*History of the Han* and Its Use of the Recording Rules of *Annals of the Spring and Autumn*]. Beijing: Zhonghua, 2019.
Pines, Yuri. *Foundations of Confucian Thought: Intellectual Life in the Chunqiu Period, 722–453 B.C.E.* Honolulu: University of Hawai'i Press, 2002.
———. "From Teachers to Subjects: Ministers Speaking to the Rulers from Yan Ying 晏嬰 to Li Si 李斯." In *Facing the Monarch: Modes of Advice in the Early Chinese Court*, edited by Garret P. S. Olberding, 87–118. Cambridge, MA: Harvard University Press, 2009.
———. "A Hero Terrorist: Adoration of Jing Ke Revisited." *Asia Major* 21, no. 2 (2008): 1–34.
———. "Speeches and the Question of Authenticity in Ancient Chinese Historical Records." In *Historical Truth, Historical Criticism and Ideology: Chinese Historiography and Historical Culture from a New Comparative Perspective*, edited by Helwig Schmidt-Glintzer, Achim Mittag, and Jörn Rüsen, 195–224. Leiden: Brill, 2005.
———. *Zhou History Unearthed: The Bamboo Manuscript "Xinian" and Early Chinese Historiography*. New York: Columbia University Press, 2020.
Prince, Gerald. "The Disnarrated." *Style* 22, no. 1 (Spring 1988): 1–8.
———. "Narrative Pragmatics, Message, and Point." *Poetics* 12, no. 6 (1983): 527–36.
———. *Narratology: The Form and Functioning of Narrative*. Janua Linguarum: Series Maior 108. Berlin: Mouton, 1982.
Puett, Michael. *The Ambivalence of Creation: Debates concerning Innovation and Artifice in Early China*. Stanford, CA: Stanford University Press, 2001.
Qian Mu 錢穆. *Zhongguo shixue mingzhu* 中國史學名著 [Masterpieces of Chinese Historiographical Works]. Beijing: Sanlian, 2000.
Qian Zhongshu 錢鍾書. *Guan Zhui Bian* 管錐編 [A Collection of Limited Views]. Beijing: Sanlian, 2001.

Raphals, Lisa Ann. *Divination and Prediction in Early China and Ancient Greece*. Cambridge: Cambridge University Press, 2013.

———. *Sharing the Light: Representations of Women and Virtue in Early China*. Albany: State University of New York Press, 1998.

Reding, Jean-Paul. *Les fondements philosophiques de la rhétorique chez les sophists grecs et chez les sophists chinois*. Bern: Peter Lang, 1985.

Richter, Matthias L. "Manuscript Formats and Textual Structure in Early China." In *Confucius and "Analects" Revisited: New Perspectives on Composition, Dating, and Authorship*, edited by Michael Hunter and Martin Kern, 187–217. Leiden: Brill, 2018.

Ruan Zhisheng 阮芝生. "Sima Qian zhi xin—Bao Ren Shaoqing shu xilun" 司馬遷之心《報任少卿書》析論 [Sima Qian's Heart—Analysis and Discussion of the *Letter in Reply to Ren Shaoqing*]. *Taida lishi xuebao* 臺大歷史學報 [Historical Inquiry: National Taiwan University] 26 (2000): 151–205.

Satō Taketoshi 佐藤武敏. *Shiba Sen no kenkyū* 司馬遷の研究 [A Study of Sima Qian]. Tokyo: Kyuko Shoin, 1997.

Schaberg, David. *The Oxford History of Historical Writing*. Vol. 1, *Beginnings to AD 600*. Edited by Andrew Feldherr and Grant Hardy. Oxford: Oxford University Press, 2011.

———. *A Patterned Past: Form and Thought in Early Chinese Historiography*. Cambridge, MA: Harvard University Asia Center, 2001.

———. "Platitude and Persona: Junzi Comments in *Zuozhuan* and Beyond." In *Historical Truth, Historical Criticism, and Ideology: Chinese Historiography and Historical Culture from a New Comparative Perspective*, edited by Helwig Schmidt-Glintzer, Achim Mittag, and Jörn Rüsen, 177–96. Boston: Brill, 2005.

———. "Remonstrance in Eastern Zhou Historiography." *Early China* 22 (1997): 133–79.

———. Review of *Worlds of Bronze and Bamboo: Sima Qian's Conquest of History*, by Grant Hardy. *Harvard Journal of Asiatic Studies* 61, no. 1 (2001): 249–59.

———. "Song and the Historical Imagination in Early China." *Harvard Journal of Asiatic Studies* 59, no. 2 (1999): 305–61.

———. "Word of Mouth and the Sources of Western Han History." In *Idle Talk: Gossip and Anecdote in Traditional China*, edited by Jack W. Chen and David Schaberg, 17–37. Berkeley: University of California Press, 2014.

Scholes, Robert, James Phelan, and Robert Kellogg. *The Nature of Narrative*. Revised and expanded ed. New York: Oxford University Press, 2006.

Selden, Raman. *The Cambridge History of Literary Criticism*. Vol. 8, *From Formalism to Poststructuralism*. Cambridge: Cambridge University Press, 1989.

Shen Qinhan 沈欽韓. *Chunqiu Zuoshi zhuan buzhu* 春秋左氏傳補注 [A Supplementary Commentary of the *Zuo Commentary on Annals of Spring and Autumn*]. Shanghai: Shanghai guji chubanshe, 1995.

Shi Ding 施丁. "Ma–Ban yitong sanlun" 班馬異同三論 [Three Discussions on the Differences between Sima Qian and Ban Gu]. In *Sima Qian yanjiu xinlun* 司馬遷研究新論 [New Essays on Sima Qian Studies], edited by Shi Ding 施丁 and Chen Keqing 陳可青, 208–368. Zhengzhou: Henan renmin chubanshe, 1982.

"Shiji" yanjiu jicheng 史記研究集成 [Collected Achievements in *Records of the Historian* Research]. Edited by Zhang Dake 張大可, An Pingqiu 安平秋, and Yu Zhanghua 俞樟華. 14 vols. Beijing: Huawen, 2005.

Shisan jing zhushu 十三經注疏 [Commentaries and Subcommentaries on the Thirteen Classics]. Taipei: Yiwen yinshuguan, 1955.

Sima Qian 司馬遷. *Shiji* 史記 [*Records of the Historian*]. Beijing: Zhonghua, 1959.

Sperber, Dan, and Deirdre Wilson. *Relevance: Communication and Cognition*. Cambridge, MA: Harvard University Press, 1986.

Sun Jingtan 孫景壇. "Dong Zhongshu de 'Tianren sance' shi Ban Gu de weizuo" 董仲舒的《天人合一》是班固的偽作 [Dong Zhongshu's "Heaven and Human Beings in Harmony as One" Is an Apocryphal Work by Ban Gu]. *Nanjing shehui kexue* 南京社會科學, no. 10 (2000): 29–35.

Sun Shaohua and Xu Jianwei 孫少華, 徐建委. *Cong wenxian dao wenben: Xian Tang Jingdian wenben de chaozhuan yu liubian* 從文獻到文本：先唐經典文本的抄撰與流變 [From Literature to Texts: The Composition and Evolution of Pre-Tang Classics Texts]. Shanghai: Shanghai guji chubanshe, 2016.

Sun Zuoyun 孫作雲. "Du *Shiji* 'Qu Yuan liezhuan'" 讀史記屈原列傳 [Reading "The Arrayed Traditions of Qu Yuan" in *Records of the Historian*]. *Shixue yuekan* 史學月刊 [Journal of Historical Science] 9 (1959): 25–29.

Takeda Taijun cho 武田泰淳. *Shiba Sen* 司馬遷 [Sima Qian]. Tokyo: Nihon Hyoronsha, 1943.

———. *Shiba Sen: Shiki no sekai* 司馬遷：史記の世界 [Sima Qian: The World of *Records of the Historian*]. Tokyo: Kodansha, 1965.

Takigawa Kametarō 瀧川龜太郎. *Shiki kaichū kōshō* 史記會注考證 [A Philological Examination of Collected Commentaries on *Records of the Historian*]. Reprint, Taipei: Hongshi, 1986.

Tong Shuye 童書業. *Chunqiu Zuozhuan yanjiu* 春秋左傳研究 [A Study of the *Zuo Commentary* on the "Annals of Spring and Autumn"]. Shanghai: Shanghai renmin chubanshe, 1980.

Tsien, Tsuen-hsuin. "Chan Kuo Ts'e 戰國策." In *Early Chinese Texts: A Bibliographical Guide*, edited by Michael Loewe, 1–11. Berkeley: University of California Press, 1993.

Turner, Karen. "War, Punishment, and the Law of Nature in Early Chinese Concepts of the State." *Harvard Journal of Asiatic Studies* 53, no. 2 (1993): 285–324.

Twitchett, D. C. "Chinese Biographical Writing." In *Historians of China and Japan*, vol. 3, edited by William G. Beasley and Edwin George Pulleyblank, 95–114. London: Oxford University Press, 1961.

van Els, Paul, and Sarah A. Queen. "Anecdotes in Early China." In *Between History and Philosophy: Anecdotes in Early China*, edited by Paul van Els and Sarah A. Queen, 1–40. Albany: State University of New York Press, 2017.
van Ess, Hans. "Praise and Slander: The Evocation of Empress Lü in the *Shiji* and the *Hanshu*." *Nan nü* 8, no. 2 (2006): 221–54.
Vankeerberghen, Griet. "Texts and Authors in the *Shiji*." In *China's Early Empires: A Re-appraisal*, edited by Michael Nylan and Michael Loewe, 461–79. University of Cambridge Oriental Publications 67. Cambridge: Cambridge University Press, 2010.
Van Norden, Bryan W. "Han Fei and Confucianism: Toward a Synthesis." In *Dao Companion to the Philosophy of Han Fei*, edited by Paul R. Goldin, 135–45. Dordrecht: Springer Netherlands, 2013.
Veyne, Paul. *Writing History: Essay on Epistemology*. Translated by Mina Moore-Rinvolucri. Middletown, CT: Wesleyan University Press, 1984.
Walsh. W. H. *An Introduction to Philosophy of History*. Reprint, London: Thoemmes Press, 1992.
Wang Chongmin 王重民. "Lun '*Qilue*' zai woguo muluxue shi shang de chengjiu he yingxiang" 論《七略》在我國目錄學史上的成就和影響 [A Discussion of the Achievements and Influence of the *Seven Categories*]. *Lishi yanjiu* 歷史研究 [Historical Research] 4 (1963): 177–90.
Wang Guowei 王國維. "Taishigong xingnian kao" 太史公行年考 [An Investigation into the Life and Activities of the Grand Historian]. In *Guantang jilin* 觀堂集林 [Collected Writings of Mr. Wang Guantang (i.e., Guowei)]. Taipei: Yiwen yinshu guan, 1956.
Wang, John C. Y. "Early Chinese Narrative: The *Tso-Chuan* as Example." In *Chinese Narrative: Critical and Theoretical Essays*, edited by Andrew H. Plaks, 3–20. Princeton: Princeton University Press, 1977.
Wang Liqi 王利器, ed. *Lüshi Chunqiu zhushu* 呂氏春秋註疏 [The Annotated *Master Lü's Annals of the Spring and Autumn*]. Chengdu: Bashu shushe, 2002.
Wang Xianshen 王先慎, ed. and comm. *Han Feizi jijie* 韓非子集解 [Collected Commentaries on *Hanfeizi*]. Xinbian zhuzi jiecheng 新編諸子集成 edition. Beijing: Zhonghua shuju, 2003.
Watson, Burton. *Early Chinese Literature*. New York: Columbia University Press, 1962.
———, trans. *Records of the Grand Historian: Han Dynasty (Han I, Han II)*. 2 vols. Hong Kong: Renditions; New York: Columbia University Press, 1993.
———, trans. *Records of the Grand Historian: Qin Dynasty (Qin)*. New York: Columbia University Press, 1993.
———, trans. *Records of the Historian: Chapters from the Shih chi of Ssu-ma Ch'ien*. New York: Columbia University Press, 1958.
———. *Ssu-ma Ch'ien: Grand Historian of China*. New York: Columbia University Press, 1958.

———. *The Tso Chuan: Selections from China's Oldest Narrative History*. New York: Columbia University Press, 1992.
Weberman, David. "Gadamer's Hermeneutics and the Question of Authorial Intention." In *The Death and Resurrection of the Author?*, edited by William Irwin, 45–64. Westport, CT: Greenwood, 2002.
White, Hayden. "Historical Pluralism." *Critical Inquiry* 12, no. 3 (1986): 480–93.
———. *Metahistory: The Historical Imagination in Nineteenth-Century Europe*. Baltimore: Johns Hopkins University Press, 2014.
———. "The Value of Narrativity." In *On Narrative*, edited by W. J. T. Mitchell, 1–24. Chicago: University of Chicago Press, 1980.
Wimsatt, W. K., Jr., and Monroe C. Beardsley. *The Verbal Icon: Studies in the Meaning of Poetry*. Lexington: University Press of Kentucky, 1954.
Xiao Tong 蕭統. *Wenxuan* 文選 [A Selection of Literary Works]. With commentary by Li Shan 李善. Beijing: Zhonghua, 1977.
Xiao Yunxiao. "Restoring Bamboo Scrolls: Observations on the Materiality of Warring States Bamboo Manuscripts." *Chinese Studies in History* 50, no. 3 (2017): 235–54.
Xu Fuguan 徐復觀. *Liang Han sixiangshi* 兩漢思想史 [The Intellectual History of the Western Han and Eastern Han]. 3 vols. Shanghai: Huadong shifan daxue chubanshe, 2001.
Xu Jianwei 徐建委. "*Shiji* Chunqiu lishi de xiezuo shijian yu wenben jiegou" 史記春秋歷史的寫作實踐與文本結構 [The Writing Practice and Textual Structure of Events in the Spring and Autumn Period in *Records of the Historian*]. *Wenxue yichan* 文學遺產 [Literary Heritage] 1 (2020): 28–43.
———. *Wenxian kaogu: Guanyu "Zuo Commentary" "Shiji" guanxi de yanjiu* 文獻考古：關於左傳史記關係的研究 [Excavating Texts: A Research on the Relationship between *Zuo Commentary* and *Records of the Historian*]. Beijing: Commercial Press, 2021.
Xu Weitong 许维通. *Lüshi Chunqiu jishi* 呂氏春秋集释 [The Assembled Commentary on *Master Lü's Annals of Spring and Autumn*]. Beijing: Zhonghua, 2009.
Xun Yue 荀悅. *Hanji* 漢紀 [Annals of the Han]. SBCK edition.
Yang Bojun 楊伯峻. *Chunqiu "Zuozhuan" zhu* 春秋左傳注 [Commentary on the *Spring and Autumn with the Zuo Commentary*]. Beijing: Zhonghua, 1981.
———. *Mengzi yizhu* 孟子譯註 [Mencius with the Yang Commentary and Annotation]. Beijing: Zhonghua, 2005.
Yang Kuan 楊寬. *Zhanguo shi* 戰國史 [A History of the Warring States]. Zonghe: Gufeng, 1986.
Yang, Lei. "From Evil Women to Dissolute Rulers: Changes in Gender Representation across *Zuozhuan*, *Guoyu*, and *Shiji*." *Journal of the Royal Asiatic Society* 3 (2020): 721–36.
Yang Xiong 揚雄. *Fayan yishu* 法言義疏 [Exemplary Sayings with Glosses and Subcommentary]. Beijing: Zhonghua, 1987.

Yu Guofan 余國藩. *Yu Guofan Xiyouji lun ji* 余國藩西遊記論集 [Anthony Yu's Critical Essays on *Journey to the West*]. Taipei: Liaojing, 1989.

Yu Jiaxi 餘嘉錫. *Gushu tongli* 古書通例 [The General Practices of Ancient Books]. Shanghai: Shanghai guji chubanshe, 1985.

Yu, Ying-shih. "The Seating Order at the Hung Men Banquet." Translated by T. C. Tang. In *The Translation of Things Past: Chinese History and Historiography*, edited by George Kao, 49–61. Hong Kong: Chinese University Press, 1982.

Zhang Dake 張大可. *"Shiji" yanjiu* 史記研究 [A Study of the *Records of the Historian*]. Lanzhou: Gansu People's Press, 1985.

Zhang Gaoping 張高評. "Shufa, Shixue, xushi, guwen yu bishi zhuci: Zhongguo chuantong xushixue zhi lilun jichu" 書法，史學，敘事，古文與比事屬辭：中國傳統敘事學之理論基礎 [Expression of Judgment, Historiography, Narration, Ancient Chinese Prose, and Comparing Events and Categorizing Phrases: The Theoretical Foundation of Traditional Chinese Narratology]. *Journal of Chinese Studies* 中國文化研究所學報64 (2017): 1–33.

Zhang Hanmo. *Authorship and Text-Making in Early China*. Boston: De Gruyter Mouton, 2018.

Zhang Xuecheng 章學誠. *Wenshi tongyi* 文史通義 [Comprehensive Principles of Prose and History]. Beijing: Zhonghua, 1956.

Zhang Yiren 張以仁. "Lun *Guoyu* yu *Zuozhuan* de guanxi" 論國語與左傳的關係 [A Discussion of the Relationship between *Discourses of the States* and *Zuo Commentary*]. *Lishi yuyan yanjiu suo jikan* 歷史語言研究所輯刊33 (1962): 233–86.

Zhou Jingjing 周晶晶. "Shiben yanjiu" 《世本》 研究 [A Study of *Roots of the Generations*]. PhD diss., Zhejiang University, 2011.

Zhu Dongrun 朱東潤 (1896–1988). *Shiji kaosuo* 史記考索 [The Examination and Searching of *Records of the Historian*]. Reprint, Hong Kong: Taiping, 1962.

Zhu Ziqing 朱自清 (1893–1948). *Jingdian changtan* 經典常談 [Frequent Discussions of the Classics]. Reprint, Hong Kong: Sanlian, 2001.

Index

Allen, Joseph R., 148n13
Anachronism and anachrony, 13, 49. *See also* analepsis, prolepsis, simultaneous order
Analepsis (flashback), 12, 17, 48–50, 75–79, 143; *Zuo Commentary* of 120; *Records of Historian* of, 75–79, 130–32
Annals of the Chu-Han Period (*Chu-Han Chunqiu*), 23, 31–32
Annals of the Spring and Autumn (*Chunqiu*), 5–7, 13; "anecdotes" of, 22; *Shiji* and, 148n11, 149n20, 154n28, 167n13; *Zuo Commentary* and, 16, 25, 109, 139
Arrayed Traditions (*liezhuan*), 10, 11, 23, 28, 154n33; chapters of, 160n2; see also *zhuan* and linear unity
authorial intent, 5–9, 13, 141
authorship, 3–4, 13, 21; multiple, 24–25

Baima zhimeng (Oath of the white horse), 103–4, 164n41
Ban Biao, 7, 151n37
Ban Gu, 7, 16, 74, 151n37, 165n56; on Empress Dowager Lü, 109; Pak Chae-u on, 160n44; Sima Qian and, 85, 109, 162n27
Ban Zhao, 151n37, 162n27

Bao Mu, 90–91, 93–94
Bao Shu (Bao Shuya), 128–32
"Basic Annals" (*benji*), 10, 23, 28, 31–32, 160n2
Beardsley, Monroe C., 8
biannian ti (writing style), 22, 154n31
biography (*zhuanji*), 11, 28, 145
Boltz, William G., 21
Book of Changes, 161n14
Book of Odes, 87, 114

Cao Wushang, 38
causality in narrative, 12, 47–50; analepsis and, 75–79; chronological order and, 50–57, 142–43; prolepsis and, 64–75
character development, 34–35, 116–17, 142
characterization, 24, 35, 43, 116–17
Chatman, Seymour, 160n1
Chavannes, Édouard, 161n10
Chen Ping, 105
Chen She, 34
Chen Wan (Tian Wan), 86–88
Chen Xi, 137
Chen Yu (Lord Cheng'an), 72–73
Chenggao, Battle of, 59–61, 64, 70, 159n36
Chengzhi 稱制, 103, 106
Chengshi (Jin), 52–55, 158n

184 | Index

chronological order, 12, 48–57, 142–43
Chu-Han Chunqiu (*Annals of the Chu-Han Period*), 23, 31–32
Chu uprising, 37–38
Chunqiu. See *Annals of the Spring and Autumn*
closed texts. See open versus closed texts
Concubine Li (Emperor Jing of Han's secondary wife), 126–28
Confucius, 5–7, 13, 114, 148n10; Hereditary House of, 27; Qu Yuan and, 154n29; Sima Qian and, 149n20, 154n28, 167n13. See also specific works
Connery, Christopher, 153n25
consorts, 117–28, 139–40

desire (motivation), 18, 111–12, Li Si of 43–45, Liu Bi's, 115, *Zuo Commentary* and *Records of the Historian* of, 118–24, 127–28, 130–32, 140
Discourses of the States (*Guoyu*), 18, 65; chronological order in, 51; writing style of, 22–23, 25–26; *Zuo Commentary* and, 152n11
Divination, 87–88, 91, 97, 120, 123; see also omen, prolepsis, and prediction
diwang zhi shu (techniques of monarchs), 41
dizhangzi (succession line), 44, 47, 49, 117–26, 140
Duan (brother of Lord Zhuang of Zheng), 83
Durant, Stephen W., 149n16, 149n20

Egan, Ronald C., 148n13
Emperor Gaozu, (Emperor of Han; King of Han), 35–36, 38–39, 59–61, 98; death of, 101; Han Xin and, 70–75; names of, 98; oath of, 103, 104; Xiang Yu and, 100; Xiao He and, 136–38; Zhang Liang and, 123–26
Emperor Hui of Han, 98–102, 104–5, 107–9, 123–26, 163n33
Emperor Jing of Han, 126–28
Emperor Wen of Han, 98, 139
Emperor Wu of Han, 2, 3, 26, 109, 150n21; Sima Qian and, 6–7, 9; Empress Chen and, 77–79, enthronement of, 126–27; Li Guang and, 139
Empress Chen (Emperor Wu's first empress) 77–79, 115, 126
Empress Lü (Empress Dowager Lü; Lü Zhi), 17, 85, 97–110, 115
external perspective, 113–14

Fan Li, 71–73
Feng Wuze (Marquis of Bocheng), 103, 104
First Emperor of Qin. See Ying Zheng
Fusu, 43–44, 156m56

Gadamer, Hans-Georg, 9
Gao Qumi, 76–77
Gao Shiqi, 24
Gao Xi, 129–31
genealogy, 22, 28
Genette, Gérard, 11–13, 48–50, 142, 151n31; on direct speech, 160n7, 161n13; on narrative speed, 81–83, 110, 160n1; on point of view, 111, 166n1
Gongshu Cuo, 66–69
Gongsun Yang. See Shang Yang
Gongzi Jiu, 128–31
Goujian (King of Yue), 72–73
Grand Princess (Emperor Jing of Han's sister), 77–79, 126–27
Guan Ying, 30, 33–34
Guan Zhong (Yiwu), 128–32

Guanzi, 22
guobie ti (writing style), 22

Han, Battle of, 25
Han Feizi, 154n28
Han Xin (Marquis of Huaiyin), 59–61, 70–75, 100, 137, 159n36, 163n35
Hanfei zi, 22
Hanshu (*History of the Han*), 4–5, 84–85, 148n12; authorship of, 16, 151n37; Empress Dowager Lü in, 97–110; *Records of Historian* versus, 15–18, 74–75, 144–45; textual recovery, 26
Hardy, Grant, 150n21
Hereditary Houses (*shijia*), 10, 23; chapters of, 160n2; chronological order in, 51–52; of Confucius, 27; writing style of, 28, 31–33
History of the Han. See *Hanshu*
Huhai (Second Emperor of Qin), 43, 44, 156nn55–56

Imitation (mimesis), 84, 166n3
internal perspective, 18, 112–14, 128, 143–44; *Records of the Historian* of, 93, 115–16, 121–22, 133–34, 136; *Zuo Commentary* of, 118, 129, 130

ji-zhuan ti (annal-tradition style), 28, 109, 154n31
Jing Ke, 61–64
jishi benmo (writing style), 24

Kan Zhi, 94–95, 96
Kern, Martin, 154nn28–29
King Huan f Zhou, 54, 157n14
King Hui of Wei, 66–69
King Li of Zhou, 32, 54
King Ling of Yan, 105–6
King Ping of Zhou, 54, 157n14

King Wen of Zhou, 32
King Xiao of Qin, 67, 69
King Xuan of Lü, 106
King You of Zhou, 32, 53, 56
King Zhuang of Chu, 25
King Zhuangxiang of Qin (Zichu), 132–36
kongwen, 139–40
Kuai Tong, 71–75

Lady Li (Jin), 118–23
Lady Qi (Concubine of Liu Bang), 99, 101, 107, 125
Lady Wang (Emperor Jing of Han's secondary wife), 126–27
Lao Ai, 134–35, 168n37
Li Guang, 84–85, 139
Li Jixiang, 157n7
Li Ling, 6
Li Shaoyong, 149n20, 155n45, 167n14
Li Si, 40–45, 116
Li, Wai-yee, 52, 161n12
Liang Qichao, 155n45
liezhuan. See Arrayed Traditions
linear unity, 19, 20, 23–28, 31, 36–39; *see also* Arrayed Traditions, *zhuan*, characterization, character development
Liu Bang. *See* Emperor Gaozu
Liu Bi, 115
Liu Fei, 101, 107
Liu Gong, 98, 100, 103, 108–9
Liu Heng. *See* Emperor Wen of Han
Liu Hong, 98, 108–9, 163n31
Liu Hui (King of Liang), 104, 106, 164n44
Liu Rong, 126
Liu Ruyi, 99, 101, 107, 123–24, 164n44
Liu Tai (Marquis of Pingchang; King of Lü), 105

Liu Xiang, 22, 26
Liu Xie, 154n31
Liu Ying. See Emperor Hui of Han
Liu You, 104, 106, 164n44
Liu Zhiji, 109, 154n31, 162n22
Long Ju, 71–72
Lord Ai of Jin, 54
Lord Dao of Qi (Yangsheng), 90, 92–94, 96, 118, 161n17
Lord E of Jin, 54
Lord Huan of Qi (Gongzi Xiaobai), 54, 56, 86–87, 128–32, 168n33
Lord Jian of Qi, 94–95
Lord Jing of Qi, 90
Lord Kang of Qi, 86
Lord Li of Zheng, 76–77
Lord Mu of Jin, 52–53, 56
Lord Mu of Qin, 25, 68–69
Lord Ping of Qi, 94–96
Lord Teng (of Han), 59
Lord Wei of Zheng (Ziwei), 76–77
Lord Wen of Jin, 25
Lord Wen of Lu, 123
Lord Wu of Jin (Wugong), 54–55
Lord Xian of Jin, 33, 118–23
Lord Xiang of Qi, 54, 76–77, 128
Lord Xiao of Jin, 52–55
Lord Xiaozi of Jin, 54
Lord Xuan of Wei, 123
Lord Xue (of Han), 60
Lord Yin of Lu, 54
Lord Zhao of Jin, 53, 55
Lord Zhao of Zheng, 54
Lord Zhuang of Lu, 87, 123
Lord Zhuang of Zheng, 24, 83, 87, 118
Lu Jia, 23, 31–32
Lü Buwei (Marquis of Wenxin), 132–36, 169n37
Lü Chan (King of Liang), 102, 105, 106
Lü Lu (Marquis of Wuxin; King of Zhao), 102, 105, 106

Lü Ping (Marquis of Fuliu), 103, 104
Lü Shizhi (Marquis of Jiancheng), 106
Lü Tai (Marquis of Li; King of Lü), 102–6
Lü Tong, 105, 106
Lü Zhong (Marquis of Pei; King of Yan), 103, 104
Lü Zhuang (King of Dongping), 105

Ma Rong, 151n37
Ma Xu, 151n37
Marquis of Weiji, 30, 33–34
Marquis of Wu'an, 30, 33–34
Master Lü's Annals of the Spring and Autumn (*Lüshi Chunqiu*), 22, 31–32, 66
measurement units, 88–89, 94–95
Mencius, 154n28
Metz, Christian, 49
Min (brother of Lord Ai of Jin), 54
Mink, Louis O., 156n1
multiple perspectives. See points of view
Munslow, Alun, 160n6

narrative, 2–3, 12; definition of, 2; "disnarrated" device in, 156n58; length differences in, 82; point of view of, 113–15; temporal orders in, 17, 48–49, 81; U-turn, 157n7; speed of, 81–85. See also causality in narrative
narrative speed (pace), 81–85, 99, 110, 160n1; ellipsis (omission) 83, 86, 99–101, 103, 106–8; pause, 83, 86–87; scene, 83, 86–88; summary, 83, 88, 99, 106–8; constant narrative speed, 89–90; uneven speed, 91, 106
narratology, 11–15, 142, 145

omen, 52–57, 64, 70–71, 161n12

omniscient author, 113–15
open versus closed texts, 3–4, 16–17, 20–21, 26–27, 34, 45
Nienhauser, William H., 151n30, 163n37

Panfu, 52, 53, 55
Pak Chae-u, 160n44
Peng Yue, 59–61, 100, 163n35
Pines, Yuri, 158n19, 168n30
points of view, 12, 18, 111–17, 142–44, 166n1; *Zuo Commentary* of, 114; 118–20; *Records of Historian* of, 115; rulers and consorts of, 121–26; rulers and ministers of 128–38; *see also* desire, speeches, internal perspective
prediction (prophecy, prognostications), 12, 56; *Zuo Commentary* of 52, 55–56, 65, 86–89, 161n12; of *Records of the Historian* of, 57, 64, 66–69, 97; *see also* divination
Prince, Gerald, 2, 24, 25, 34–35
prolepsis, 12, 17, 48, 50, 64–75, 143. *See also* prediction and divination
Proust, Marcel, 151n31
Pudie (Records of the Families), 22
Puett, Michael, 149n20

Qian Zhongshu, 115
Qin dynasty, 3, 7, 117, 132, 150n29; Chu uprising against, 36–38
Qin-Han transition, 3, *benji* chapters 10; writing freedom and use of materials, 27, 34, 65; composed accounts in *Records of the Historian* 8, 23, 27, 112–13
Qin Wuyang, 62
Qing Bu, 137–38
Qu Yuan, 27, 116, 151n34, 154n29

reading order, 16, 19, 21, 33, 48–49
Records of the Historian. *See Shiji*

rulers: consorts and, 117–28, 139–40; ministers and, 128–40. *See also specific names*

Sanguo yanyi (*Romance of the Three Kingdoms*), 145
Schaberg, David, 161n13
Scribe of Zhou, 87, 91
Shang Yang (Gongsun Yang; Zhongshuzi), 66–70
Shao Hu, 128–131
Shen Buhai, 159n35
Shiben (*Roots of the Generations*), 22–23, 153n13
Shifu (Jin), 52–56
Shiji (*Records of the Historian*), 1–9, 15, 26–34, 141–45; analepsis in, 75–79; character development in, 34–45, 116–17, 142; chronological order in, 12, 48–57, 142–43; contradictions in, 27, 151n1; divisions of, 10, 23; *Hanshu* versus, 15–18, 144–45; historical context of, 20–26; points of view in, 111–17, 144, 166n1; predecessors of, 4; prolepsis in, 66–70; Shang Yang in, 66–69; sources of, 150n24; succession struggles in, 117–18; synchrony in, 57–64; temporal order in, 47–50; textual unity of, 19–20, 19–20; title of, 147n1; *Zuo Commentary* versus, 15–18, 57, 65, 86–97, 144
Shiji studies, 2
shijia. *See* Hereditary Houses
shu (Treatises), 10
Shu Xiang, 88–89
Shuihu zhuan (*Water Margin*), 145
Sima Qian, 1–3, 141–45; Ban Gu and, 85; biographical events in *Shiji* of, 5–9, 142, 144; castration of, 6, 20; Confucius and, 149n20, 154n28, 167n13; legacy of, 14, 155n45; Pak

Sima Qian *(continued)*
  Chae-u on, 160n44; on Qin dynasty sources, 132
Sima Tan, 6, 26
simultaneous order, 48–50, 57–64
speeches, on direct speech, 83–84, 93, 115, 160n7, 161n13; on indirect speeches, 83, 115; *see also* characterization and point of view
struggle between Jin branches, 51–57
Six Dynasties, 26, 141
Song Yi, 37–38
Spring and Autumn period, 58, 112, 117–18, 123, 129. See also *Annals of the Spring and Autumn*
Stratagems of Warring States (Zhanguo ce), 22, 31, 58; chronological order in, 51; Shang Yang in, 66–67; writing style of, 25–26, 66–67. See also *Text of the Strategists in Warring States (Zhangguo zonghengjia shu)*
succession line *(dizhangzi)*, 44, 47, 49, 117–26, 140

Tables *(biao)*, 10, 58–59
Taishigong shu. See *Shiji*
Takigawa Kametarō, 151n1
Tang dynasty, 141
temporal order, 17, 47–50, 81; *see also* anachronism and anachrony
Text of the Strategists in Warring States (Zhangguo zonghengjia shu), 23, 31–32
Tian lineage, 17, 85–97, 102, 110, 161n11
Tian Chang, 87, 91, 94–97, 162n22
Tian He, 86
Tian Qi (Tian Xizi), 87, 90–97, 161n17
Tian Wan (Chen Wan), 86–88
Tian Xuwu, 91
Tong Shuye, 158n20

U-turn narratives *(zhuanshu)*, 157n7

van Ess, Hans, 109, 162n28, 163n37

Wang, John C. Y., 148n13
Wang Feng, 1, 141
Wang Ling, 103, 106
Wang Mang, 16
Warring States period, 1, 112, 117, 134, texts composed in, 21–23, narration in *Records of the Historian* of, 58, 65–66, 70. See also *Stratagems of Warring States*
Watson, Burton, 149n20, 150n21, 156n45
Wei Changjun, 78
Wei Qing, 78
Wei Wuji (Noble Scion of Wei), 29–30, 33, 134
Wei Zifu, 77–79
Wen Zhong, 72–73, 159n36
White, Hayden, 11, 23
Wimsatt, William K., Jr., 8
Wu She, 71, 73, 74
Wu Zixu, 32, 139

Xia Wuju 63–64
Xiang Yu (King Xiang; King of Chu), 35–39, 59–61; Liu Bang and, 100, 136; suicide of, 39, 116
Xia Yue, 71–72
Xiao He, 136–38
xiaoshuo (fiction), 14
xingming (performance and title), 159n35
Xiongnu, 6, 84, 155n33
Xiqi, 118–19, 121–22
Xunzi, 41, 43

Yan Ying (Master Yan), 88–89, 92
Yang Kuan, 168n37
Yang Xiong, 7

Yang Yun, 149n16
Yanzi Chunqiu, 22
Yao, Battle of, 25
Yi clan (Chen), 87, 91
Ying Zheng (First Emperor of Qin), 7–9, 36, 40–44, 62–64, 132–36, 150n21, 150n29
Yu, Anthony C. (Yu Guofan), 166n3
yuanlüe jinxiang (narrative speed difference), 82

Zhai Zhong, 76–77
Zhang Biqiang, 101–2
Zhang Er, 59, 72–73
Zhang Liang (Marquis of Liu), 101–2, 123–26
Zhang Mai (Marquis of Nangong), 104
Zhao Gao, 43–45, 156n56
Zhao Ping, 137
Zheng Zhong, 60
zhuan (traditions) literary form, 27–32, 36, 109
Zhuangbo (Jin) 54–55
zhuanji (biography), 11, 28, 145
zhuanshu (U-turn narratives), 157n7
Zhushu jinian (*Bamboo Annals*), 158n21
Zuo Commentary (*Zuozhuan*), 4–5, 15–18; *Annals of the Spring and Autumn*, 16, 25, 109, 139; author-observer perspective of, 114; authors of, 24–25; *Book of Changes* and, 161n14; chronological order in, 50–53; *Discourses of the States* and, 152n11; Gao Shiqi's rearrangement of, 24; narrative speed in, 84; *Shiji* and, 15–18, 57, 65, 86–97, 144; succession struggles in, 117–18; writing style of, 22, 25, 31–32, 65; Lord Zhuang of Zheng in, 83

www.ingramcontent.com/pod-product-compliance
Lightning Source LLC
Chambersburg PA
CBHW030826230426
43667CB00008B/1405